DOMINION

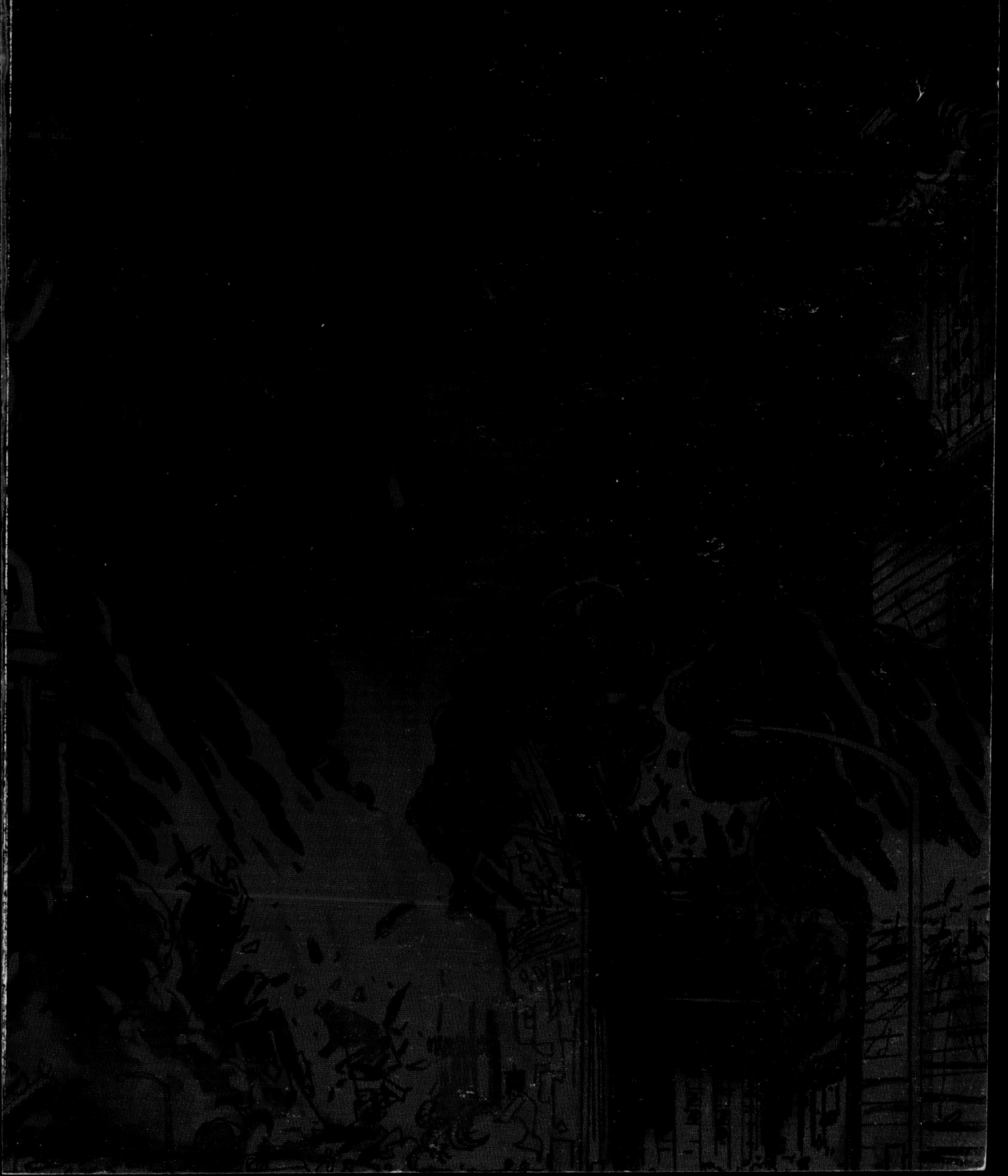

DOMINION

ROSS RICHIE AND KEITH GIFFEN
CONCEPT

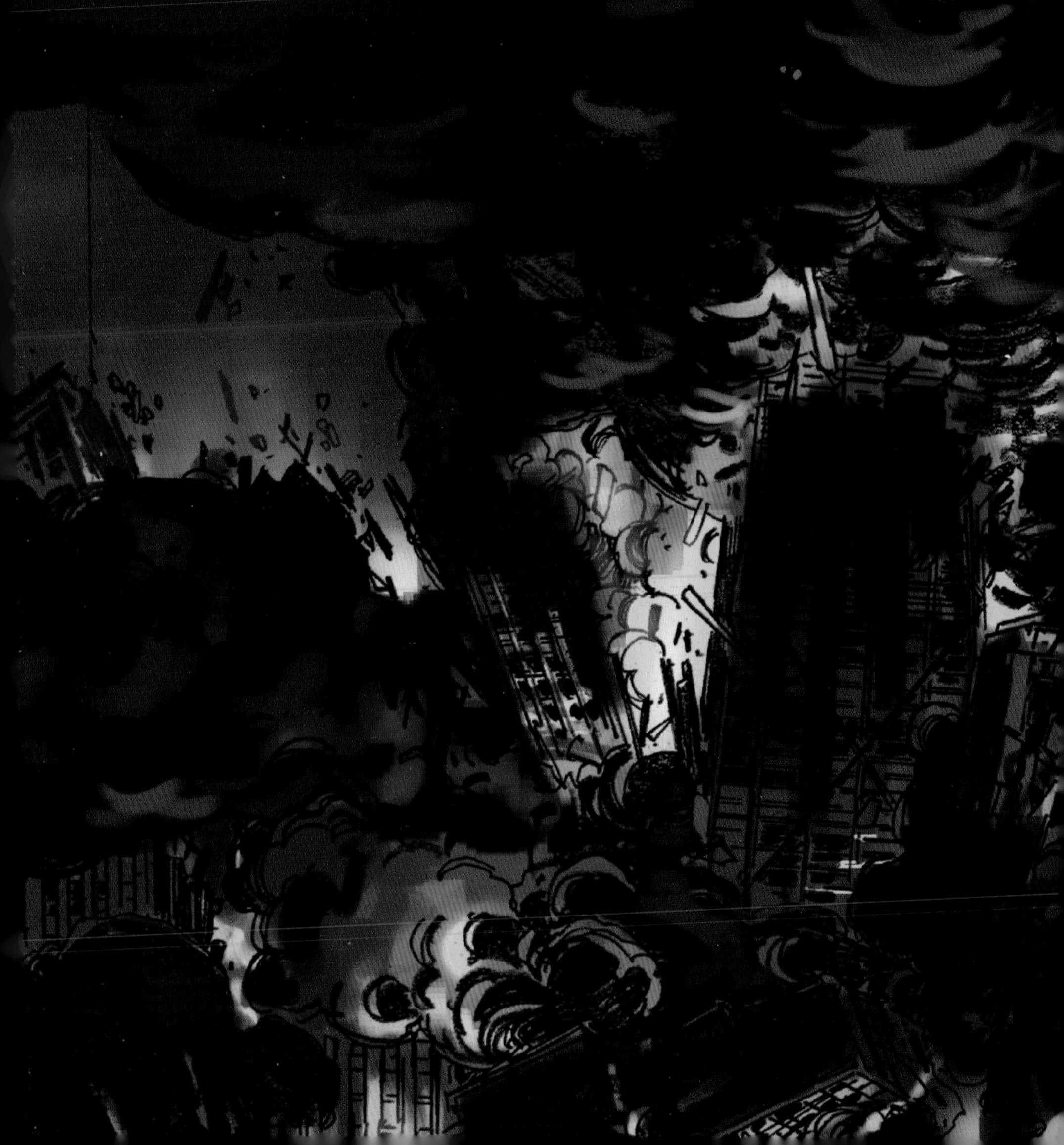

MICHAEL ALAN NELSON
WRITER

TIM HAMILTON
ARTIST

FRAN GAMBOA AND PABLO QUILIGOTTI
COLORISTS

MARSHALL DILLON
LETTERER AND MANAGING EDITOR

JOYCE EL HAYEK
ASSISTANT EDITOR

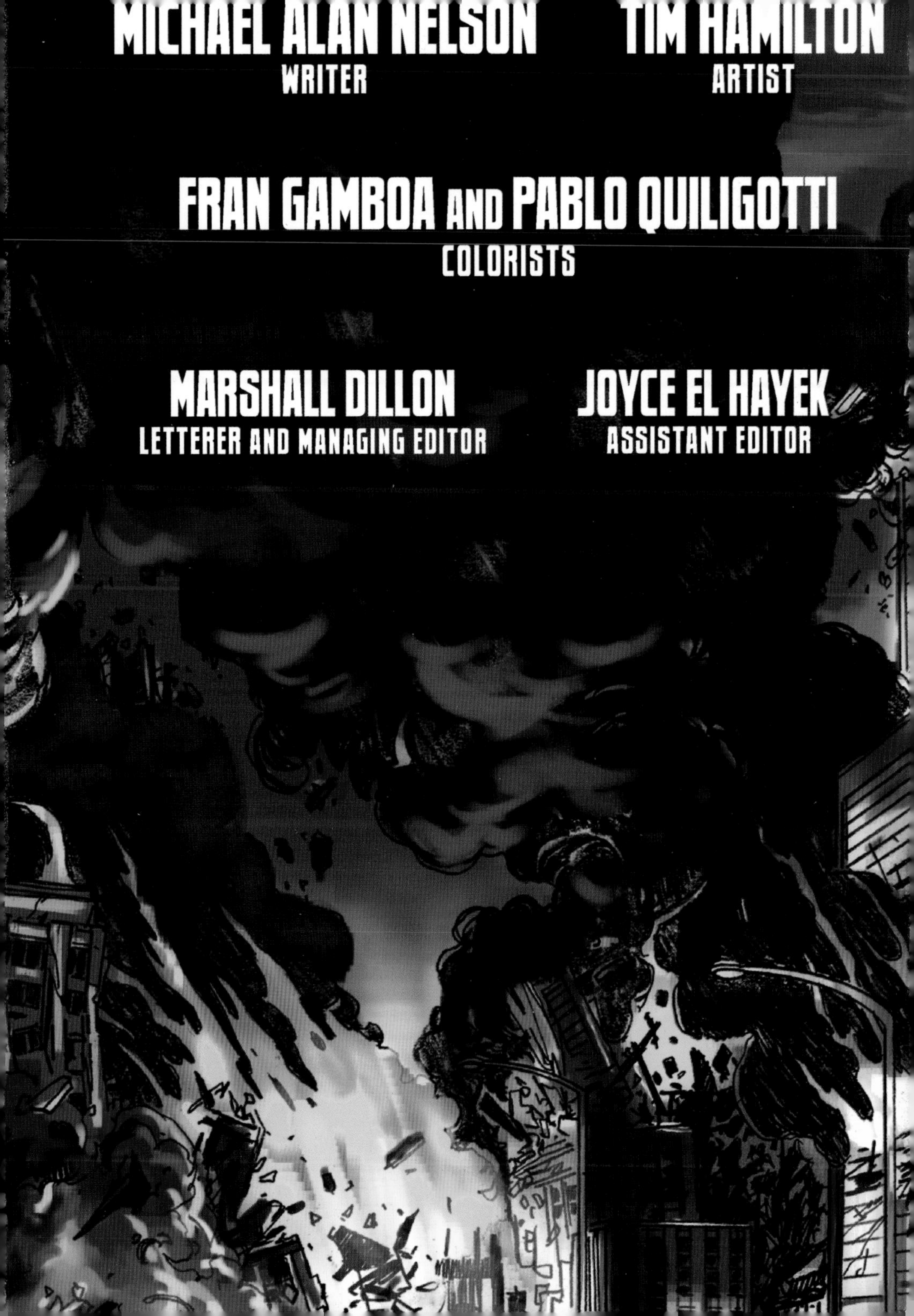

ANDREW COSBY
ROSS RICHIE
founders

MARK WAID
editor-in-chief

WENDY WALLACE
general manager

ADAM FORTIER
vice president,
new business

CHIP MOSHER
marketing &
sales director

ED DUKESHIRE
designer

Dominion — published by Boom! Studios. Dominion is copyright © Boom Entertainment, Inc. and Keith Giffen. Boom! Studios ™ and the Boom! logo are trademarks of Boom Entertainment, Inc., registered in various countries and categories. All rights reserved. The characters and events depicted herein are fictional. Any similarity to actual persons, demons, anti-Christs, aliens, vampires, face-suckers or political figures, whether living, dead or undead, or to any actual or supernatural events is coincidental and unintentional. So don't come whining to us.

Office of publication: 6310 San Vicente Blvd, Ste 404, Los Angeles, CA 90048-5457.

First Edition: June 2008

10 9 8 7 6 5 4 3 2 1
PRINTED IN KOREA

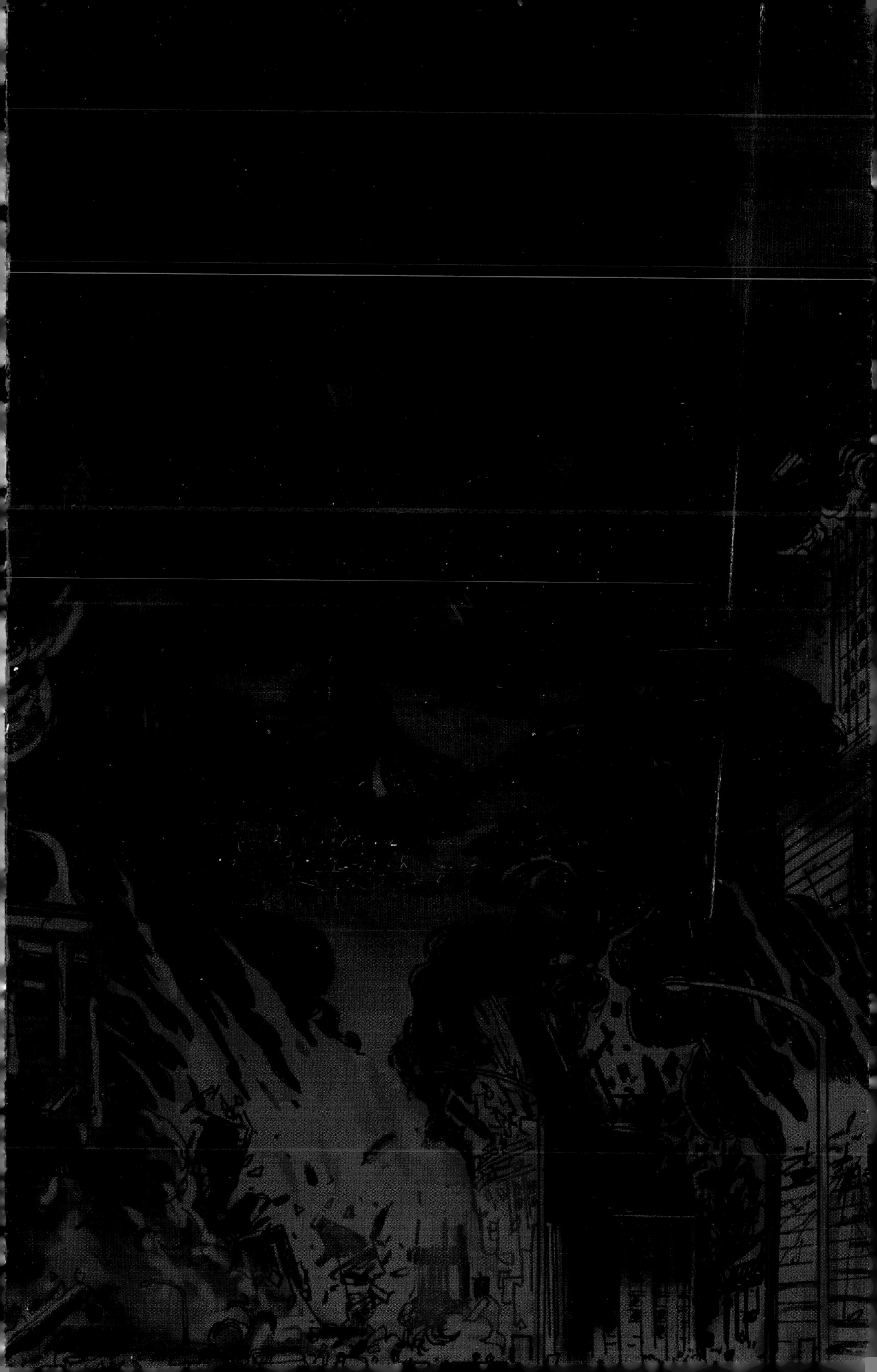

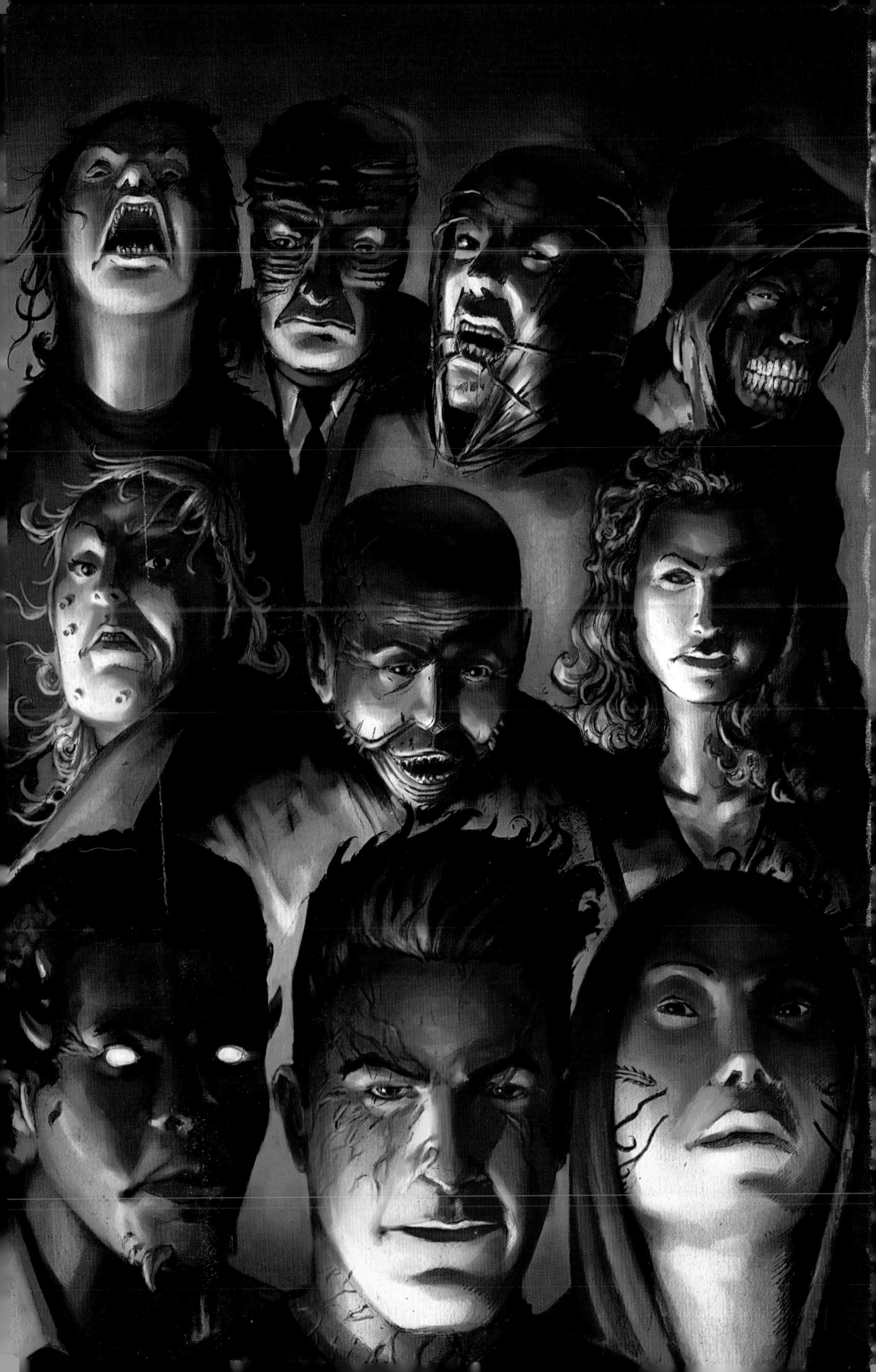

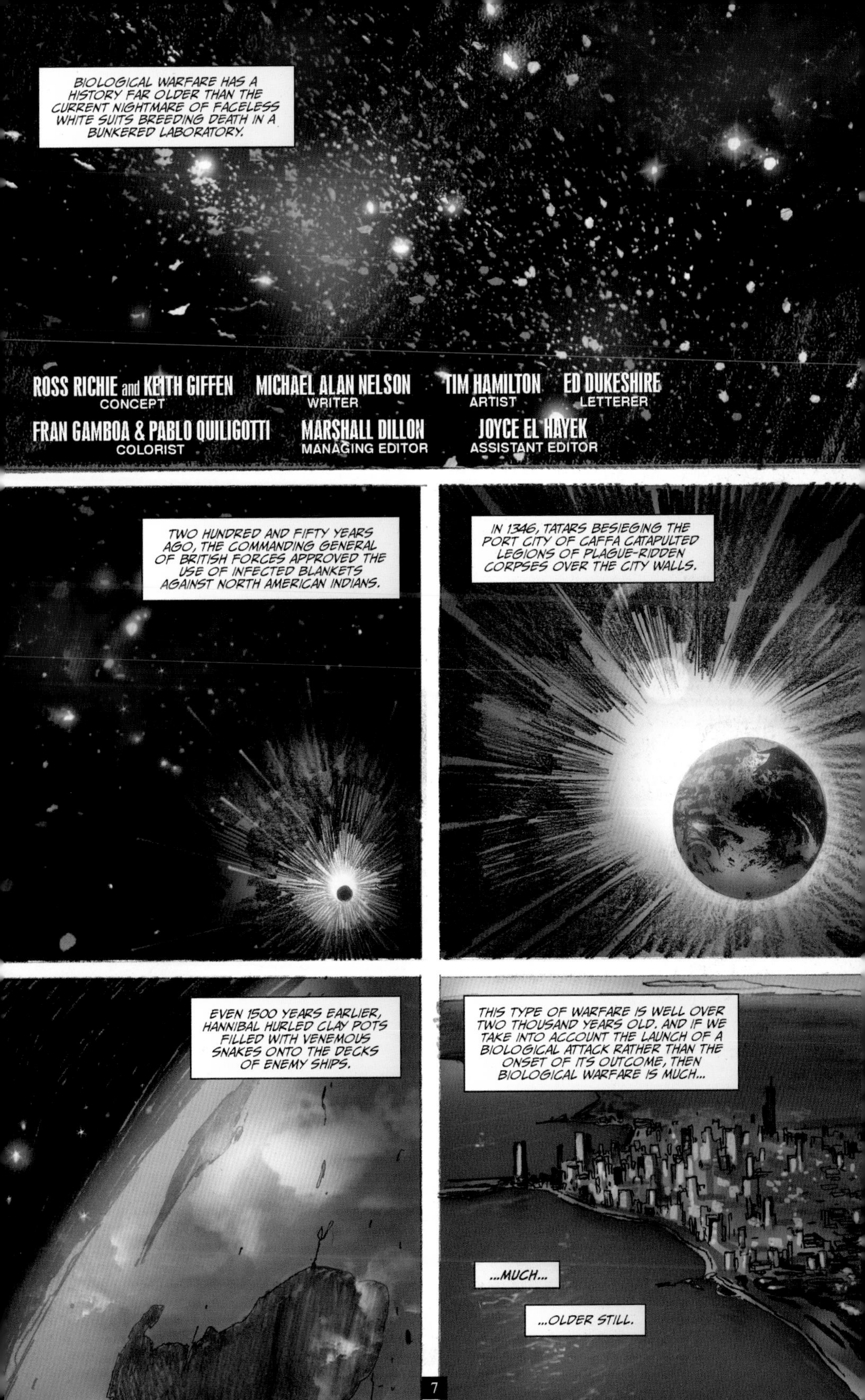
BIOLOGICAL WARFARE HAS A HISTORY FAR OLDER THAN THE CURRENT NIGHTMARE OF FACELESS WHITE SUITS BREEDING DEATH IN A BUNKERED LABORATORY.
ROSS RICHIE and KEITH GIFFEN
CONCEPT
MICHAEL ALAN NELSON
WRITER
TIM HAMILTON
ARTIST
ED DUKESHIRE
LETTERER
FRAN GAMBOA & PABLO QUILIGOTTI
COLORIST
MARSHALL DILLON
MANAGING EDITOR
JOYCE EL HAYEK
ASSISTANT EDITOR
TWO HUNDRED AND FIFTY YEARS AGO, THE COMMANDING GENERAL OF BRITISH FORCES APPROVED THE USE OF INFECTED BLANKETS AGAINST NORTH AMERICAN INDIANS.
IN 1346, TATARS BESIEGING THE PORT CITY OF CAFFA CATAPULTED LEGIONS OF PLAGUE-RIDDEN CORPSES OVER THE CITY WALLS.
EVEN 1500 YEARS EARLIER, HANNIBAL HURLED CLAY POTS FILLED WITH VENEMOUS SNAKES ONTO THE DECKS OF ENEMY SHIPS.
THIS TYPE OF WARFARE IS WELL OVER TWO THOUSAND YEARS OLD. AND IF WE TAKE INTO ACCOUNT THE LAUNCH OF A BIOLOGICAL ATTACK RATHER THAN THE ONSET OF ITS OUTCOME, THEN BIOLOGICAL WARFARE IS MUCH...
...MUCH...
...OLDER STILL.

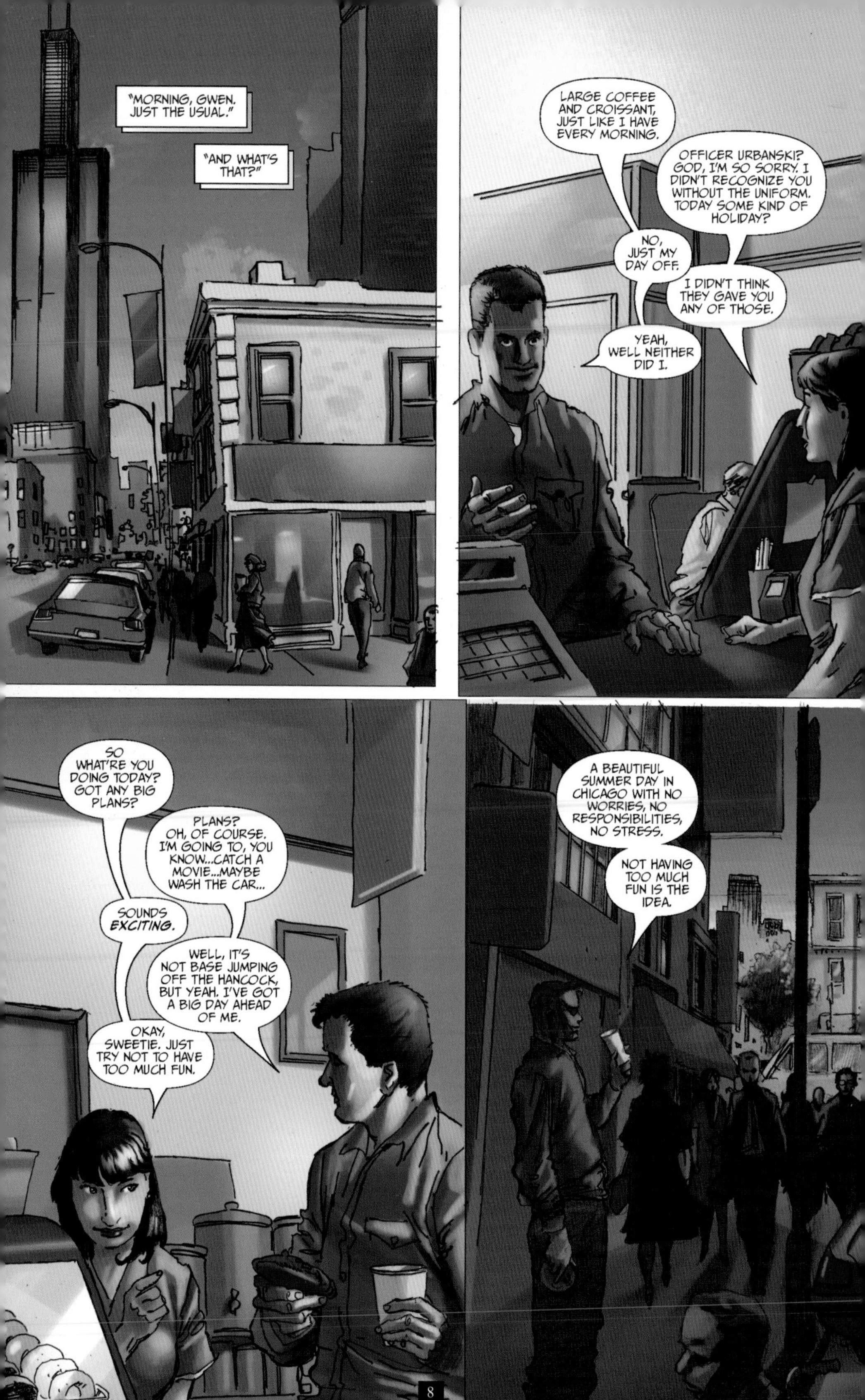
"MORNING, GWEN. JUST THE USUAL."
"AND WHAT'S THAT?"
LARGE COFFEE AND CROISSANT, JUST LIKE I HAVE EVERY MORNING.
OFFICER URBANSKI? GOD, I'M SO SORRY. I DIDN'T RECOGNIZE YOU WITHOUT THE UNIFORM. TODAY SOME KIND OF HOLIDAY?
NO, JUST MY DAY OFF.
I DIDN'T THINK THEY GAVE YOU ANY OF THOSE.
YEAH, WELL NEITHER DID I.
SO WHAT'RE YOU DOING TODAY? GOT ANY BIG PLANS?
PLANS? OH, OF COURSE. I'M GOING TO, YOU KNOW...CATCH A MOVIE...MAYBE WASH THE CAR...
SOUNDS *EXCITING*.
WELL, IT'S NOT BASE JUMPING OFF THE HANCOCK, BUT YEAH. I'VE GOT A BIG DAY AHEAD OF ME.
OKAY, SWEETIE. JUST TRY NOT TO HAVE TOO MUCH FUN.
A BEAUTIFUL SUMMER DAY IN CHICAGO WITH NO WORRIES, NO RESPONSIBILITIES, NO STRESS.
NOT HAVING TOO MUCH FUN IS THE IDEA.

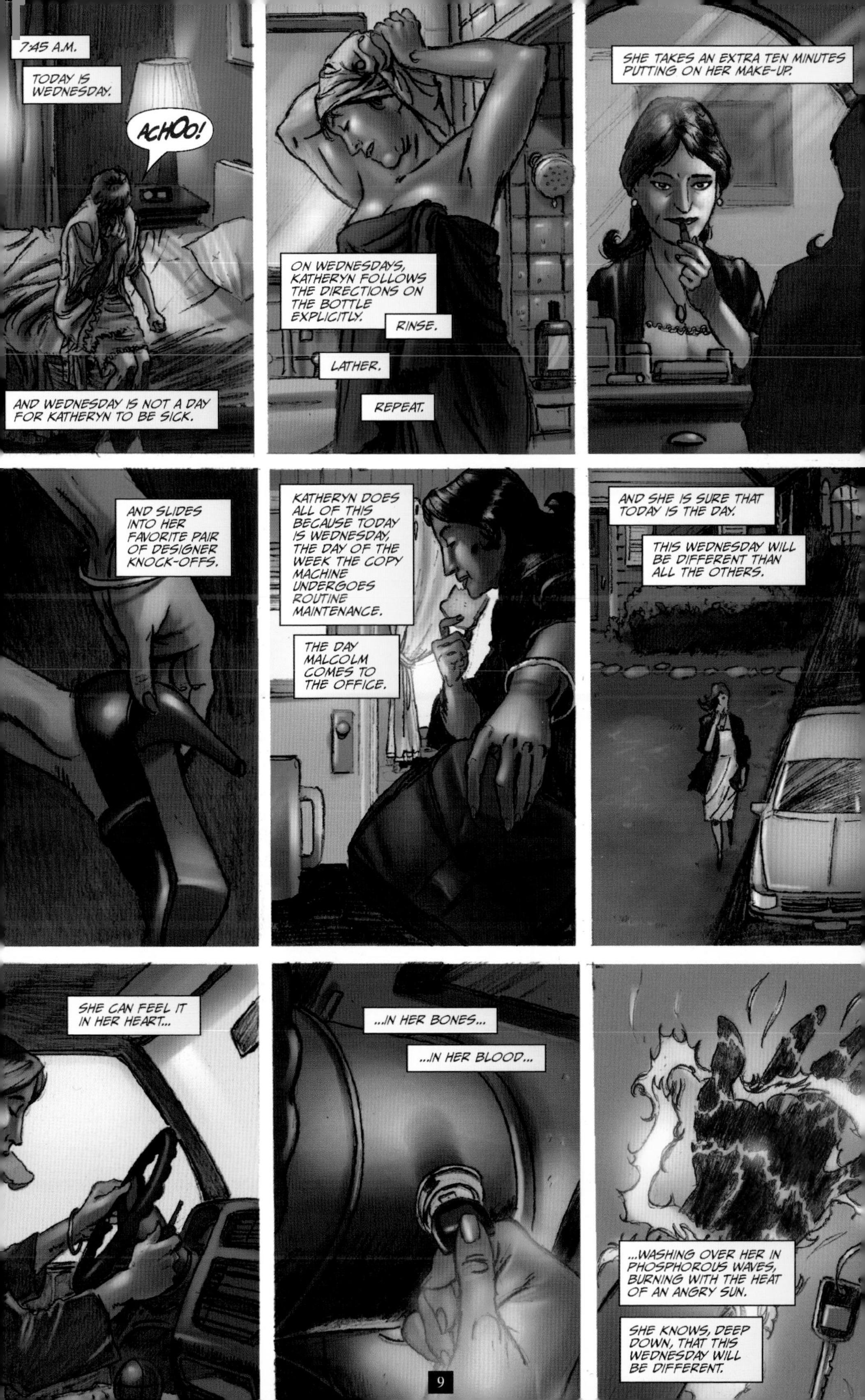
7:45 A.M.
TODAY IS WEDNESDAY.
ACHOO!
AND WEDNESDAY IS NOT A DAY FOR KATHERYN TO BE SICK.
ON WEDNESDAYS, KATHERYN FOLLOWS THE DIRECTIONS ON THE BOTTLE EXPLICITLY.
RINSE.
LATHER.
REPEAT.
SHE TAKES AN EXTRA TEN MINUTES PUTTING ON HER MAKE-UP.
AND SLIDES INTO HER FAVORITE PAIR OF DESIGNER KNOCK-OFFS.
KATHERYN DOES ALL OF THIS BECAUSE TODAY IS WEDNESDAY, THE DAY OF THE WEEK THE COPY MACHINE UNDERGOES ROUTINE MAINTENANCE.
THE DAY MALCOLM COMES TO THE OFFICE.
AND SHE IS SURE THAT TODAY IS THE DAY.
THIS WEDNESDAY WILL BE DIFFERENT THAN ALL THE OTHERS.
SHE CAN FEEL IT IN HER HEART...
...IN HER BONES...
...IN HER BLOOD...
...WASHING OVER HER IN PHOSPHOROUS WAVES, BURNING WITH THE HEAT OF AN ANGRY SUN.
SHE KNOWS, DEEP DOWN, THAT THIS WEDNESDAY WILL BE DIFFERENT.

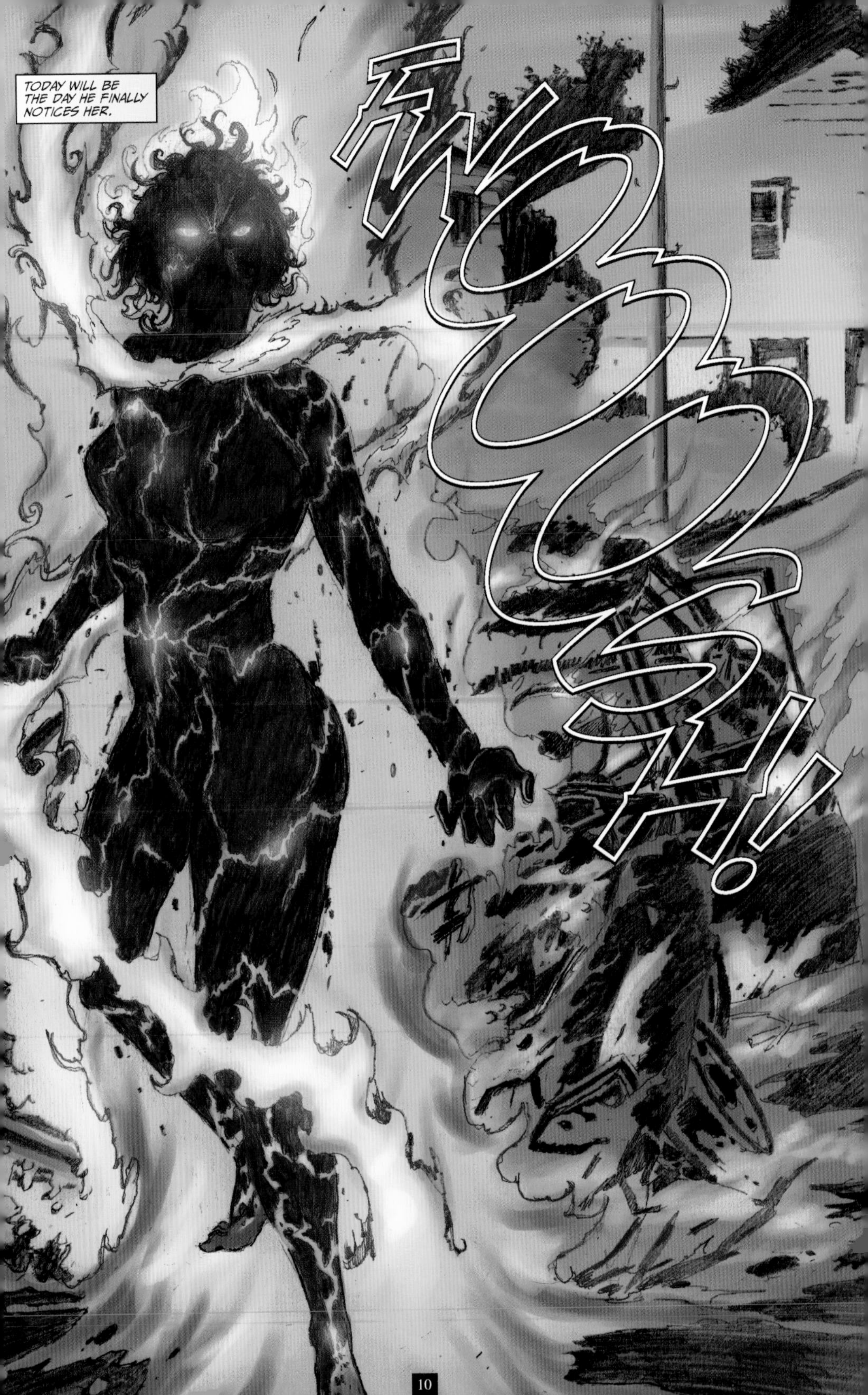
TODAY WILL BE THE DAY HE FINALLY NOTICES HER.
FWOOOOSSH!!

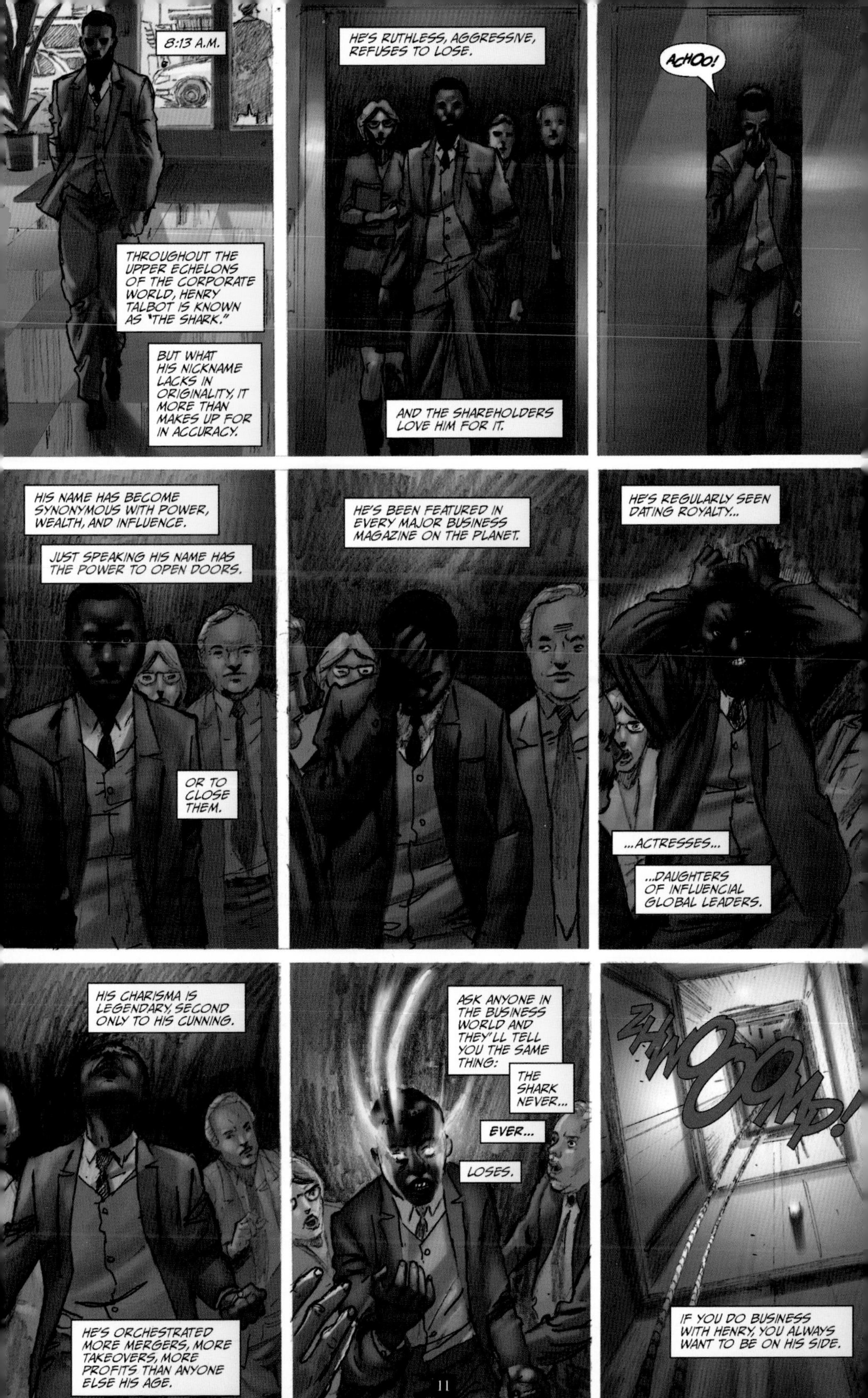
8:13 A.M.
THROUGHOUT THE UPPER ECHELONS OF THE CORPORATE WORLD, HENRY TALBOT IS KNOWN AS "THE SHARK."
BUT WHAT HIS NICKNAME LACKS IN ORIGINALITY, IT MORE THAN MAKES UP FOR IN ACCURACY.
HE'S RUTHLESS, AGGRESSIVE, REFUSES TO LOSE.
AND THE SHAREHOLDERS LOVE HIM FOR IT.
ACHOO!
HIS NAME HAS BECOME SYNONYMOUS WITH POWER, WEALTH, AND INFLUENCE.
JUST SPEAKING HIS NAME HAS THE POWER TO OPEN DOORS.
OR TO CLOSE THEM.
HE'S BEEN FEATURED IN EVERY MAJOR BUSINESS MAGAZINE ON THE PLANET.
HE'S REGULARLY SEEN DATING ROYALTY...
...ACTRESSES...
...DAUGHTERS OF INFLUENCIAL GLOBAL LEADERS.
HIS CHARISMA IS LEGENDARY, SECOND ONLY TO HIS CUNNING.
HE'S ORCHESTRATED MORE MERGERS, MORE TAKEOVERS, MORE PROFITS THAN ANYONE ELSE HIS AGE.
ASK ANYONE IN THE BUSINESS WORLD AND THEY'LL TELL YOU THE SAME THING:
THE SHARK NEVER...
EVER...
LOSES.
ZHWOOOMP!
IF YOU DO BUSINESS WITH HENRY, YOU ALWAYS WANT TO BE ON HIS SIDE.

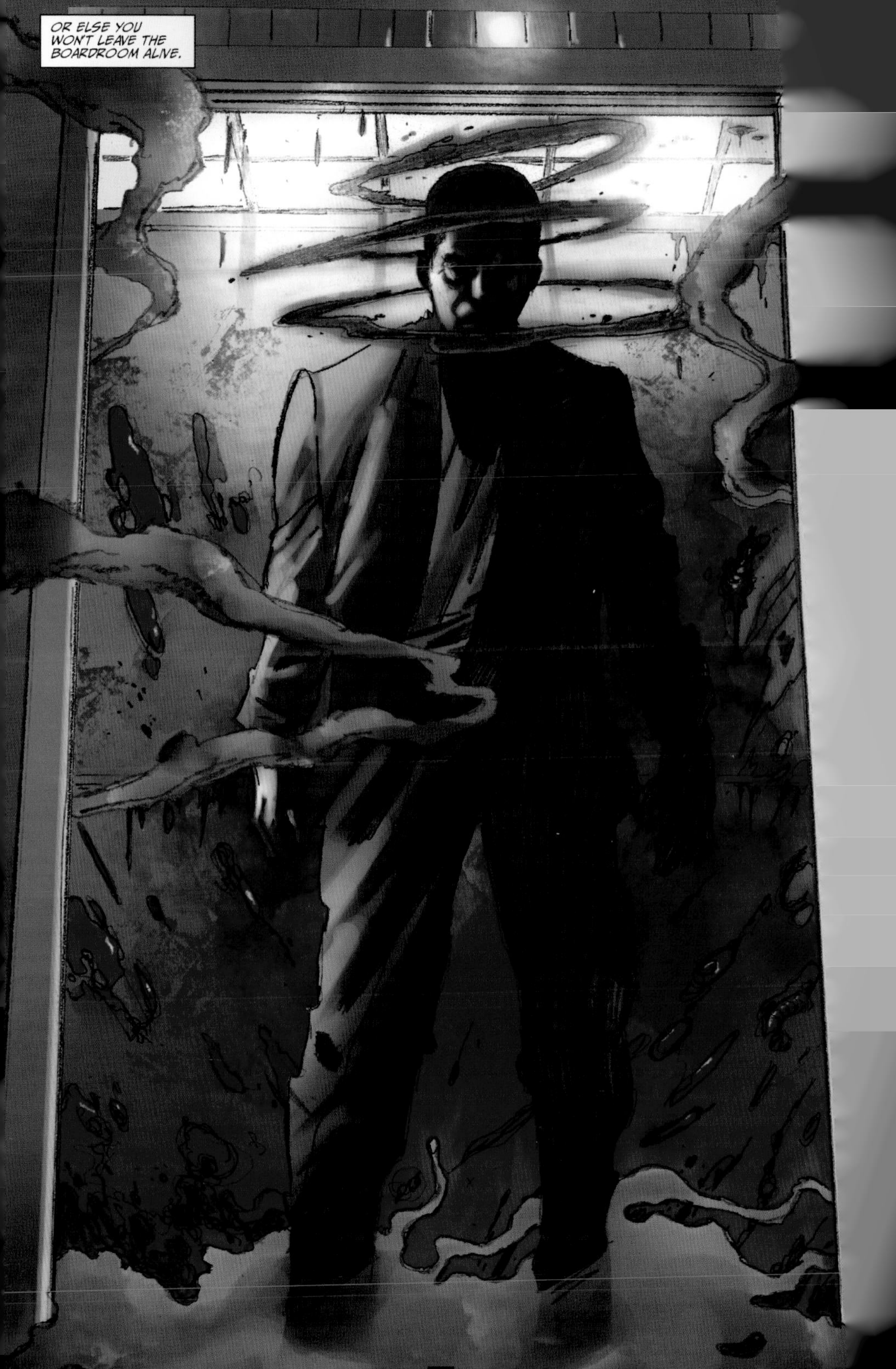
OR ELSE YOU WON'T LEAVE THE BOARDROOM ALIVE.

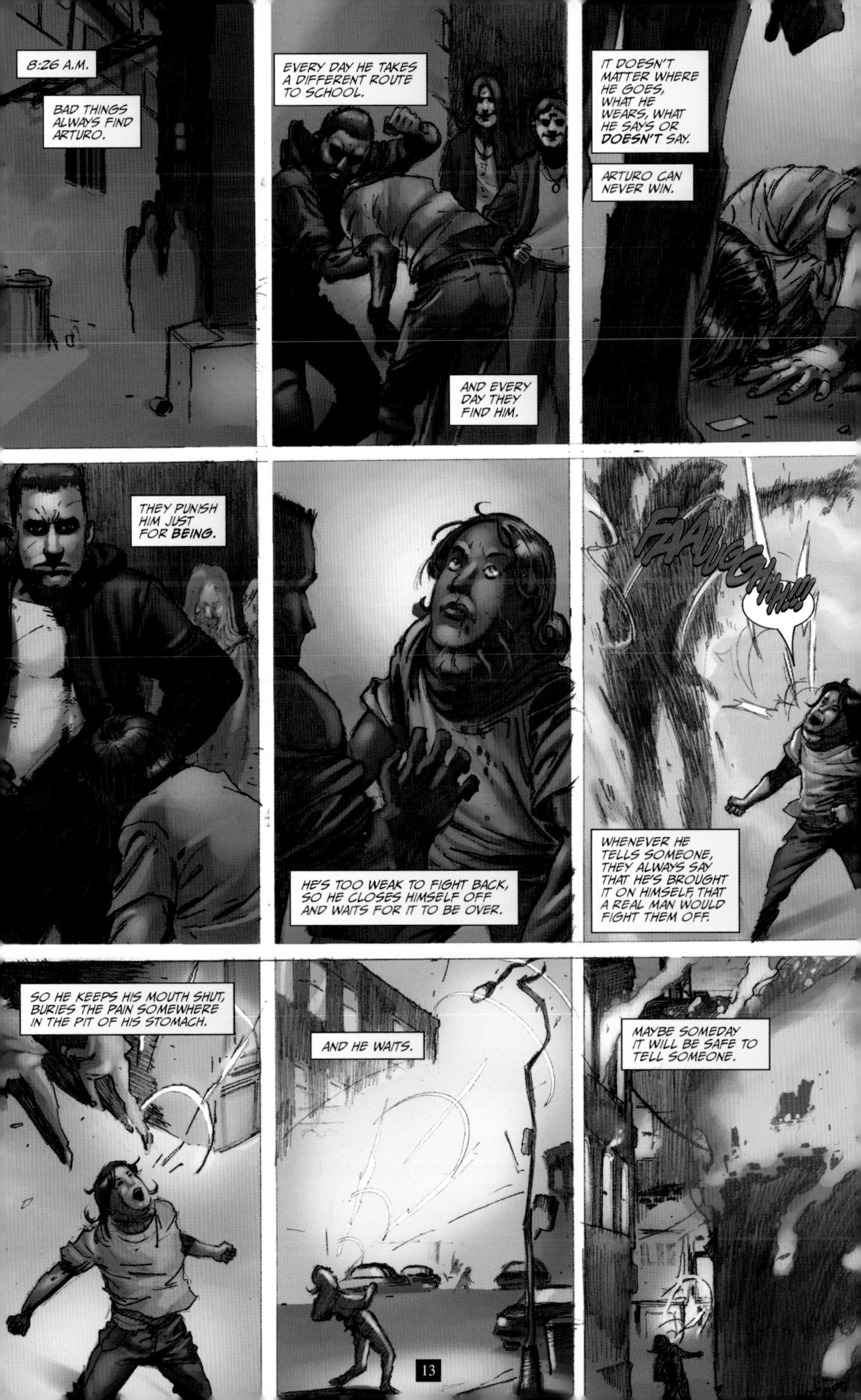
8:26 A.M.
BAD THINGS ALWAYS FIND ARTURO.
EVERY DAY HE TAKES A DIFFERENT ROUTE TO SCHOOL.
AND EVERY DAY THEY FIND HIM.
IT DOESN'T MATTER WHERE HE GOES, WHAT HE WEARS, WHAT HE SAYS OR DOESN'T SAY.
ARTURO CAN NEVER WIN.
THEY PUNISH HIM JUST FOR BEING.
HE'S TOO WEAK TO FIGHT BACK, SO HE CLOSES HIMSELF OFF AND WAITS FOR IT TO BE OVER.
FAAUGGHHH!!
WHENEVER HE TELLS SOMEONE, THEY ALWAYS SAY THAT HE'S BROUGHT IT ON HIMSELF, THAT A REAL MAN WOULD FIGHT THEM OFF.
SO HE KEEPS HIS MOUTH SHUT, BURIES THE PAIN SOMEWHERE IN THE PIT OF HIS STOMACH.
AND HE WAITS.
MAYBE SOMEDAY IT WILL BE SAFE TO TELL SOMEONE.

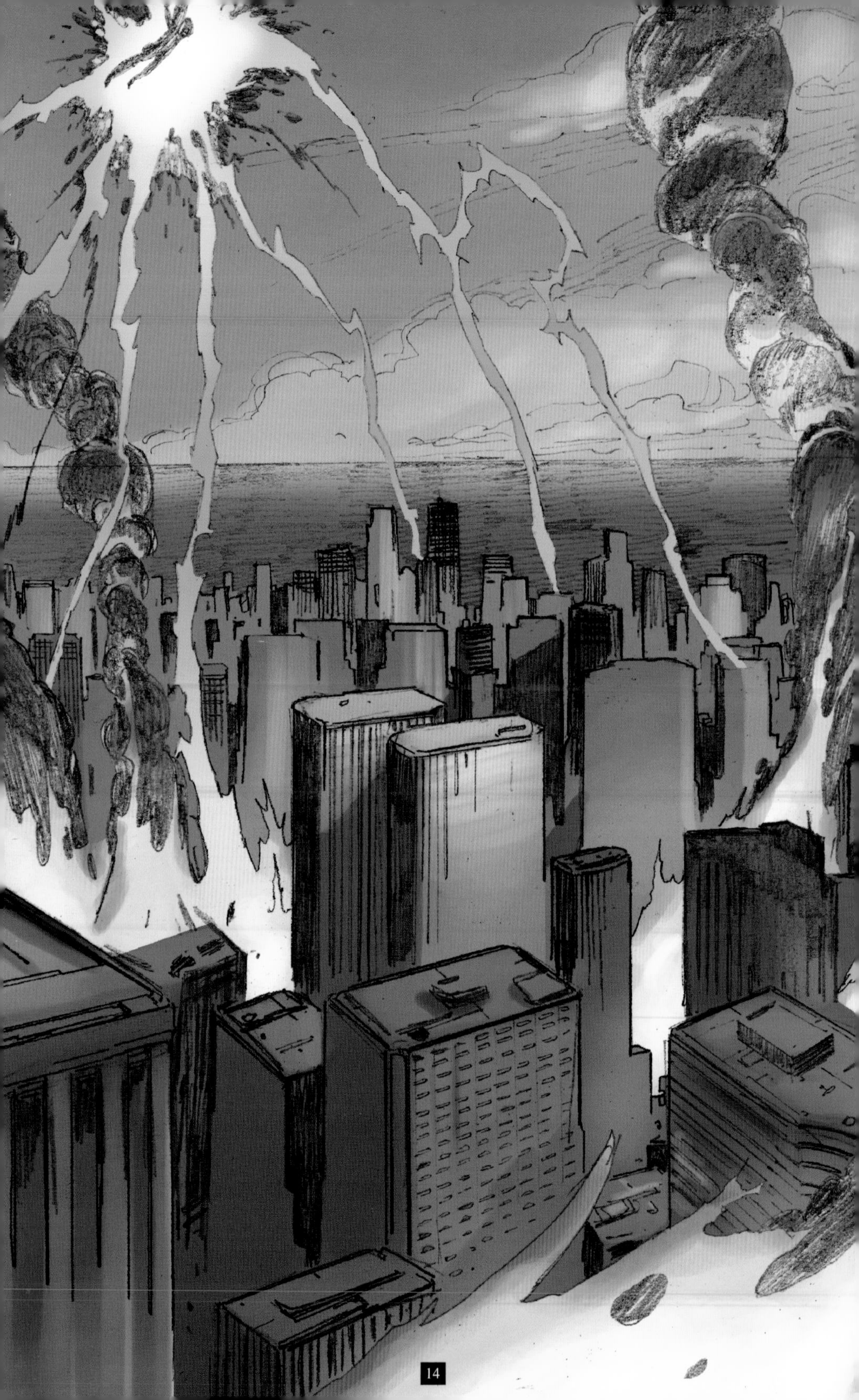

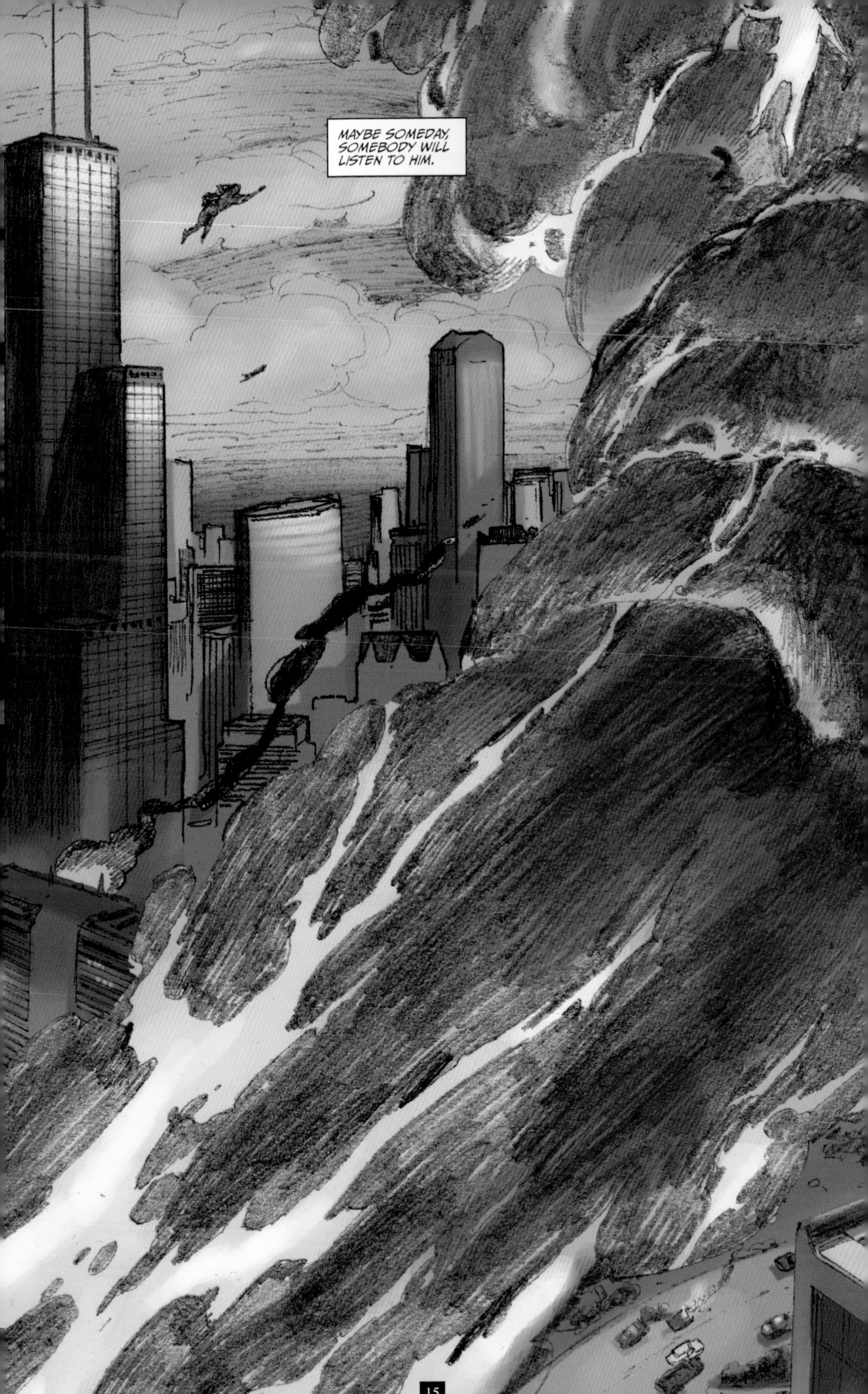
MAYBE SOMEDAY, SOMEBODY WILL LISTEN TO HIM.

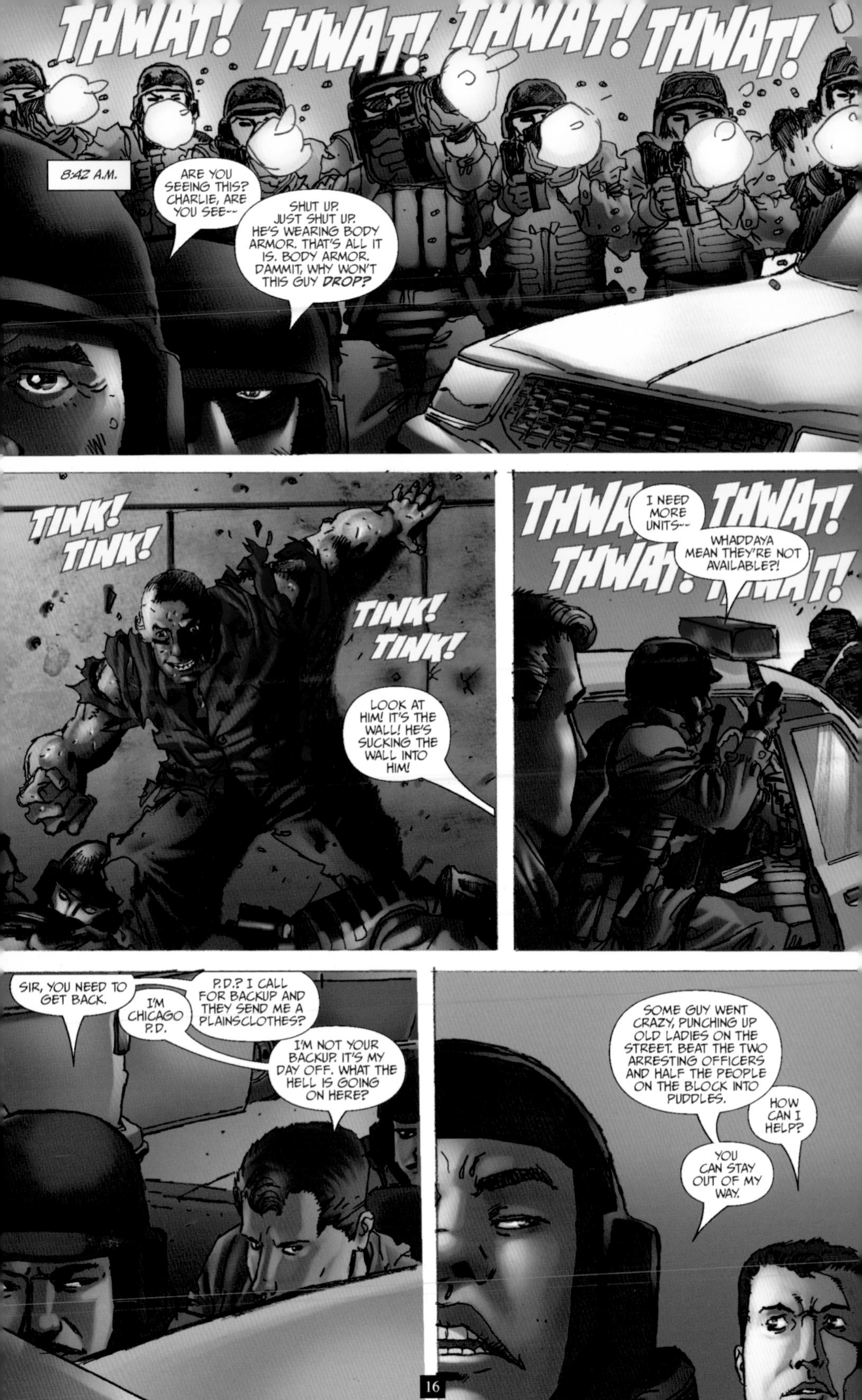

THWAT! THWAT! THWAT! THWAT!
8:42 A.M.
ARE YOU SEEING THIS? CHARLIE, ARE YOU SEE--
SHUT UP. JUST SHUT UP. HE'S WEARING BODY ARMOR. THAT'S ALL IT IS. BODY ARMOR. DAMMIT, WHY WON'T THIS GUY DROP?
TINK! TINK!
TINK! TINK!
LOOK AT HIM! IT'S THE WALL! HE'S SUCKING THE WALL INTO HIM!
THWAT! THWAT!
I NEED MORE UNITS--
WHADDAYA MEAN THEY'RE NOT AVAILABLE?!
SIR, YOU NEED TO GET BACK.
I'M CHICAGO P.D.
P.D.? I CALL FOR BACKUP AND THEY SEND ME A PLAINSCLOTHES?
I'M NOT YOUR BACKUP. IT'S MY DAY OFF. WHAT THE HELL IS GOING ON HERE?
SOME GUY WENT CRAZY, PUNCHING UP OLD LADIES ON THE STREET. BEAT THE TWO ARRESTING OFFICERS AND HALF THE PEOPLE ON THE BLOCK INTO PUDDLES.
HOW CAN I HELP?
YOU CAN STAY OUT OF MY WAY.

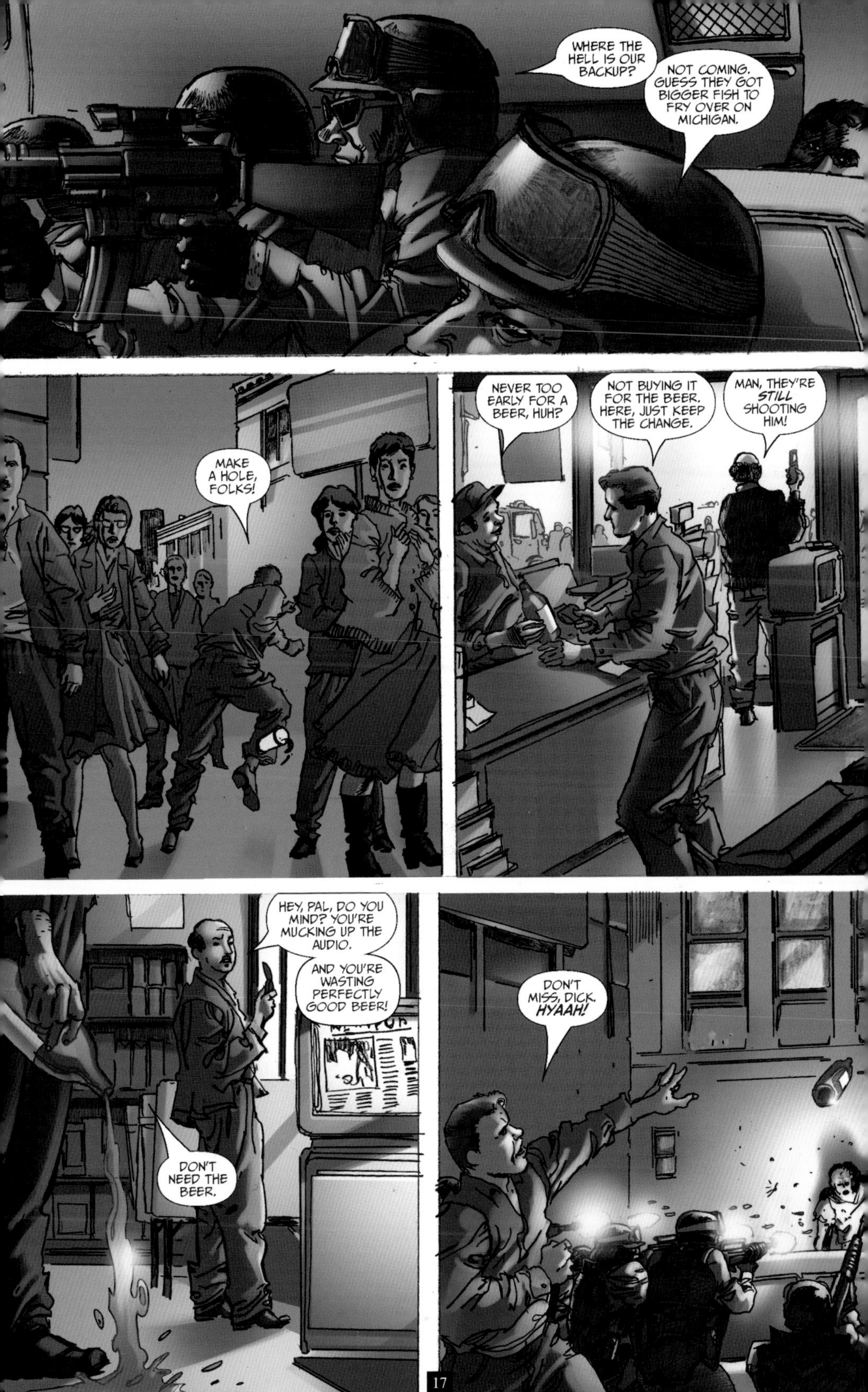
WHERE THE HELL IS OUR BACKUP?
NOT COMING. GUESS THEY GOT BIGGER FISH TO FRY OVER ON MICHIGAN.
MAKE A HOLE, FOLKS!
NEVER TOO EARLY FOR A BEER, HUH?
NOT BUYING IT FOR THE BEER. HERE, JUST KEEP THE CHANGE.
MAN, THEY'RE *STILL* SHOOTING HIM!
HEY, PAL, DO YOU MIND? YOU'RE MUCKING UP THE AUDIO.
AND YOU'RE WASTING PERFECTLY GOOD BEER!
DON'T NEED THE BEER.
DON'T MISS, DICK. ***HYAAH!***

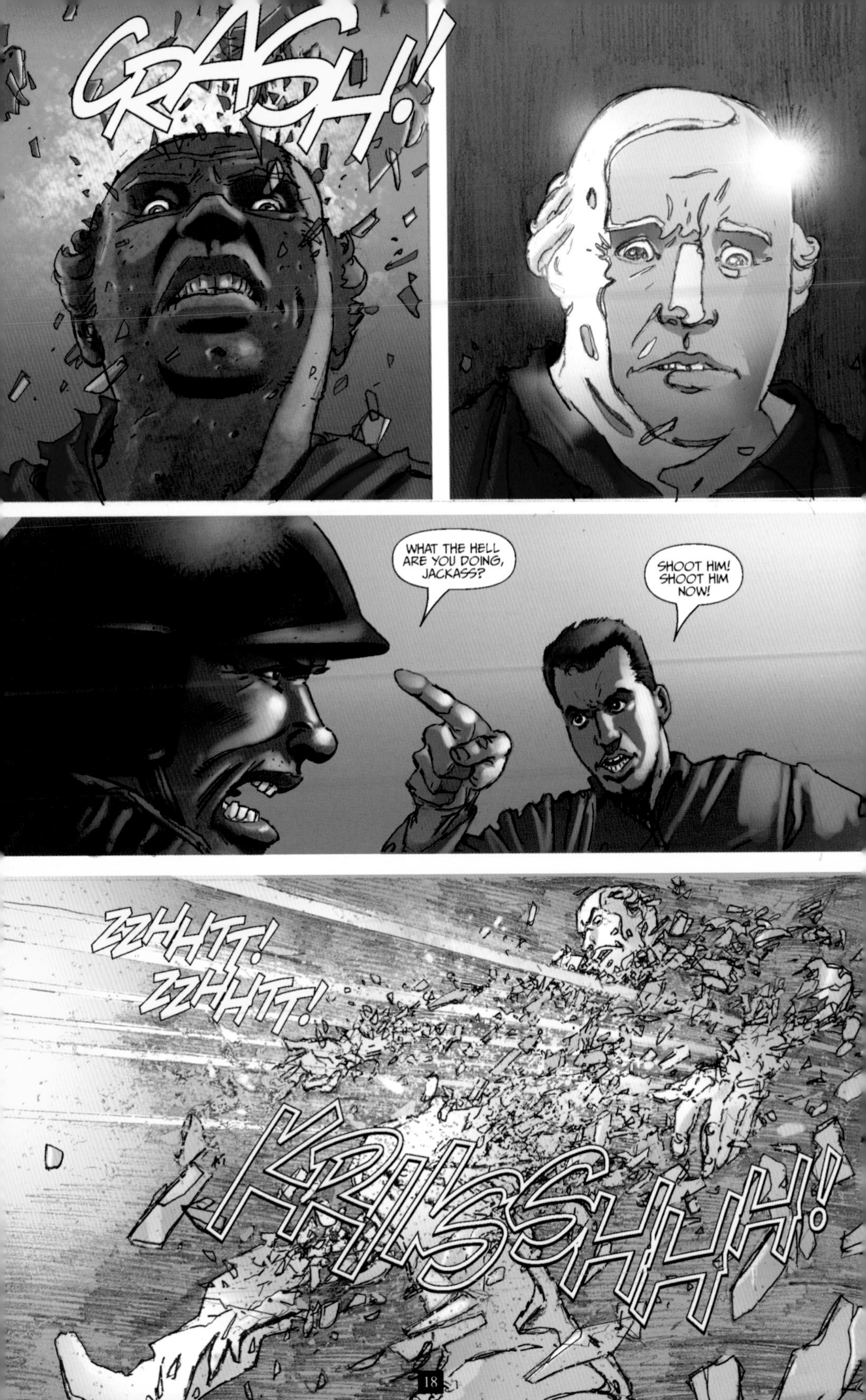
CRASH!!
WHAT THE HELL ARE YOU DOING, JACKASS?
SHOOT HIM! SHOOT HIM NOW!
ZZHHTT!
ZZHHTT!
KRHSSHH!

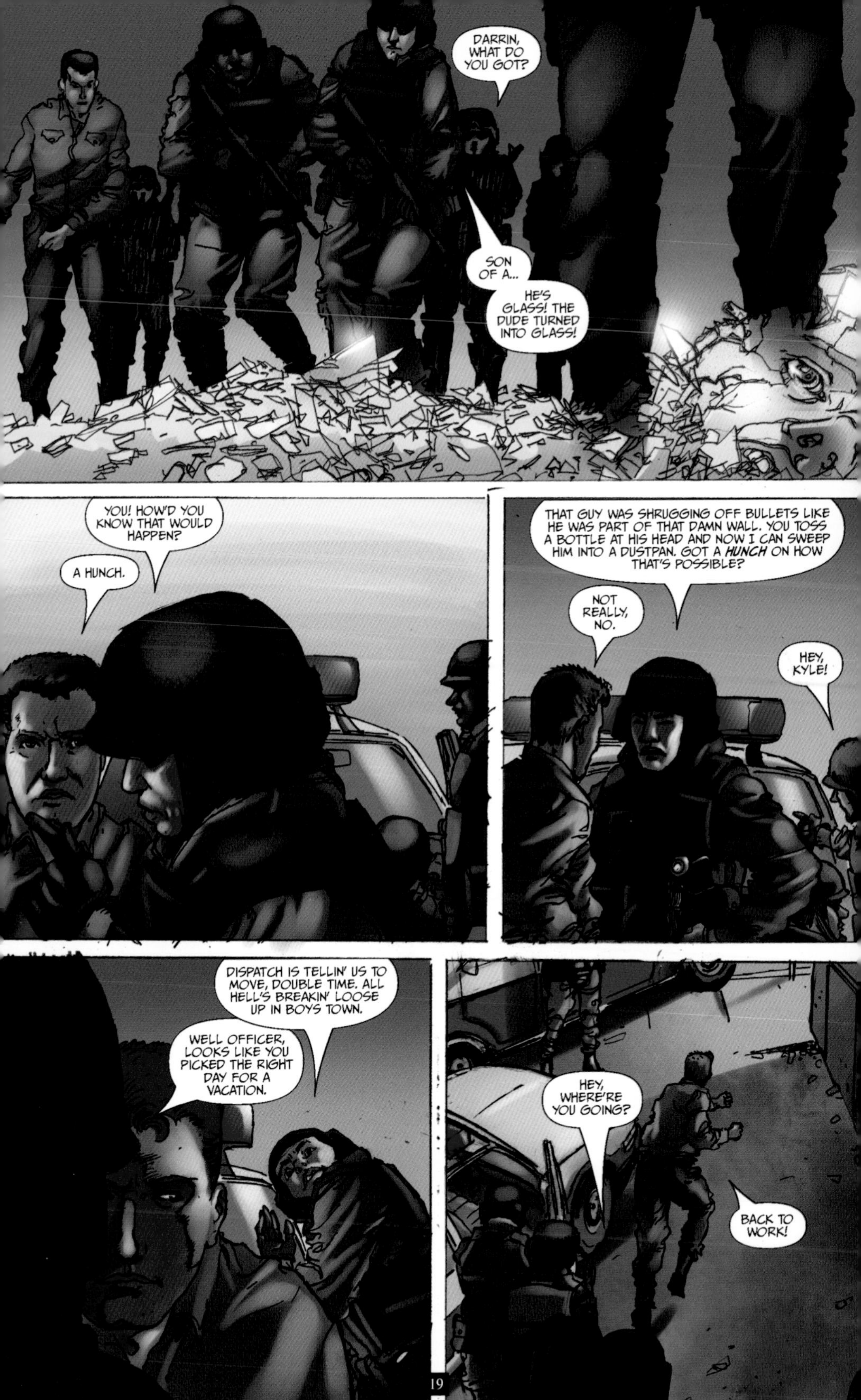
DARRIN, WHAT DO YOU GOT?
SON OF A...
HE'S GLASS! THE DUDE TURNED INTO GLASS!
YOU! HOW'D YOU KNOW THAT WOULD HAPPEN?
A HUNCH.
THAT GUY WAS SHRUGGING OFF BULLETS LIKE HE WAS PART OF THAT DAMN WALL. YOU TOSS A BOTTLE AT HIS HEAD AND NOW I CAN SWEEP HIM INTO A DUSTPAN. GOT A *HUNCH* ON HOW THAT'S POSSIBLE?
NOT REALLY, NO.
HEY, KYLE!
DISPATCH IS TELLIN' US TO MOVE, DOUBLE TIME. ALL HELL'S BREAKIN' LOOSE UP IN BOYS TOWN.
WELL OFFICER, LOOKS LIKE YOU PICKED THE RIGHT DAY FOR A VACATION.
HEY, WHERE'RE YOU GOING?
BACK TO WORK!

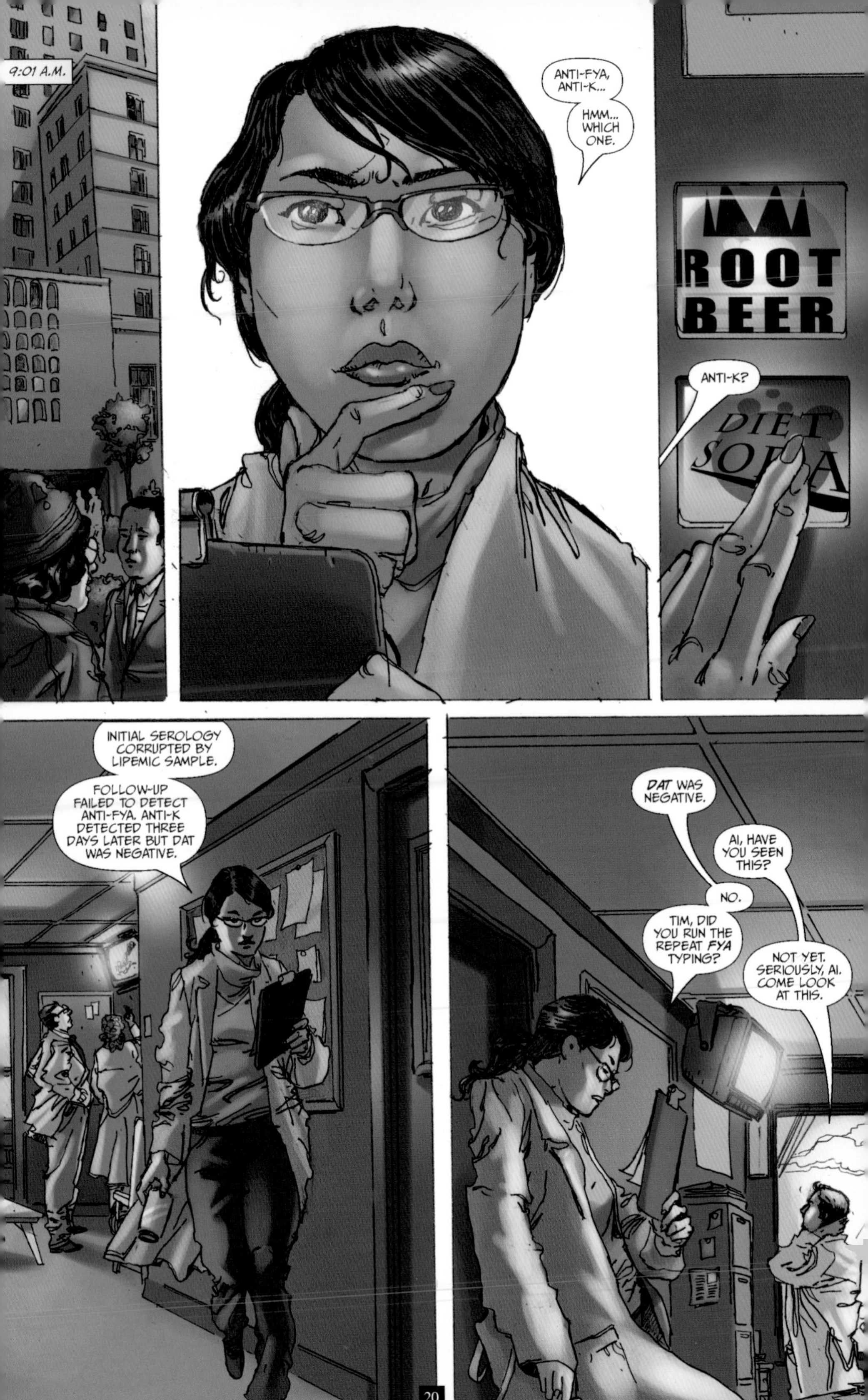
9:01 A.M.
ANTI-FYA, ANTI-K...
HMM... WHICH ONE.
ROOT BEER
DIET SODA
ANTI-K?
INITIAL SEROLOGY CORRUPTED BY LIPEMIC SAMPLE.
FOLLOW-UP FAILED TO DETECT ANTI-FYA. ANTI-K DETECTED THREE DAYS LATER BUT DAT WAS NEGATIVE.
DAT WAS NEGATIVE.
AI, HAVE YOU SEEN THIS?
NO.
TIM, DID YOU RUN THE REPEAT FYA TYPING?
NOT YET. SERIOUSLY, AI. COME LOOK AT THIS.

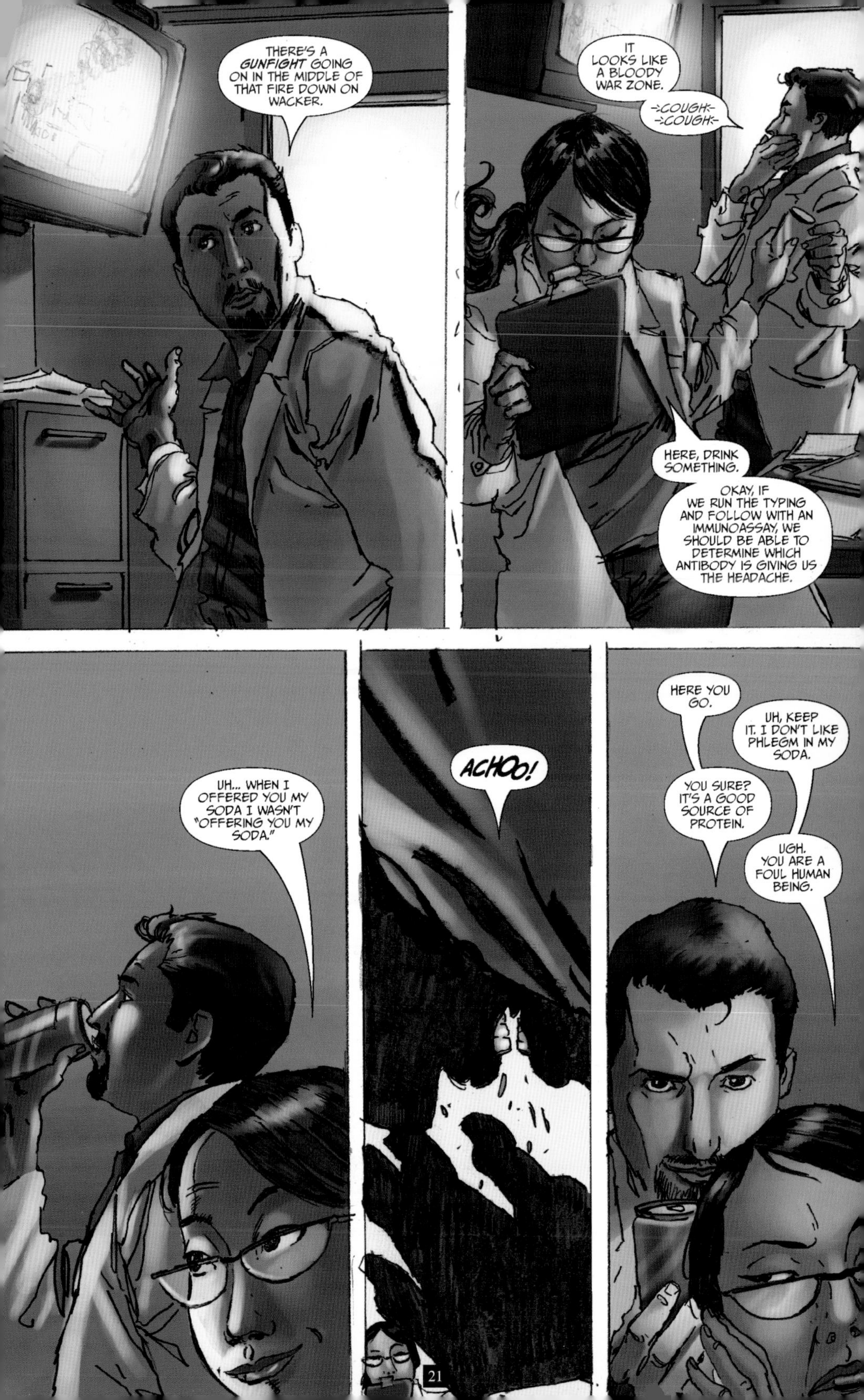

THERE'S A GUNFIGHT GOING ON IN THE MIDDLE OF THAT FIRE DOWN ON WACKER.
IT LOOKS LIKE A BLOODY WAR ZONE.
-COUGH- -COUGH-
HERE, DRINK SOMETHING.
OKAY, IF WE RUN THE TYPING AND FOLLOW WITH AN IMMUNOASSAY, WE SHOULD BE ABLE TO DETERMINE WHICH ANTIBODY IS GIVING US THE HEADACHE.
UH... WHEN I OFFERED YOU MY SODA I WASN'T "OFFERING YOU MY SODA."
ACHOO!
HERE YOU GO.
UH, KEEP IT. I DON'T LIKE PHLEGM IN MY SODA.
YOU SURE? IT'S A GOOD SOURCE OF PROTEIN.
UGH. YOU ARE A FOUL HUMAN BEING.

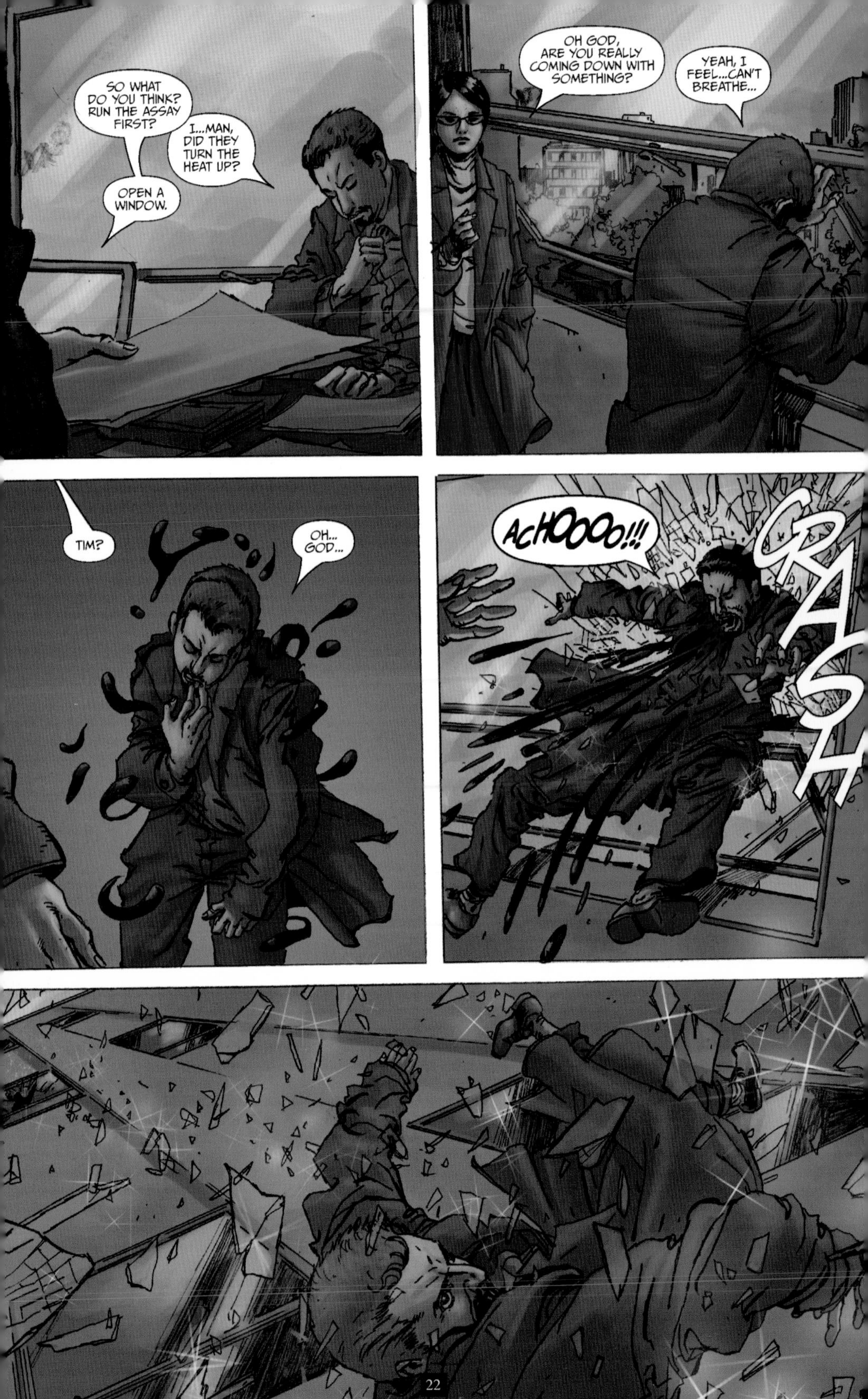
SO WHAT DO YOU THINK? RUN THE ASSAY FIRST?
OPEN A WINDOW.
I...MAN, DID THEY TURN THE HEAT UP?
OH GOD, ARE YOU REALLY COMING DOWN WITH SOMETHING?
YEAH, I FEEL...CAN'T BREATHE...
TIM?
OH... GOD...
ACHOOOO!!!
CRASH

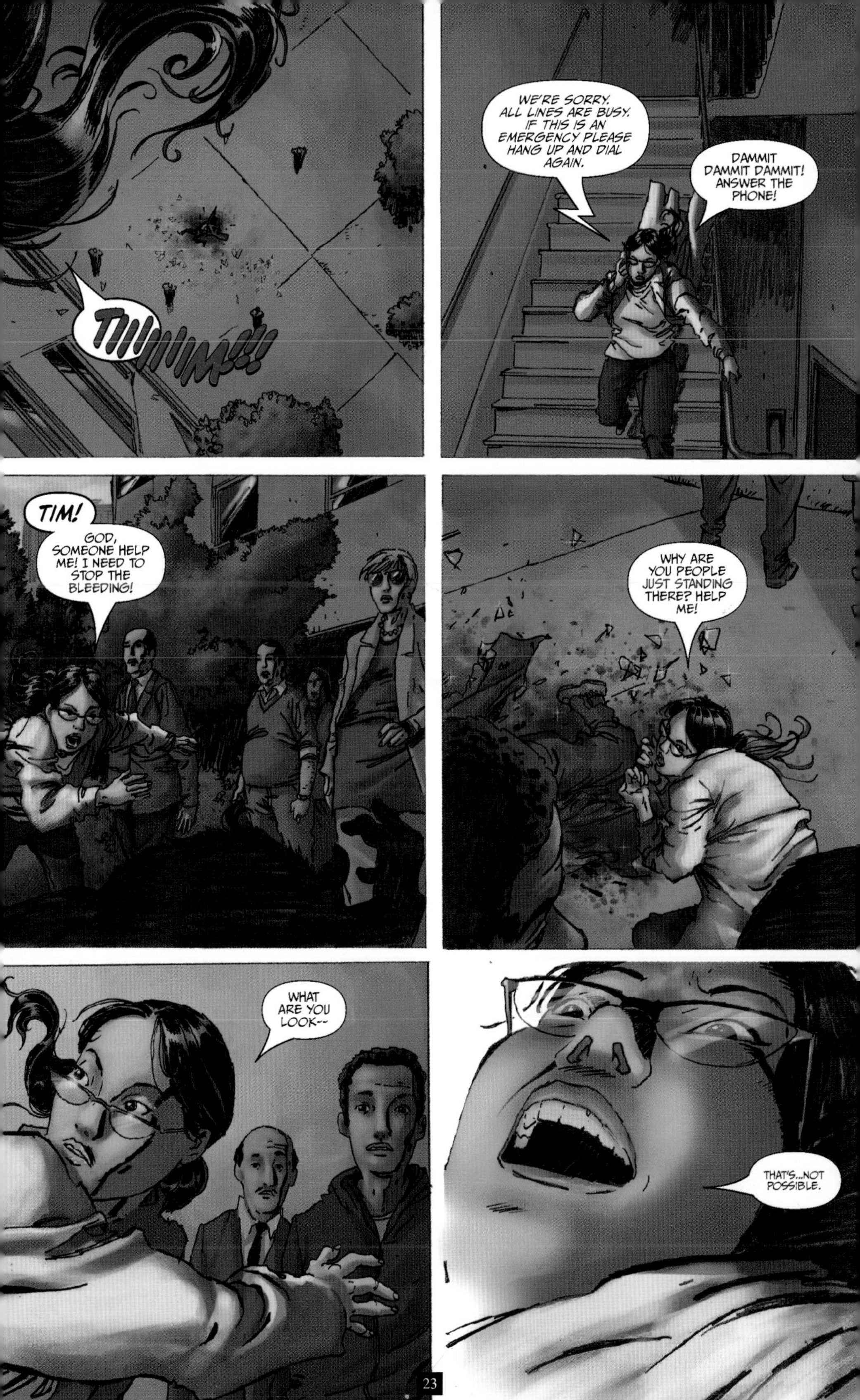
TIIIIIIIM!!!
WE'RE SORRY. ALL LINES ARE BUSY. IF THIS IS AN EMERGENCY PLEASE HANG UP AND DIAL AGAIN.
DAMMIT DAMMIT DAMMIT! ANSWER THE PHONE!
TIM!
GOD, SOMEONE HELP ME! I NEED TO STOP THE BLEEDING!
WHY ARE YOU PEOPLE JUST STANDING THERE? HELP ME!
WHAT ARE YOU LOOK--
THAT'S...NOT POSSIBLE.

9:16 A.M.

...IN THE SKY! C'MON!

...SWEAR TO GOD I SAW IT HAPPEN!

...RIGHT OUT OF HIS HEAD!

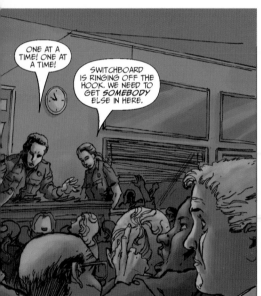

ONE AT A TIME! ONE AT A TIME!

SWITCHBOARD IS RINGING OFF THE HOOK. WE NEED TO GET *SOMEBODY* ELSE IN HERE.

EXCUSE ME, FOLKS.

...IS BURNING AND THERE AIN'T NO COPS NOWHERE!

...RIGHT THROUGH THE WALL, I'M TELLING YOU. AND WALTER'S BEEN IN THAT WHEELCHAIR FOR TEN YEARS!

URBANSKI!

...GONE. JUST GONE!

WHERE THE HELL HAVE YOU BEEN? WE'VE BEEN CALLIN' YOU IN ALL MORNING!

I RAN INTO S.W.A.T. ON GRAND AVENUE. WHAT'S GOING ON?

EITHER IT'S JUDGEMENT DAY OR SOMEONE LEFT THEIR LIGHTBRITE ON THE EL TRAIN.

EITHER WAY, THE CIRCUS IS IN TOWN.

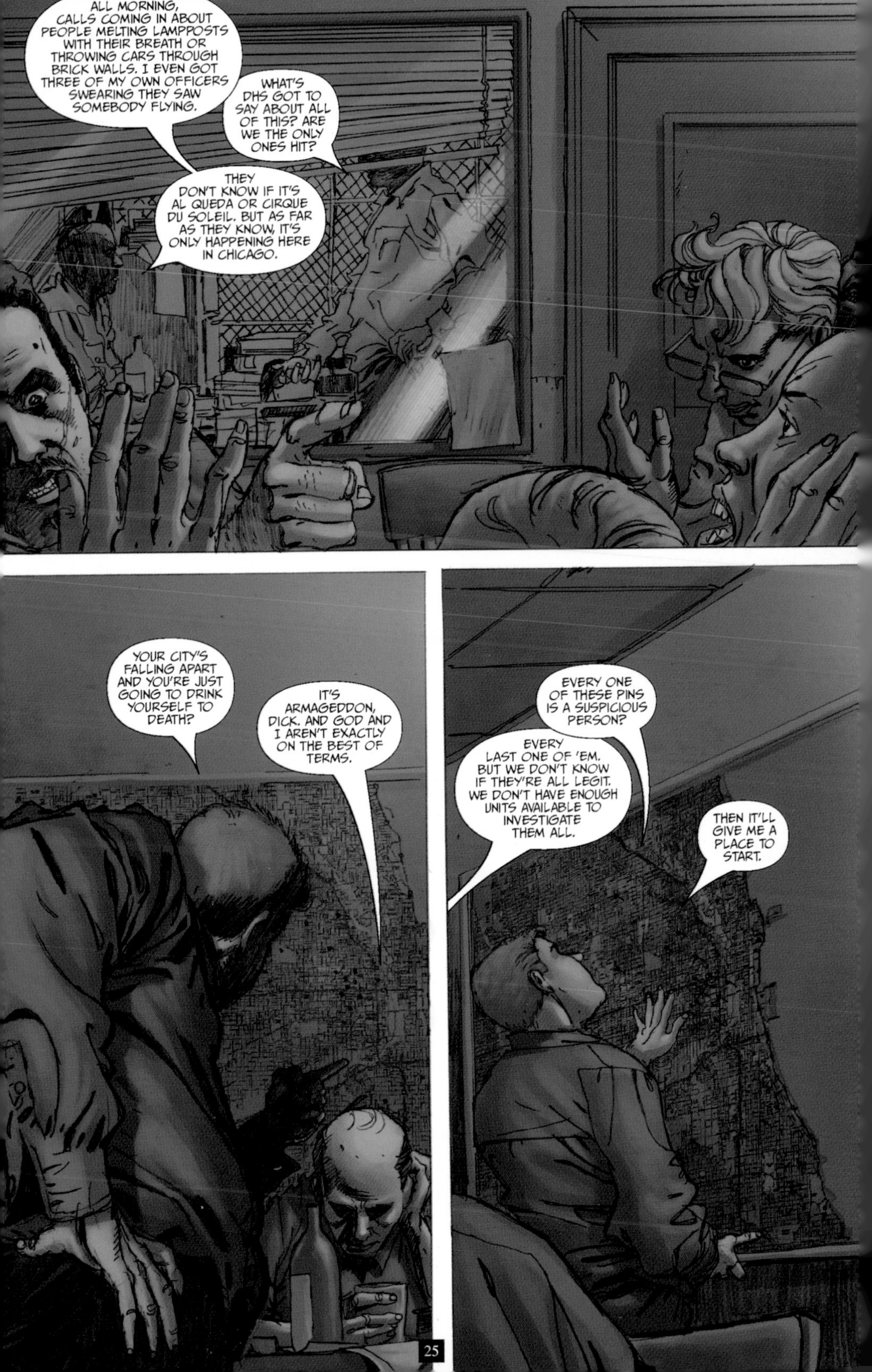
ALL MORNING, CALLS COMING IN ABOUT PEOPLE MELTING LAMPPOSTS WITH THEIR BREATH OR THROWING CARS THROUGH BRICK WALLS. I EVEN GOT THREE OF MY OWN OFFICERS SWEARING THEY SAW SOMEBODY FLYING.
WHAT'S DHS GOT TO SAY ABOUT ALL OF THIS? ARE WE THE ONLY ONES HIT?
THEY DON'T KNOW IF IT'S AL QUEDA OR CIRQUE DU SOLEIL. BUT AS FAR AS THEY KNOW, IT'S ONLY HAPPENING HERE IN CHICAGO.
YOUR CITY'S FALLING APART AND YOU'RE JUST GOING TO DRINK YOURSELF TO DEATH?
IT'S ARMAGEDDON, DICK. AND GOD AND I AREN'T EXACTLY ON THE BEST OF TERMS.
EVERY ONE OF THESE PINS IS A SUSPICIOUS PERSON?
EVERY LAST ONE OF 'EM. BUT WE DON'T KNOW IF THEY'RE ALL LEGIT. WE DON'T HAVE ENOUGH UNITS AVAILABLE TO INVESTIGATE THEM ALL.
THEN IT'LL GIVE ME A PLACE TO START.

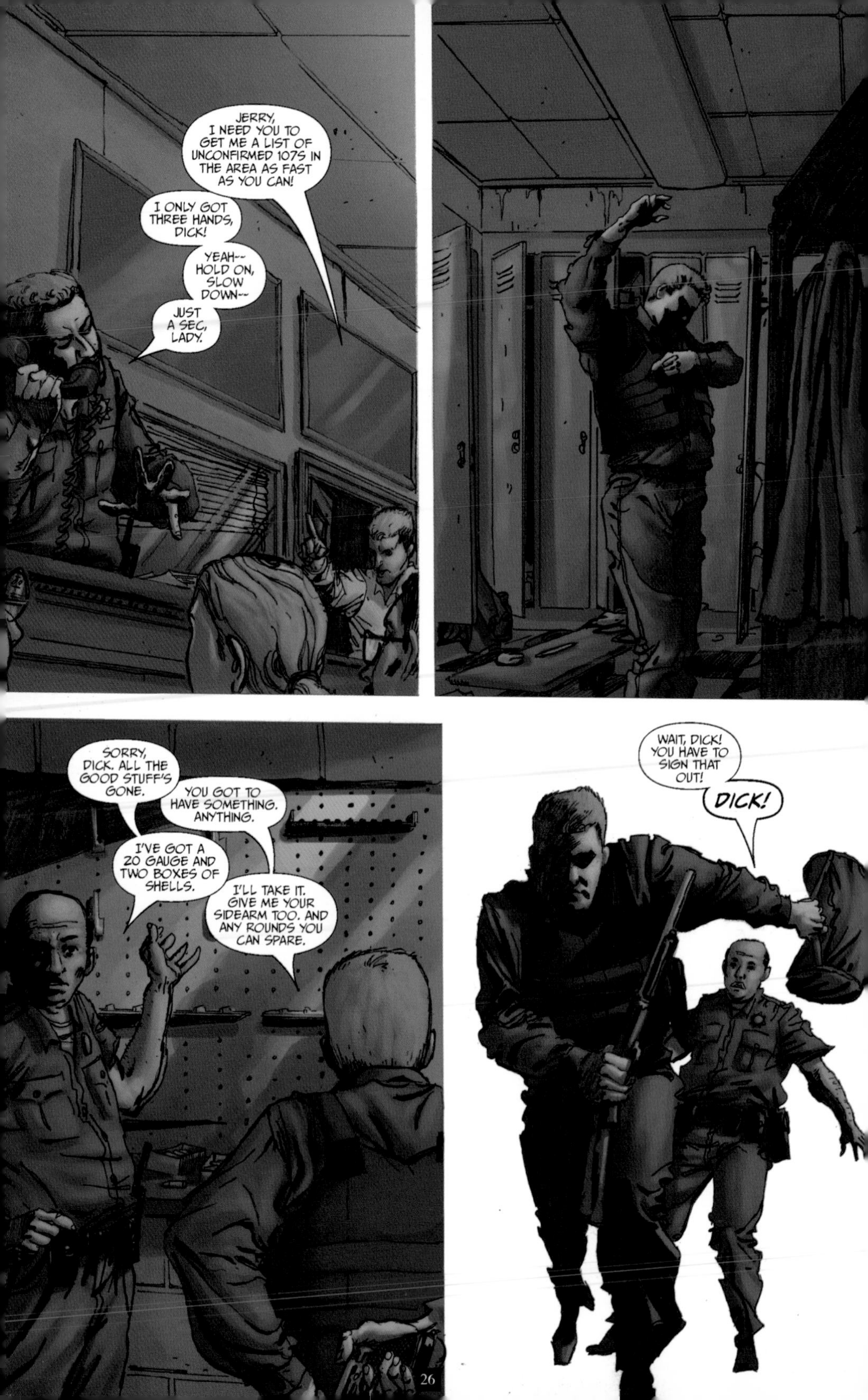
JERRY, I NEED YOU TO GET ME A LIST OF UNCONFIRMED 107S IN THE AREA AS FAST AS YOU CAN!
I ONLY GOT THREE HANDS, DICK!
YEAH-- HOLD ON, SLOW DOWN--
JUST A SEC, LADY.
SORRY, DICK. ALL THE GOOD STUFF'S GONE.
YOU GOT TO HAVE SOMETHING. ANYTHING.
I'VE GOT A 20 GAUGE AND TWO BOXES OF SHELLS.
I'LL TAKE IT. GIVE ME YOUR SIDEARM TOO. AND ANY ROUNDS YOU CAN SPARE.
WAIT, DICK! YOU HAVE TO SIGN THAT OUT!
DICK!

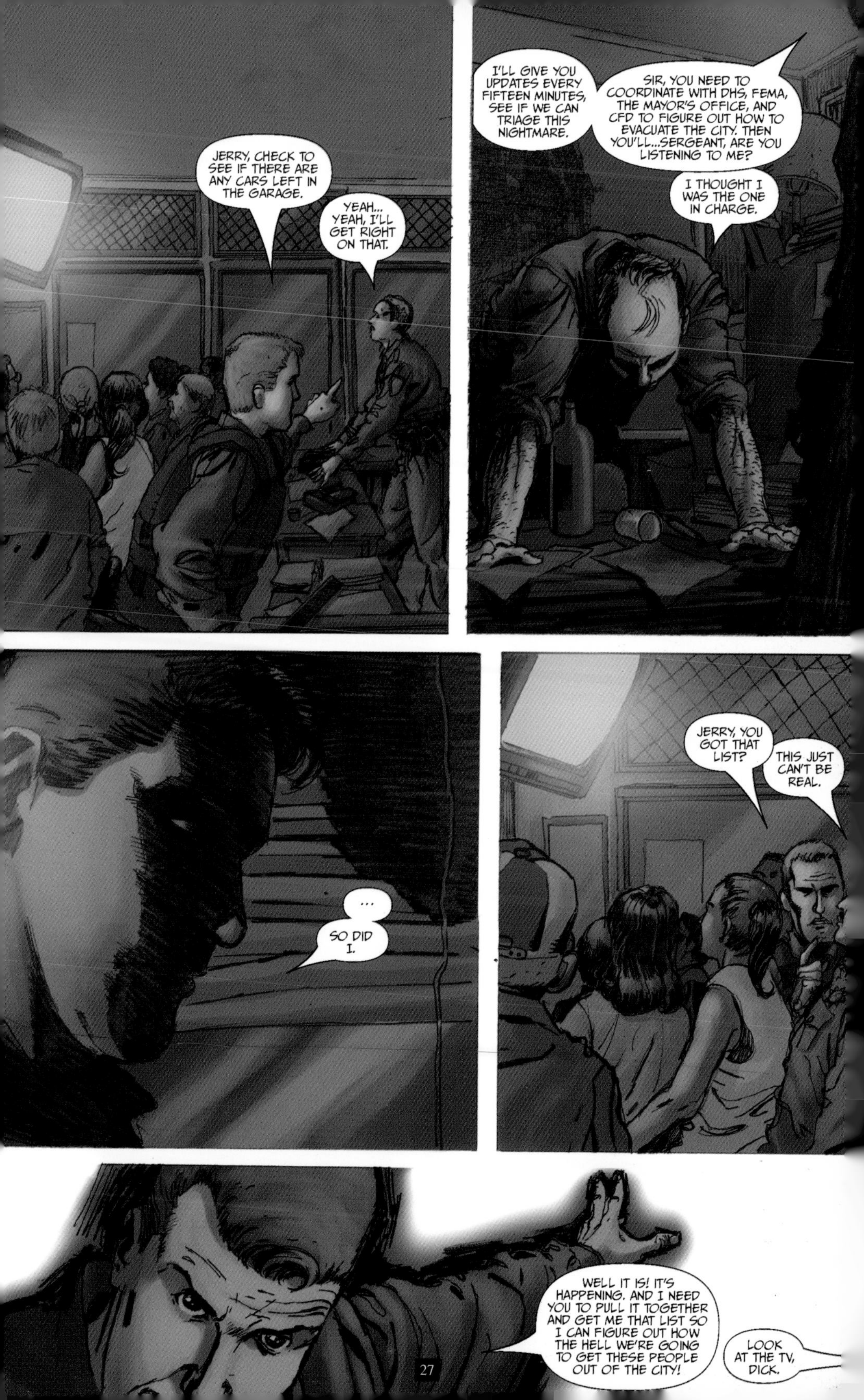
JERRY, CHECK TO SEE IF THERE ARE ANY CARS LEFT IN THE GARAGE.
YEAH... YEAH, I'LL GET RIGHT ON THAT.
I'LL GIVE YOU UPDATES EVERY FIFTEEN MINUTES, SEE IF WE CAN TRIAGE THIS NIGHTMARE.
SIR, YOU NEED TO COORDINATE WITH DHS, FEMA, THE MAYOR'S OFFICE, AND CFD TO FIGURE OUT HOW TO EVACUATE THE CITY. THEN YOU'LL...SERGEANT, ARE YOU LISTENING TO ME?
I THOUGHT I WAS THE ONE IN CHARGE.
...
SO DID I.
JERRY, YOU GOT THAT LIST?
THIS JUST CAN'T BE REAL.
WELL IT IS! IT'S HAPPENING. AND I NEED YOU TO PULL IT TOGETHER AND GET ME THAT LIST SO I CAN FIGURE OUT HOW THE HELL WE'RE GOING TO GET THESE PEOPLE OUT OF THE CITY!
LOOK AT THE TV, DICK.

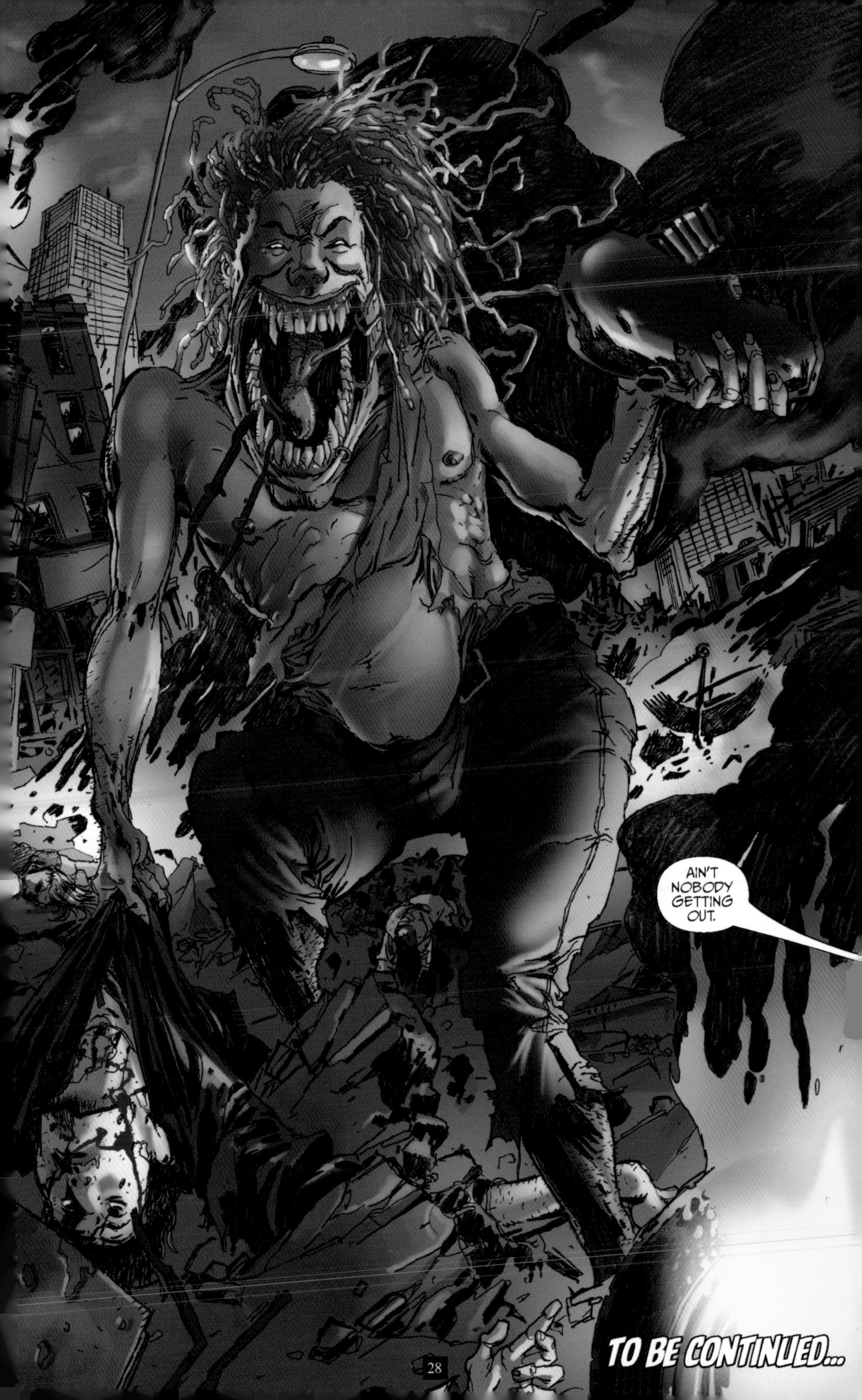
AIN'T NOBODY GETTING OUT.
TO BE CONTINUED...

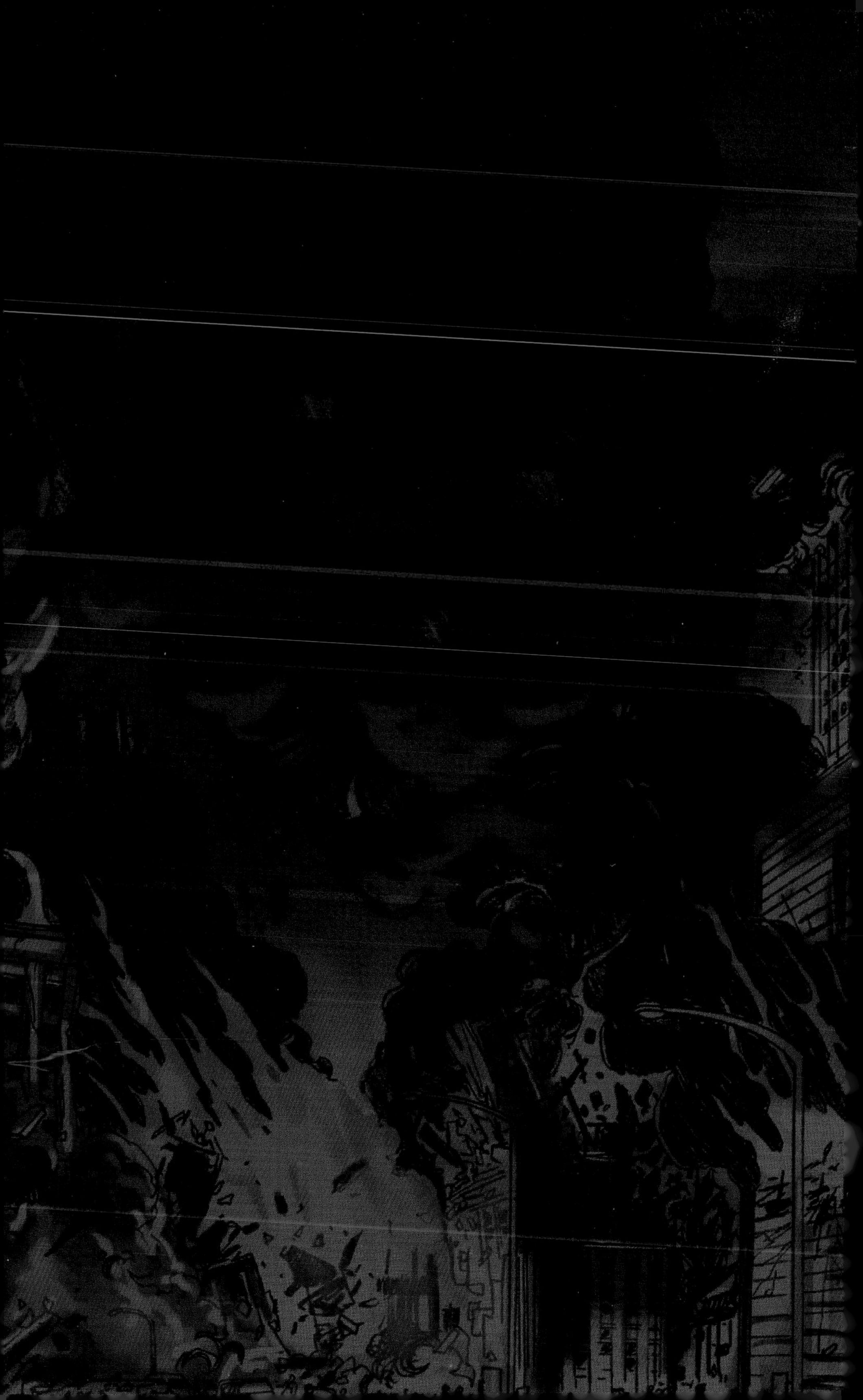

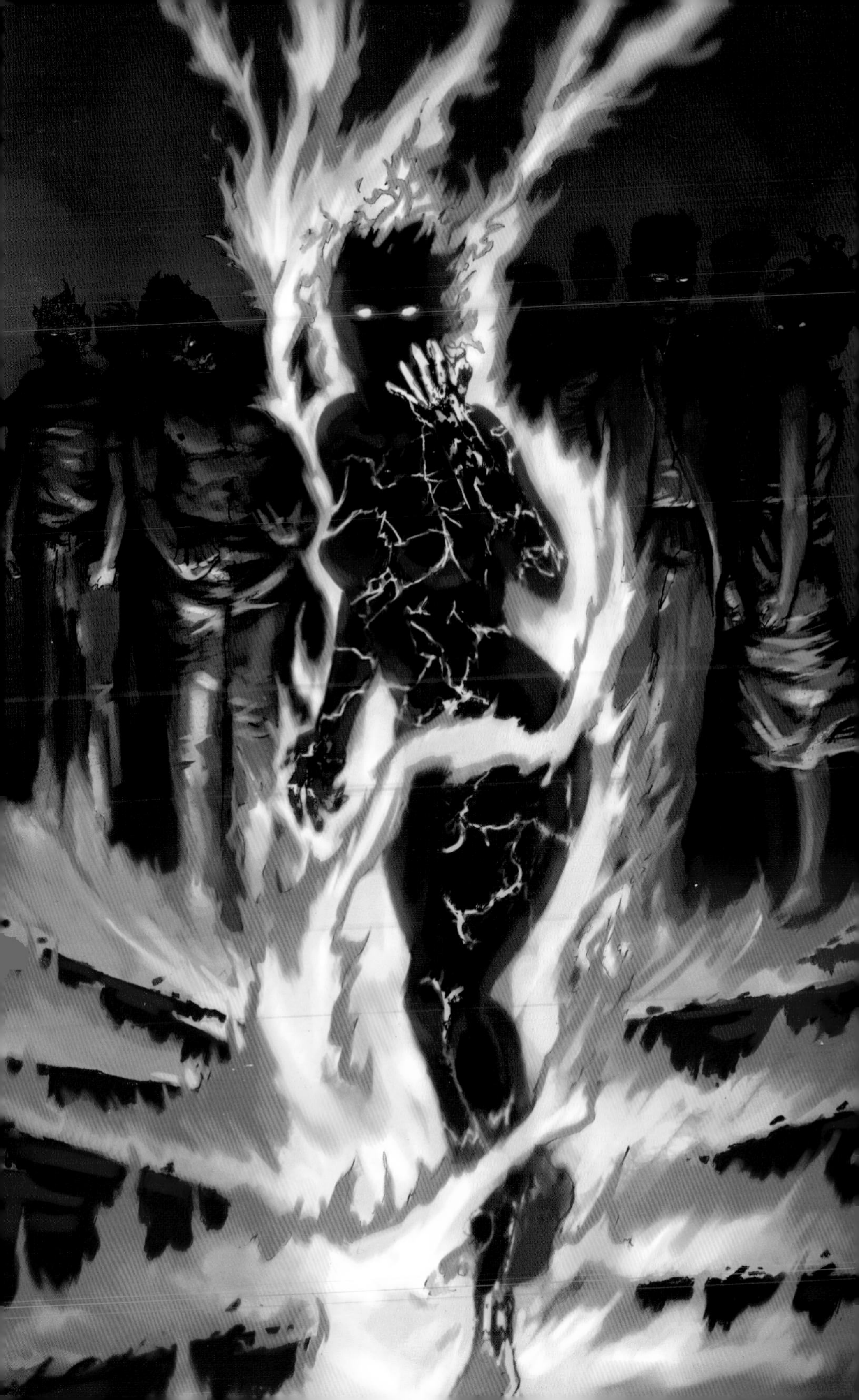

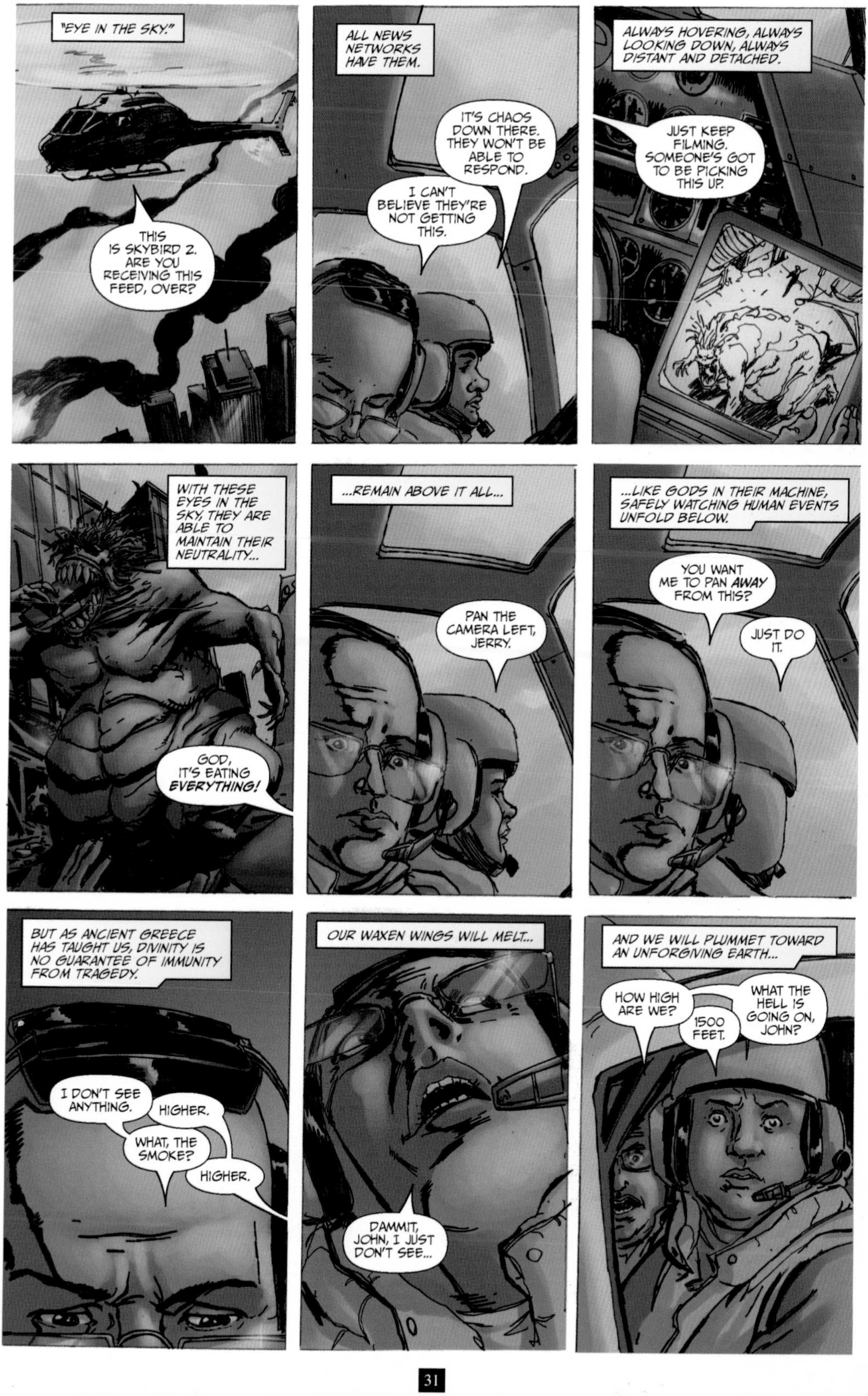
"EYE IN THE SKY."
THIS IS SKYBIRD 2. ARE YOU RECEIVING THIS FEED, OVER?
ALL NEWS NETWORKS HAVE THEM.
IT'S CHAOS DOWN THERE. THEY WON'T BE ABLE TO RESPOND.
I CAN'T BELIEVE THEY'RE NOT GETTING THIS.
ALWAYS HOVERING, ALWAYS LOOKING DOWN, ALWAYS DISTANT AND DETACHED.
JUST KEEP FILMING. SOMEONE'S GOT TO BE PICKING THIS UP.
WITH THESE EYES IN THE SKY, THEY ARE ABLE TO MAINTAIN THEIR NEUTRALITY...
GOD, IT'S EATING ***EVERYTHING!***
...REMAIN ABOVE IT ALL...
PAN THE CAMERA LEFT, JERRY.
...LIKE GODS IN THEIR MACHINE, SAFELY WATCHING HUMAN EVENTS UNFOLD BELOW.
YOU WANT ME TO PAN ***AWAY*** FROM THIS?
JUST DO IT.
BUT AS ANCIENT GREECE HAS TAUGHT US, DIVINITY IS NO GUARANTEE OF IMMUNITY FROM TRAGEDY.
I DON'T SEE ANYTHING.
HIGHER.
WHAT, THE SMOKE?
HIGHER.
OUR WAXEN WINGS WILL MELT...
DAMMIT, JOHN, I JUST DON'T SEE...
AND WE WILL PLUMMET TOWARD AN UNFORGIVING EARTH...
HOW HIGH ARE WE?
1500 FEET.
WHAT THE HELL IS GOING ON, JOHN?

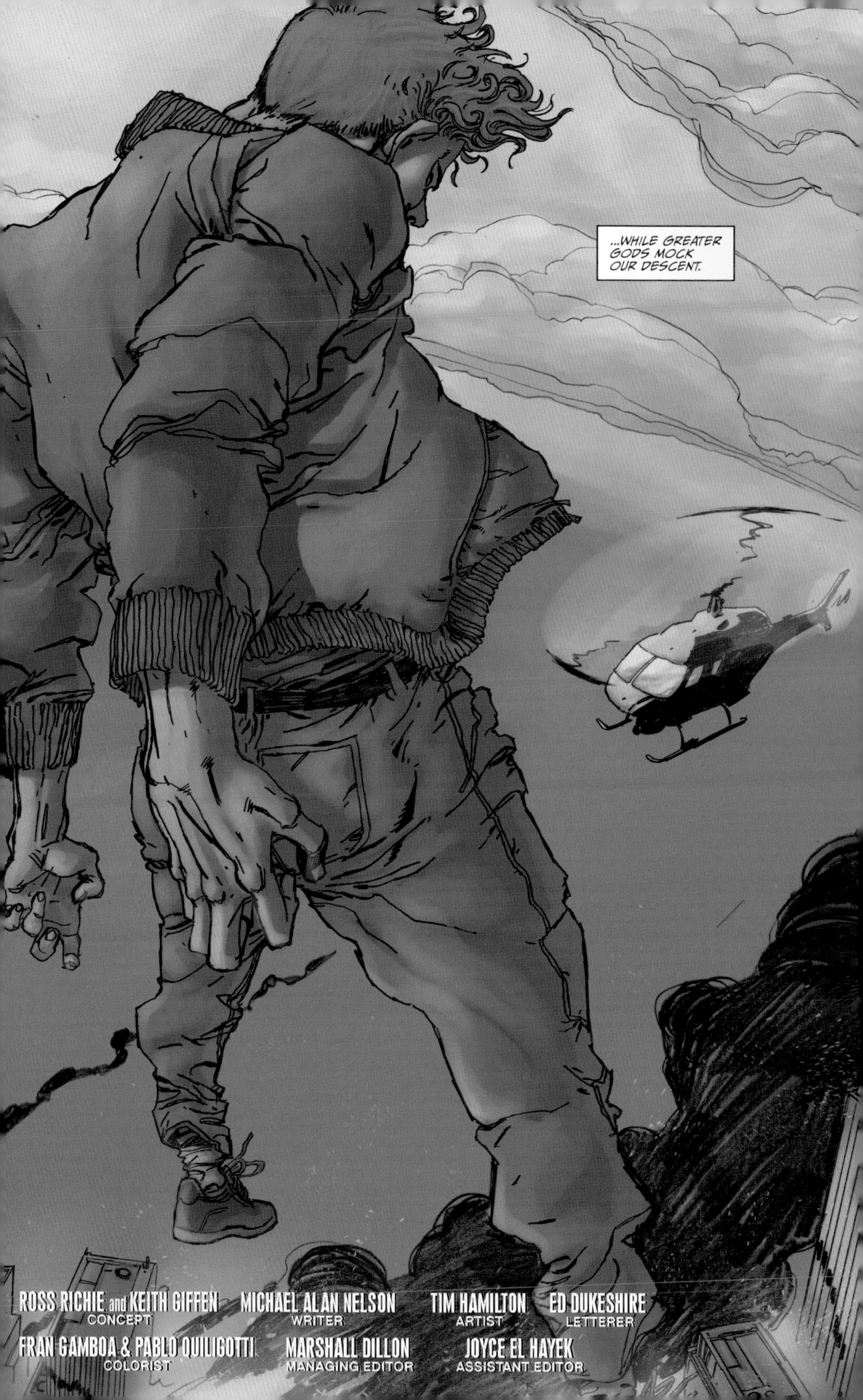
...WHILE GREATER GODS MOCK OUR DESCENT.
ROSS RICHIE and KEITH GIFFEN
CONCEPT
MICHAEL ALAN NELSON
WRITER
TIM HAMILTON
ARTIST
ED DUKESHIRE
LETTERER
FRAN GAMBOA & PABLO QUILIGOTTI
COLORIST
MARSHALL DILLON
MANAGING EDITOR
JOYCE EL HAYEK
ASSISTANT EDITOR

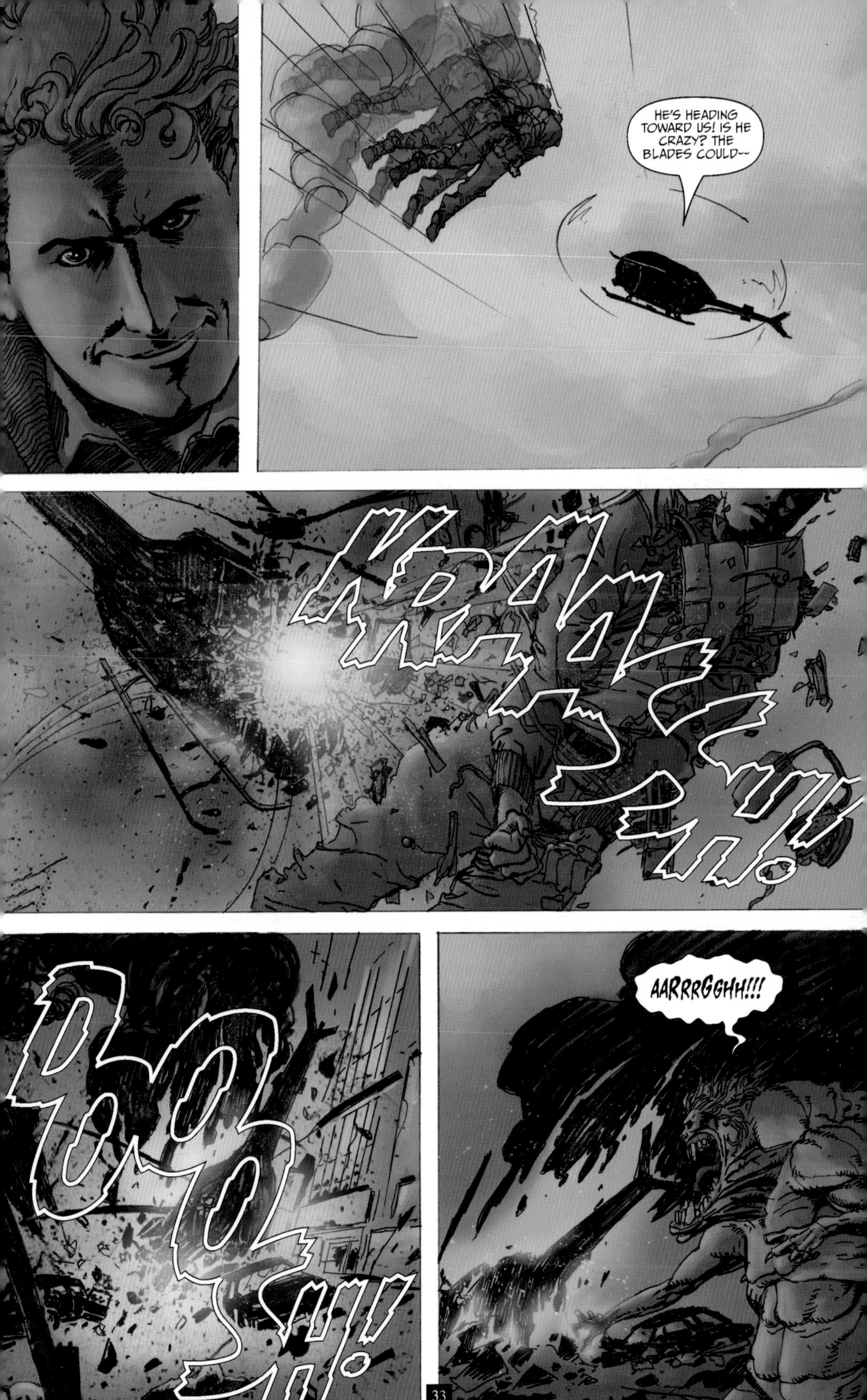
HE'S HEADING TOWARD US! IS HE CRAZY? THE BLADES COULD--
AARRRGGHH!!!

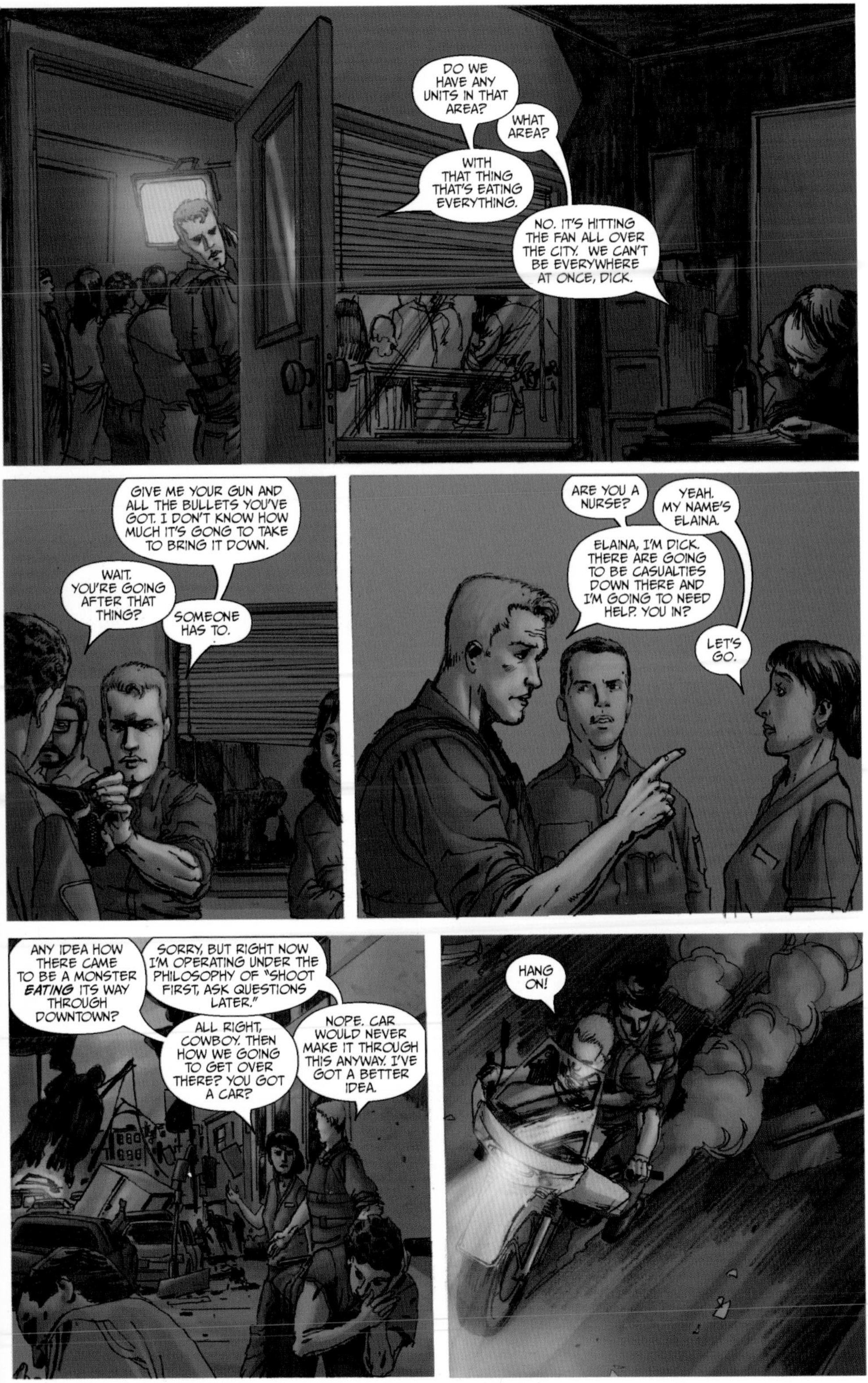
DO WE HAVE ANY UNITS IN THAT AREA?
WHAT AREA?
WITH THAT THING THAT'S EATING EVERYTHING.
NO. IT'S HITTING THE FAN ALL OVER THE CITY. WE CAN'T BE EVERYWHERE AT ONCE, DICK.
GIVE ME YOUR GUN AND ALL THE BULLETS YOU'VE GOT. I DON'T KNOW HOW MUCH IT'S GONG TO TAKE TO BRING IT DOWN.
WAIT. YOU'RE GOING AFTER THAT THING?
SOMEONE HAS TO.
ARE YOU A NURSE?
YEAH. MY NAME'S ELAINA.
ELAINA, I'M DICK. THERE ARE GOING TO BE CASUALTIES DOWN THERE AND I'M GOING TO NEED HELP. YOU IN?
LET'S GO.
ANY IDEA HOW THERE CAME TO BE A MONSTER *EATING* ITS WAY THROUGH DOWNTOWN?
SORRY, BUT RIGHT NOW I'M OPERATING UNDER THE PHILOSOPHY OF "SHOOT FIRST, ASK QUESTIONS LATER."
ALL RIGHT, COWBOY. THEN HOW WE GOING TO GET OVER THERE? YOU GOT A CAR?
NOPE. CAR WOULD NEVER MAKE IT THROUGH THIS ANYWAY. I'VE GOT A BETTER IDEA.
HANG ON!

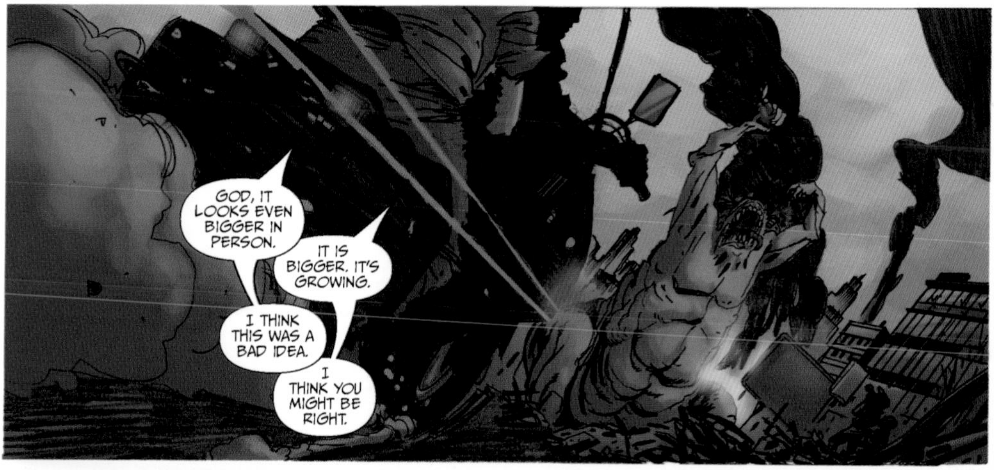
GOD, IT LOOKS EVEN BIGGER IN PERSON.
IT IS BIGGER. IT'S GROWING.
I THINK THIS WAS A BAD IDEA.
I THINK YOU MIGHT BE RIGHT.

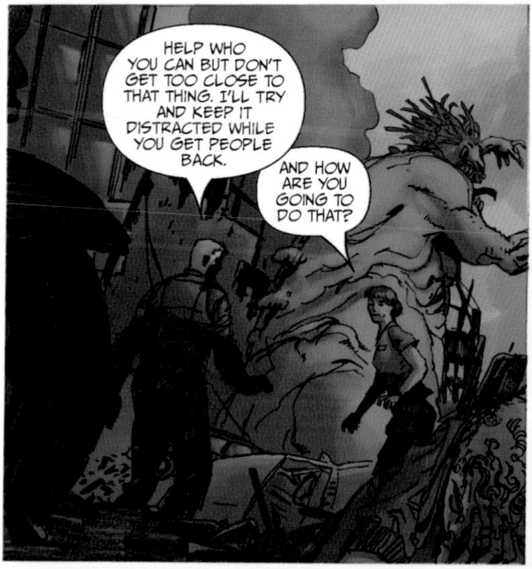
HELP WHO YOU CAN BUT DON'T GET TOO CLOSE TO THAT THING. I'LL TRY AND KEEP IT DISTRACTED WHILE YOU GET PEOPLE BACK.
AND HOW ARE YOU GOING TO DO THAT?

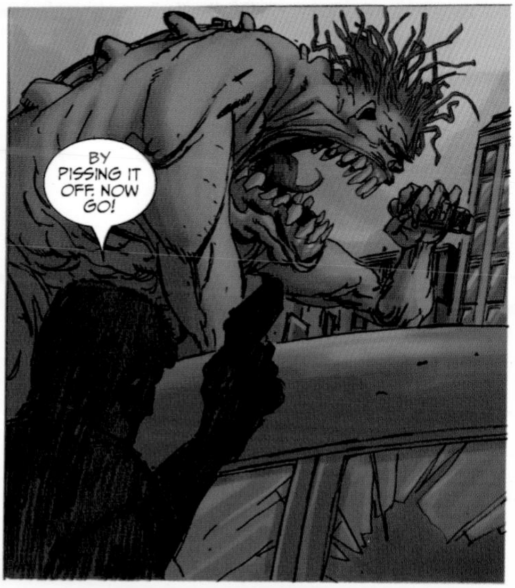
BY PISSING IT OFF. NOW GO!

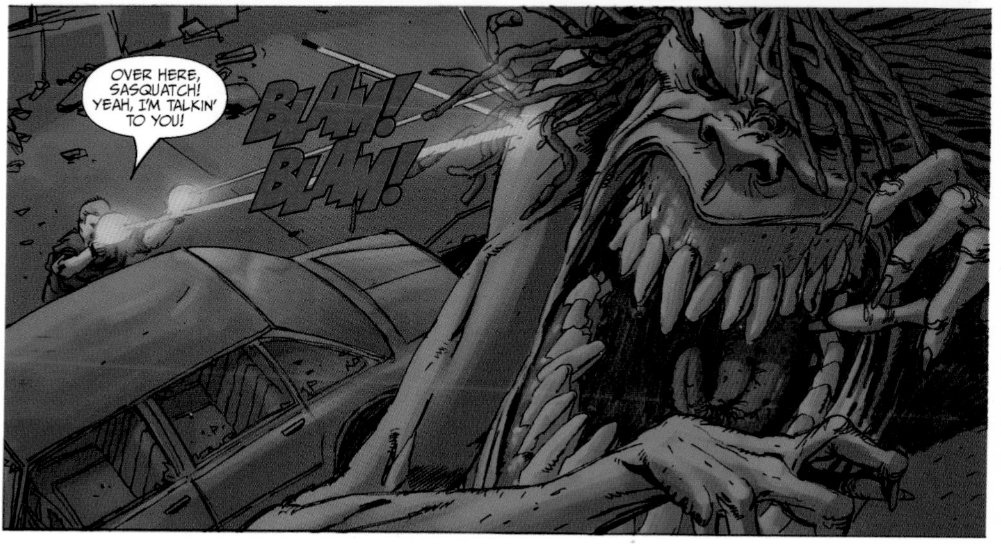
OVER HERE, SASQUATCH! YEAH, I'M TALKIN' TO YOU!
BLAM! BLAM!

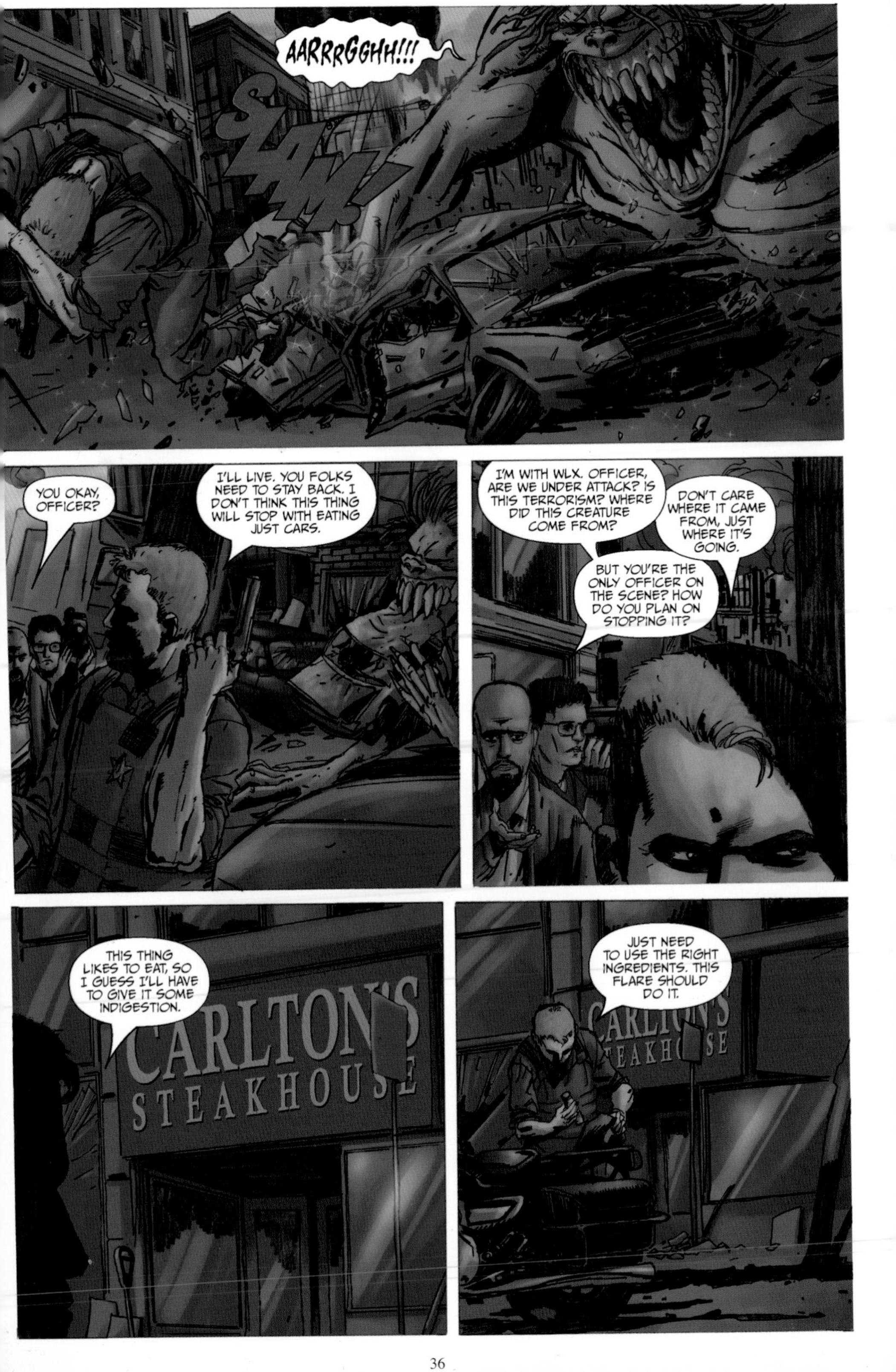
AARRRGGHH!!!
SHAM!
YOU OKAY, OFFICER?
I'LL LIVE. YOU FOLKS NEED TO STAY BACK. I DON'T THINK THIS THING WILL STOP WITH EATING JUST CARS.
I'M WITH WLX. OFFICER, ARE WE UNDER ATTACK? IS THIS TERRORISM? WHERE DID THIS CREATURE COME FROM?
DON'T CARE WHERE IT CAME FROM, JUST WHERE IT'S GOING.
BUT YOU'RE THE ONLY OFFICER ON THE SCENE? HOW DO YOU PLAN ON STOPPING IT?
THIS THING LIKES TO EAT, SO I GUESS I'LL HAVE TO GIVE IT SOME INDIGESTION.
CARLTON'S STEAKHOUSE
JUST NEED TO USE THE RIGHT INGREDIENTS. THIS FLARE SHOULD DO IT.
CARLTON'S STEAKHOUSE

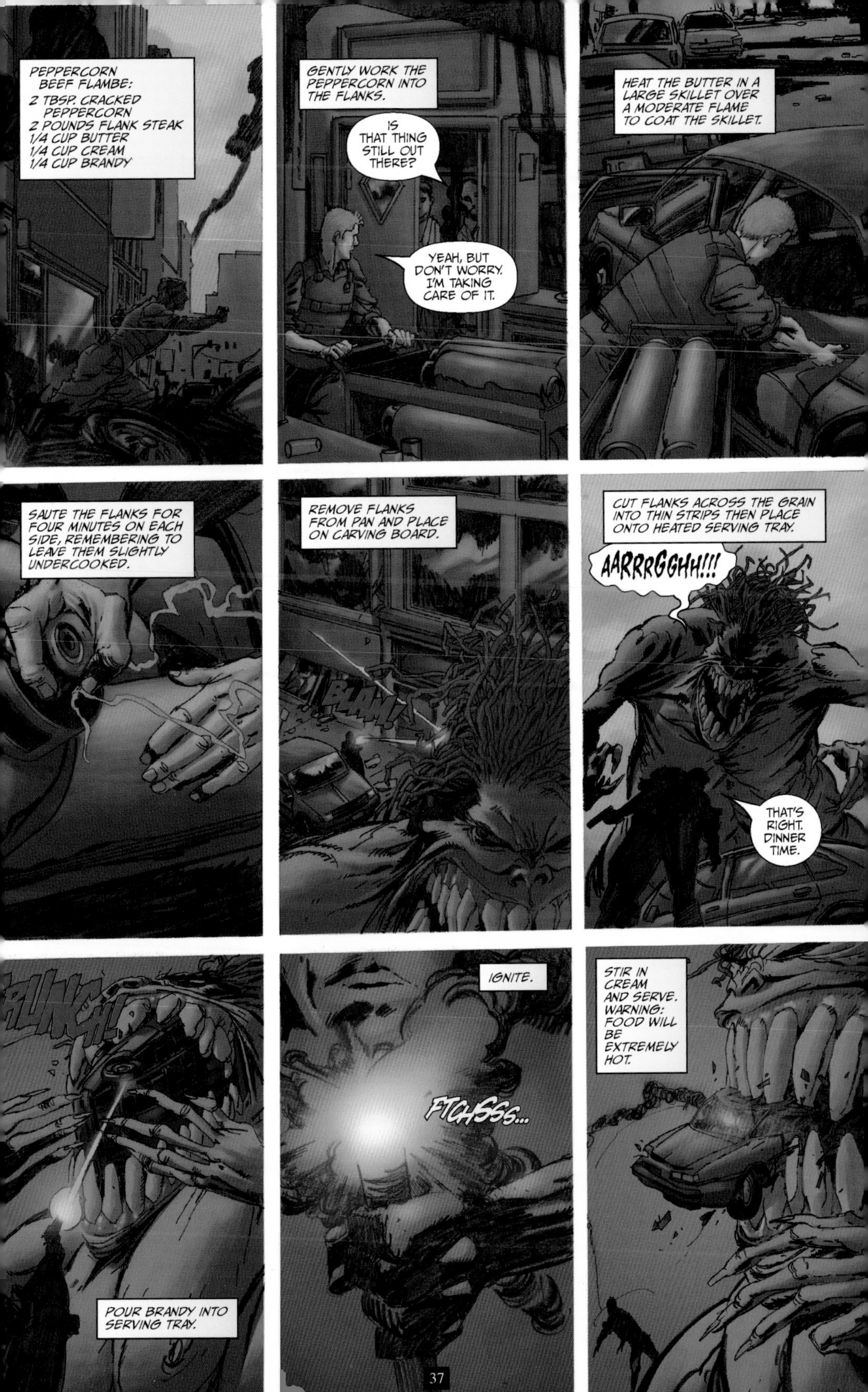
PEPPERCORN BEEF FLAMBE:
2 TBSP. CRACKED PEPPERCORN
2 POUNDS FLANK STEAK
1/4 CUP BUTTER
1/4 CUP CREAM
1/4 CUP BRANDY
GENTLY WORK THE PEPPERCORN INTO THE FLANKS.
IS THAT THING STILL OUT THERE?
YEAH, BUT DON'T WORRY. I'M TAKING CARE OF IT.
HEAT THE BUTTER IN A LARGE SKILLET OVER A MODERATE FLAME TO COAT THE SKILLET.
SAUTE THE FLANKS FOR FOUR MINUTES ON EACH SIDE, REMEMBERING TO LEAVE THEM SLIGHTLY UNDERCOOKED.
REMOVE FLANKS FROM PAN AND PLACE ON CARVING BOARD.
BLAM!
CUT FLANKS ACROSS THE GRAIN INTO THIN STRIPS THEN PLACE ONTO HEATED SERVING TRAY.
AARRRGGHH!!!
THAT'S RIGHT. DINNER TIME.
CRUNCH!
POUR BRANDY INTO SERVING TRAY.
IGNITE.
FTCHSSS...
STIR IN CREAM AND SERVE. WARNING: FOOD WILL BE EXTREMELY HOT.

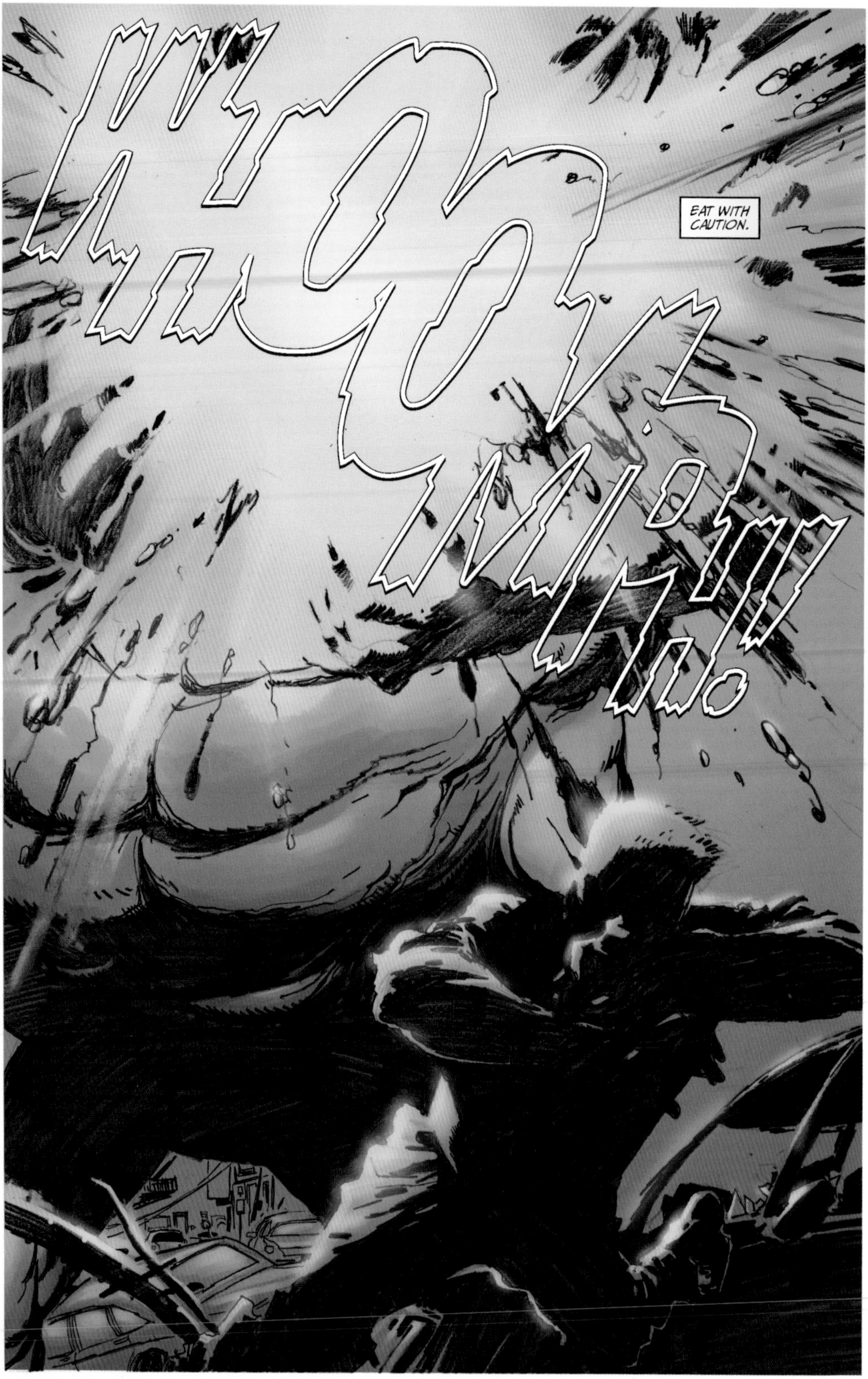
EAT WITH CAUTION.

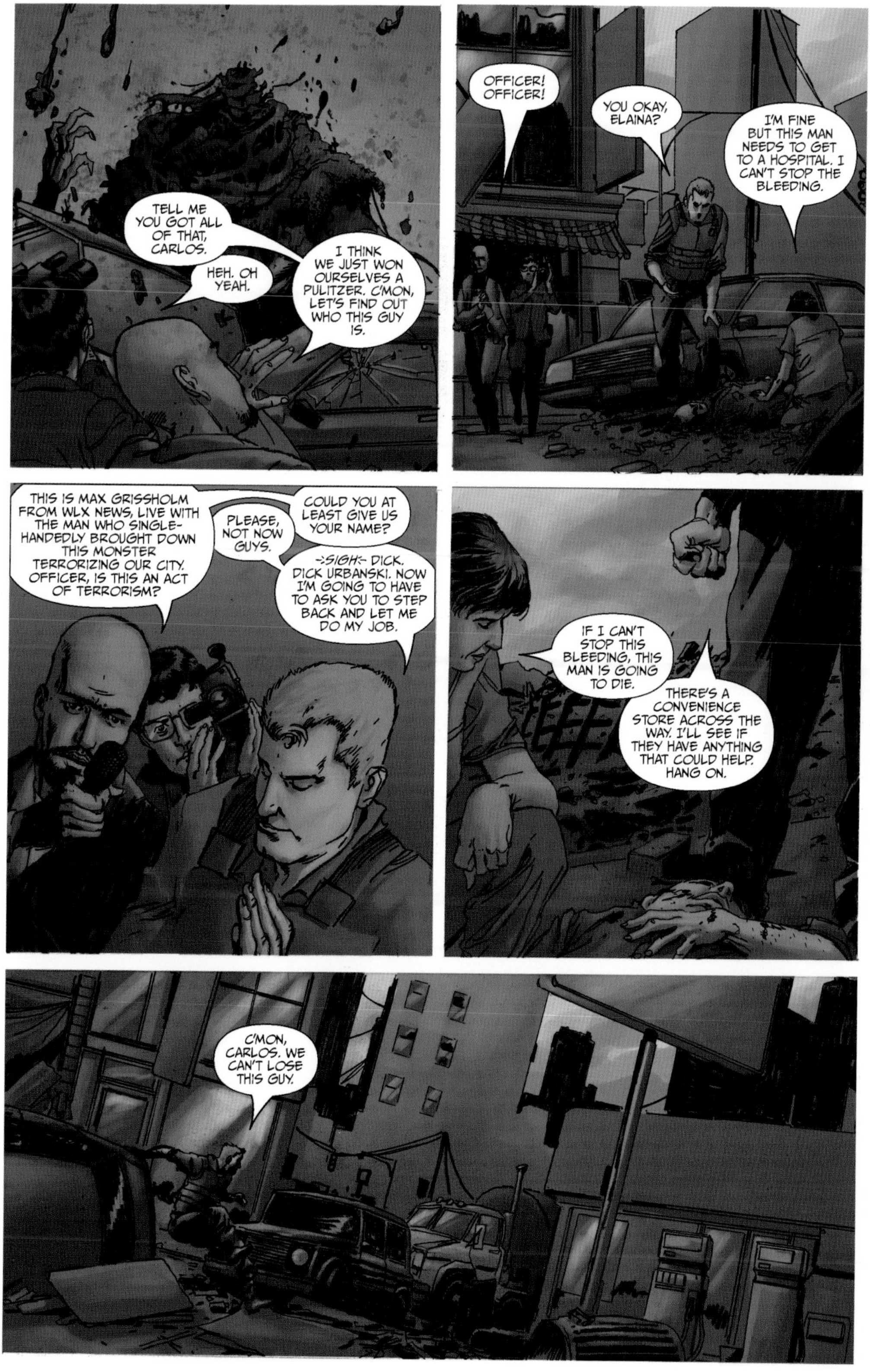
TELL ME YOU GOT ALL OF THAT, CARLOS.
HEH. OH YEAH.
I THINK WE JUST WON OURSELVES A PULITZER. C'MON, LET'S FIND OUT WHO THIS GUY IS.
OFFICER! OFFICER!
YOU OKAY, ELAINA?
I'M FINE BUT THIS MAN NEEDS TO GET TO A HOSPITAL. I CAN'T STOP THE BLEEDING.
THIS IS MAX GRISSHOLM FROM WLX NEWS, LIVE WITH THE MAN WHO SINGLE-HANDEDLY BROUGHT DOWN THIS MONSTER TERRORIZING OUR CITY. OFFICER, IS THIS AN ACT OF TERRORISM?
PLEASE, NOT NOW GUYS.
COULD YOU AT LEAST GIVE US YOUR NAME?
-SIGH- DICK. DICK URBANSKI. NOW I'M GOING TO HAVE TO ASK YOU TO STEP BACK AND LET ME DO MY JOB.
IF I CAN'T STOP THIS BLEEDING, THIS MAN IS GOING TO DIE.
THERE'S A CONVENIENCE STORE ACROSS THE WAY. I'LL SEE IF THEY HAVE ANYTHING THAT COULD HELP. HANG ON.
C'MON, CARLOS. WE CAN'T LOSE THIS GUY.

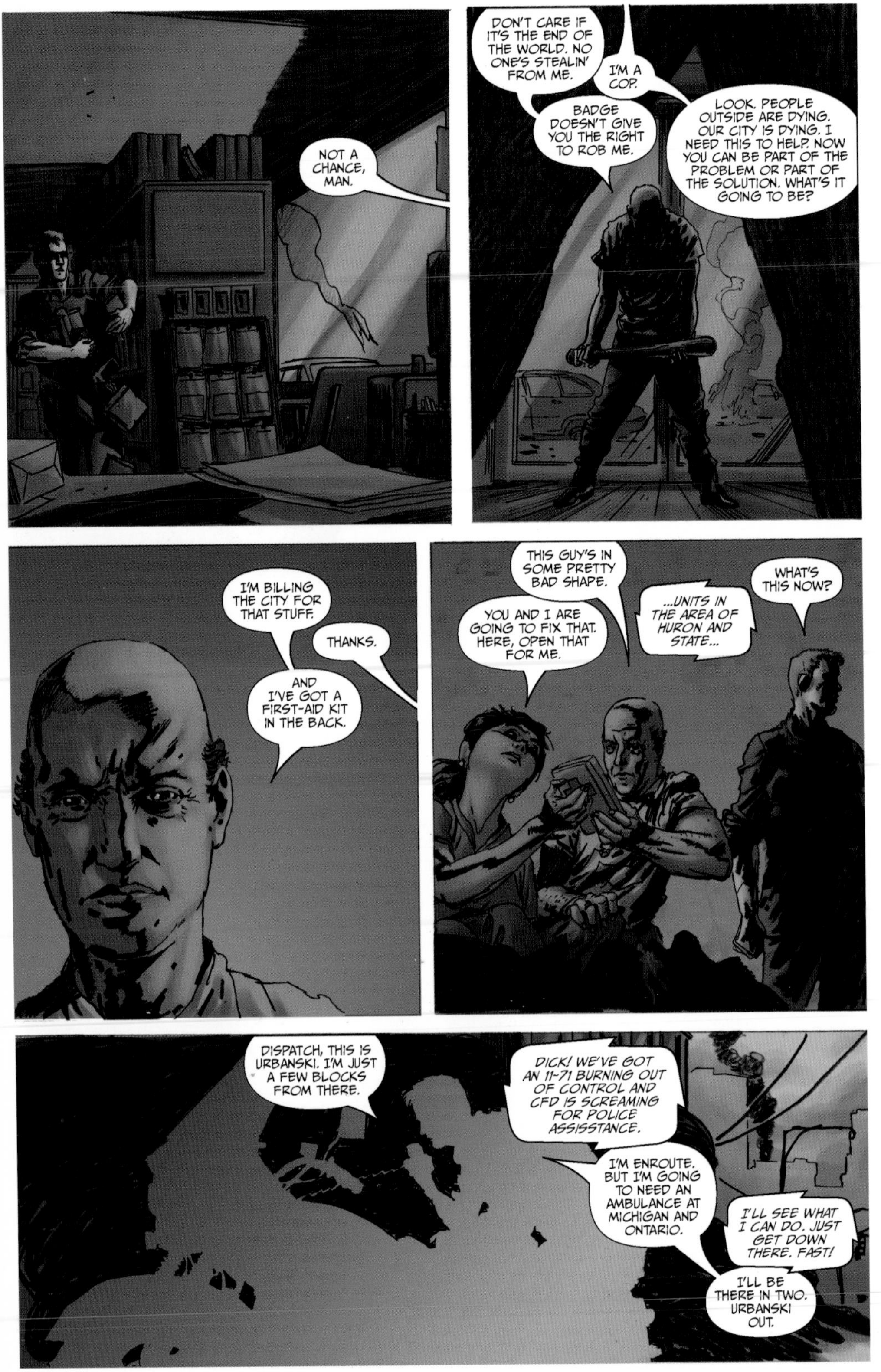

NOT A CHANCE, MAN.
DON'T CARE IF IT'S THE END OF THE WORLD. NO ONE'S STEALIN' FROM ME.
I'M A COP.
BADGE DOESN'T GIVE YOU THE RIGHT TO ROB ME.
LOOK. PEOPLE OUTSIDE ARE DYING. OUR CITY IS DYING. I NEED THIS TO HELP. NOW YOU CAN BE PART OF THE PROBLEM OR PART OF THE SOLUTION. WHAT'S IT GOING TO BE?
I'M BILLING THE CITY FOR THAT STUFF.
THANKS.
AND I'VE GOT A FIRST-AID KIT IN THE BACK.
THIS GUY'S IN SOME PRETTY BAD SHAPE.
YOU AND I ARE GOING TO FIX THAT. HERE, OPEN THAT FOR ME.
...UNITS IN THE AREA OF HURON AND STATE...
WHAT'S THIS NOW?
DISPATCH, THIS IS URBANSKI. I'M JUST A FEW BLOCKS FROM THERE.
DICK! WE'VE GOT AN 11-71 BURNING OUT OF CONTROL AND CFD IS SCREAMING FOR POLICE ASSISSTANCE.
I'M ENROUTE. BUT I'M GOING TO NEED AN AMBULANCE AT MICHIGAN AND ONTARIO.
I'LL SEE WHAT I CAN DO. JUST GET DOWN THERE. FAST!
I'LL BE THERE IN TWO. URBANSKI OUT.

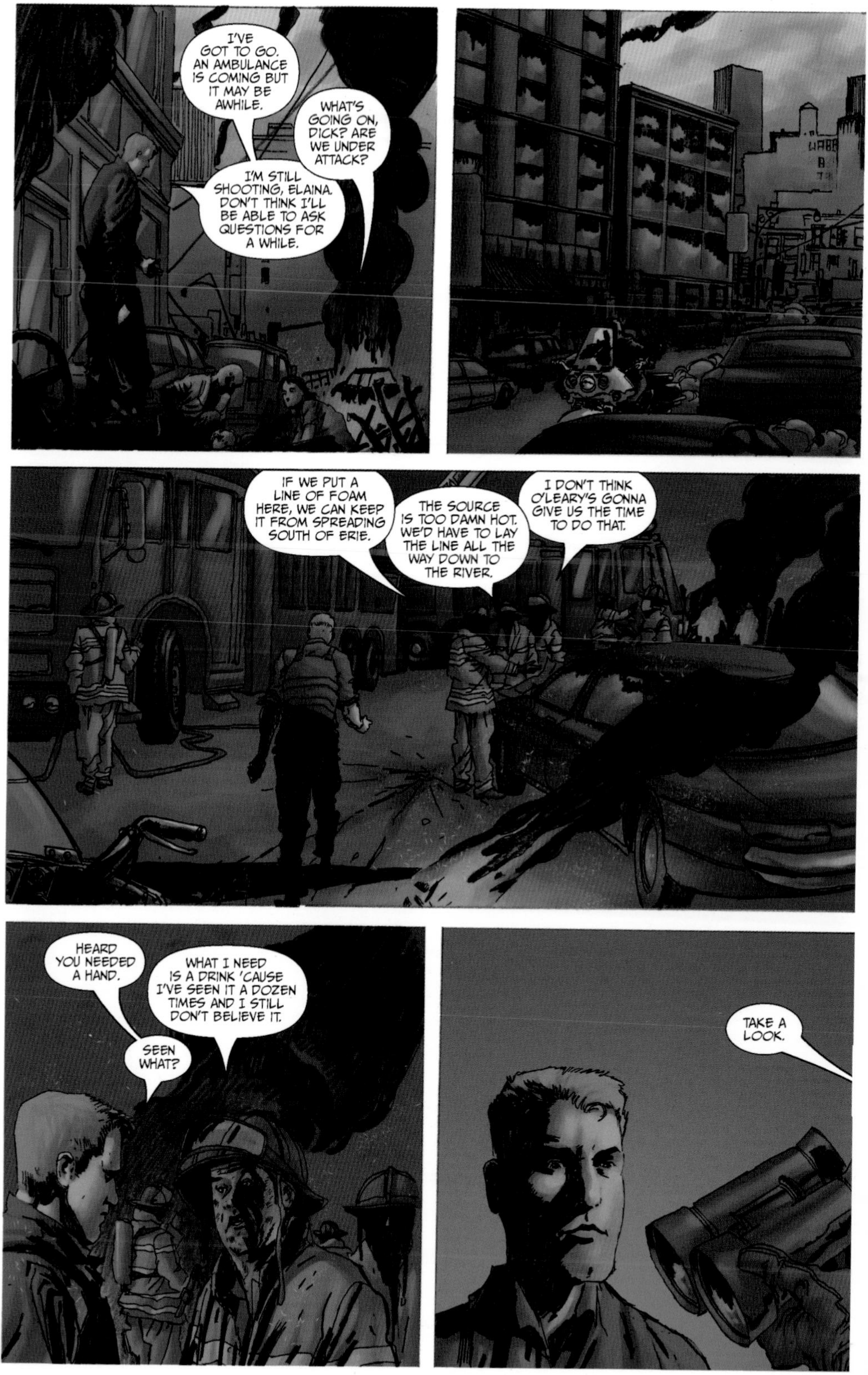
I'VE GOT TO GO. AN AMBULANCE IS COMING BUT IT MAY BE AWHILE.
WHAT'S GOING ON, DICK? ARE WE UNDER ATTACK?
I'M STILL SHOOTING, ELAINA. DON'T THINK I'LL BE ABLE TO ASK QUESTIONS FOR A WHILE.
IF WE PUT A LINE OF FOAM HERE, WE CAN KEEP IT FROM SPREADING SOUTH OF ERIE.
THE SOURCE IS TOO DAMN HOT. WE'D HAVE TO LAY THE LINE ALL THE WAY DOWN TO THE RIVER.
I DON'T THINK O'LEARY'S GONNA GIVE US THE TIME TO DO THAT.
HEARD YOU NEEDED A HAND.
WHAT I NEED IS A DRINK 'CAUSE I'VE SEEN IT A DOZEN TIMES AND I STILL DON'T BELIEVE IT.
SEEN WHAT?
TAKE A LOOK.

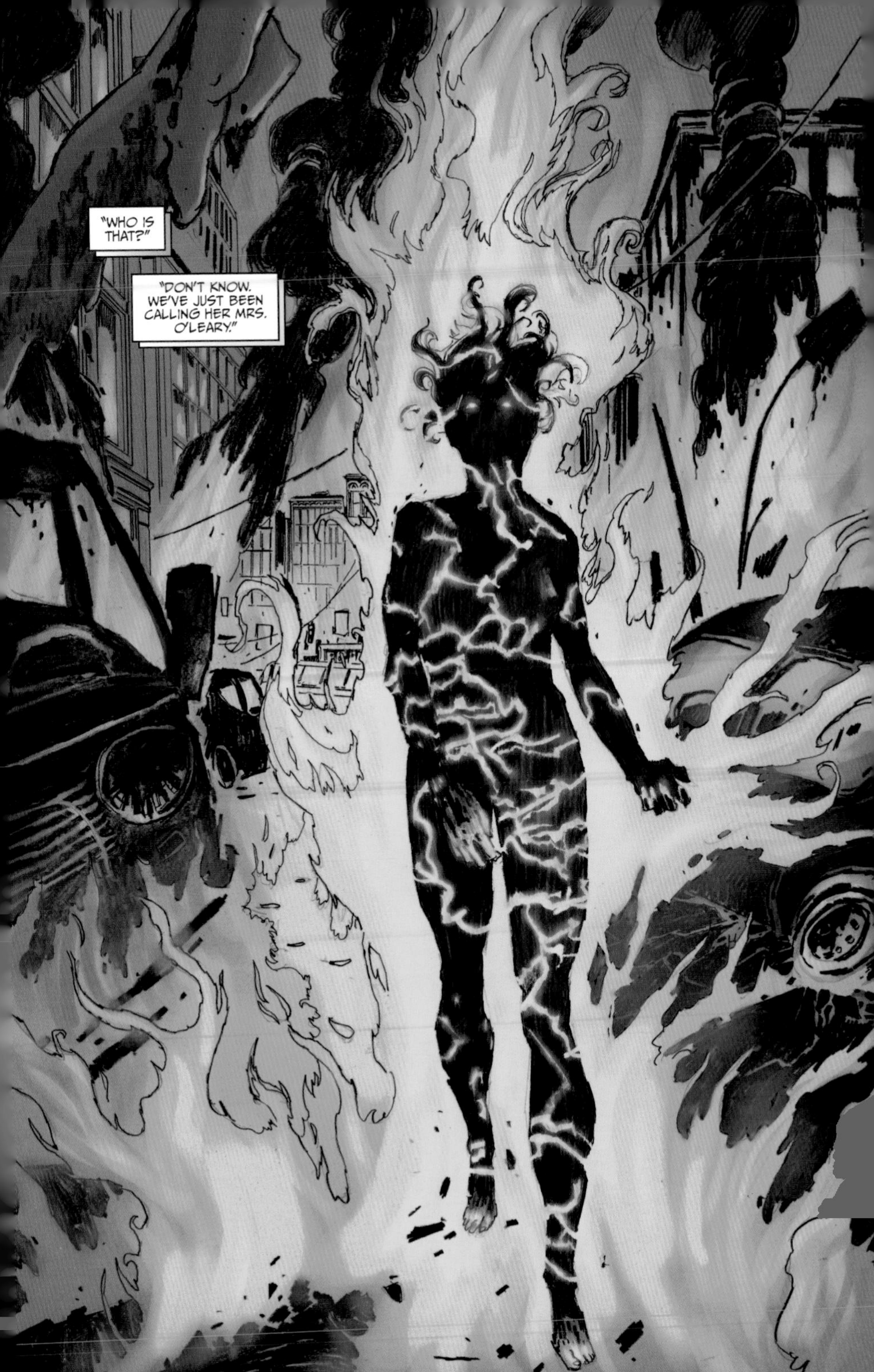
"WHO IS THAT?"
"DON'T KNOW. WE'VE JUST BEEN CALLING HER MRS. O'LEARY."

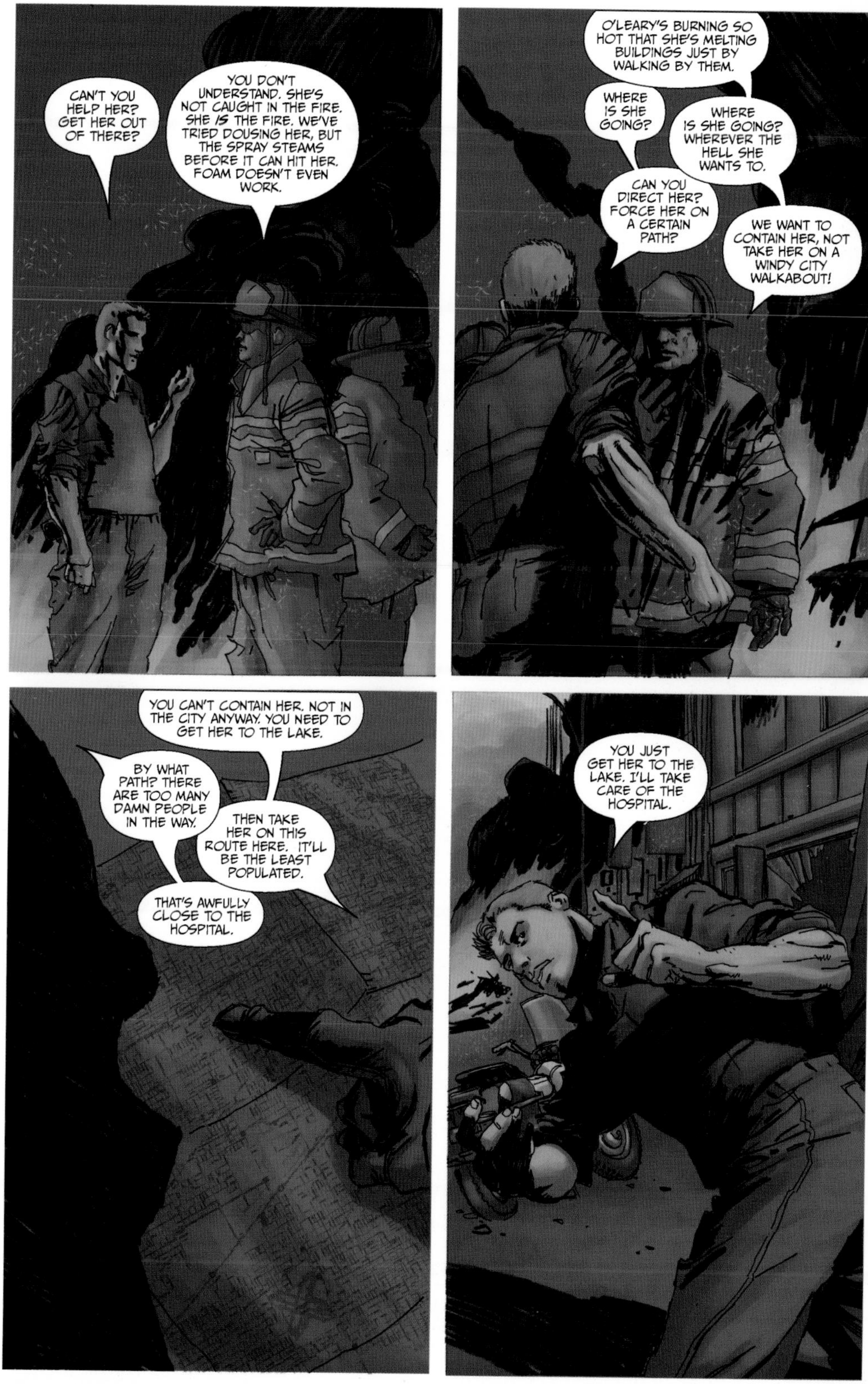
CAN'T YOU HELP HER? GET HER OUT OF THERE?
YOU DON'T UNDERSTAND. SHE'S NOT CAUGHT IN THE FIRE. SHE *IS* THE FIRE. WE'VE TRIED DOUSING HER, BUT THE SPRAY STEAMS BEFORE IT CAN HIT HER. FOAM DOESN'T EVEN WORK.
O'LEARY'S BURNING SO HOT THAT SHE'S MELTING BUILDINGS JUST BY WALKING BY THEM.
WHERE IS SHE GOING?
WHERE IS SHE GOING? WHEREVER THE HELL SHE WANTS TO.
CAN YOU DIRECT HER? FORCE HER ON A CERTAIN PATH?
WE WANT TO CONTAIN HER, NOT TAKE HER ON A WINDY CITY WALKABOUT!
YOU CAN'T CONTAIN HER. NOT IN THE CITY ANYWAY. YOU NEED TO GET HER TO THE LAKE.
BY WHAT PATH? THERE ARE TOO MANY DAMN PEOPLE IN THE WAY.
THEN TAKE HER ON THIS ROUTE HERE. IT'LL BE THE LEAST POPULATED.
THAT'S AWFULLY CLOSE TO THE HOSPITAL.
YOU JUST GET HER TO THE LAKE. I'LL TAKE CARE OF THE HOSPITAL.

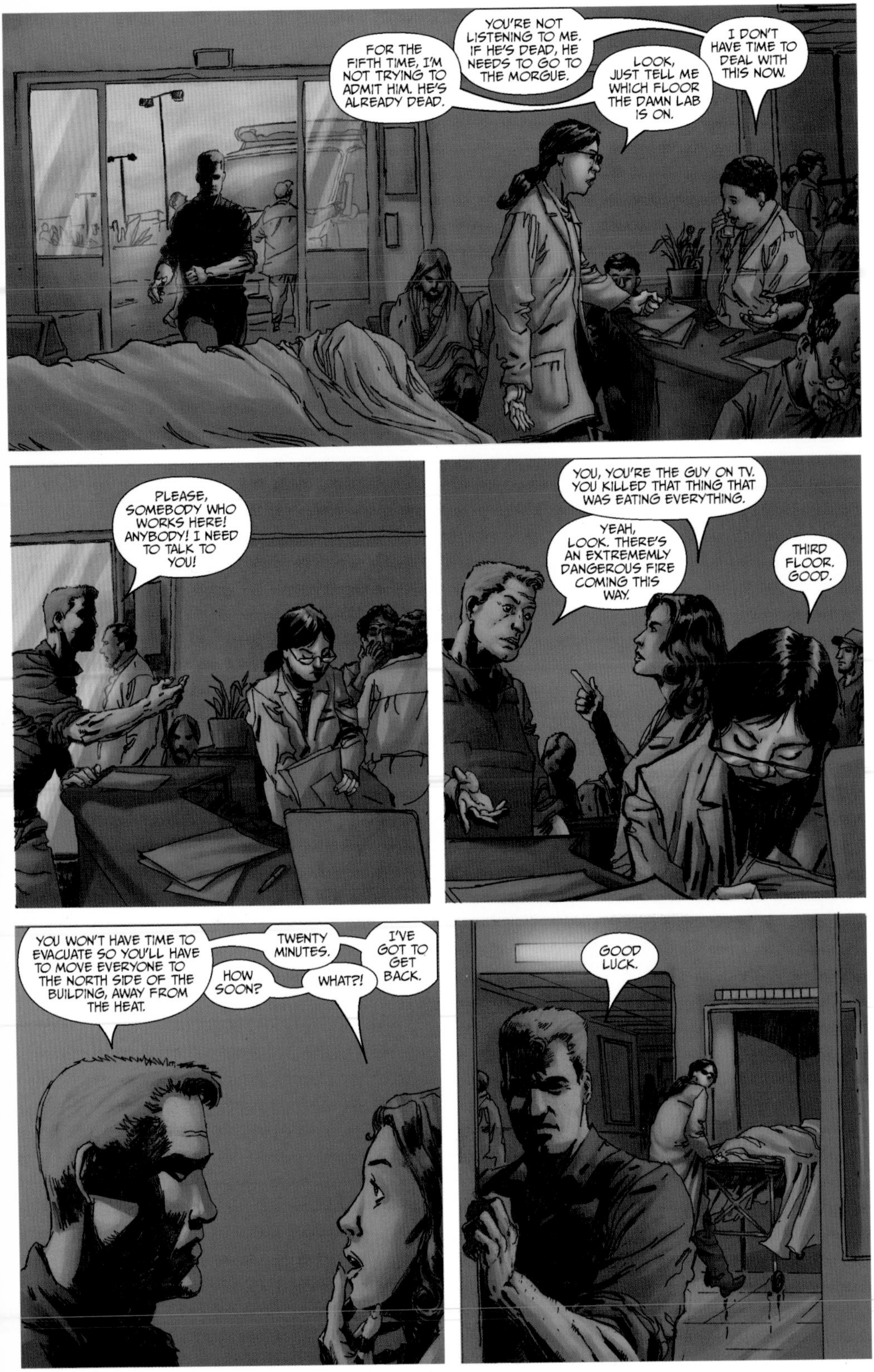

FOR THE FIFTH TIME, I'M NOT TRYING TO ADMIT HIM. HE'S ALREADY DEAD.
YOU'RE NOT LISTENING TO ME. IF HE'S DEAD, HE NEEDS TO GO TO THE MORGUE.
I DON'T HAVE TIME TO DEAL WITH THIS NOW.
LOOK, JUST TELL ME WHICH FLOOR THE DAMN LAB IS ON.
PLEASE, SOMEBODY WHO WORKS HERE! ANYBODY! I NEED TO TALK TO YOU!
YOU, YOU'RE THE GUY ON TV. YOU KILLED THAT THING THAT WAS EATING EVERYTHING.
YEAH, LOOK. THERE'S AN EXTREMEMLY DANGEROUS FIRE COMING THIS WAY.
THIRD FLOOR. GOOD.
YOU WON'T HAVE TIME TO EVACUATE SO YOU'LL HAVE TO MOVE EVERYONE TO THE NORTH SIDE OF THE BUILDING, AWAY FROM THE HEAT.
HOW SOON?
TWENTY MINUTES.
WHAT?!
I'VE GOT TO GET BACK.
GOOD LUCK.

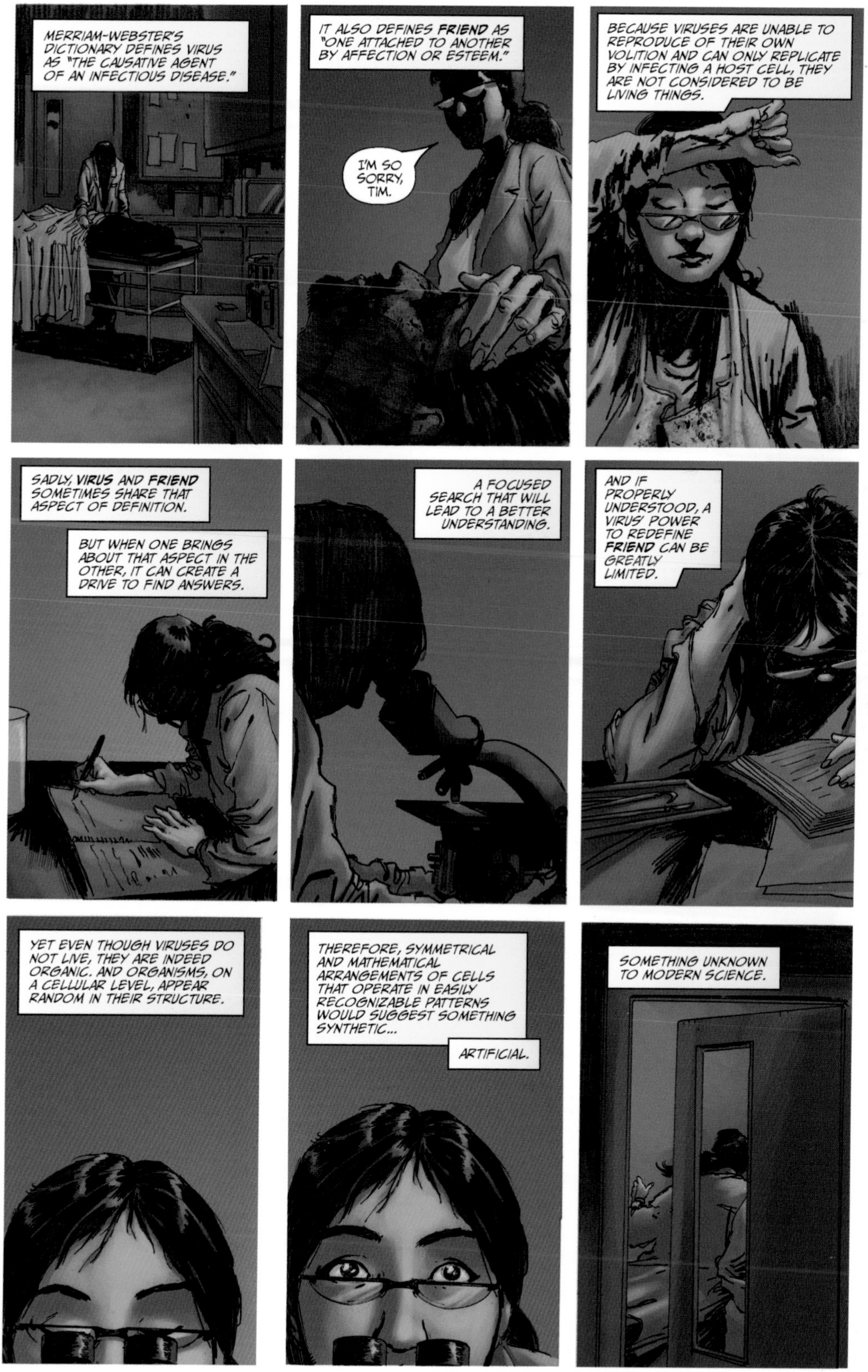
MERRIAM-WEBSTER'S DICTIONARY DEFINES VIRUS AS "THE CAUSATIVE AGENT OF AN INFECTIOUS DISEASE."
IT ALSO DEFINES **FRIEND** AS "ONE ATTACHED TO ANOTHER BY AFFECTION OR ESTEEM."
I'M SO SORRY, TIM.
BECAUSE VIRUSES ARE UNABLE TO REPRODUCE OF THEIR OWN VOLITION AND CAN ONLY REPLICATE BY INFECTING A HOST CELL, THEY ARE NOT CONSIDERED TO BE LIVING THINGS.
SADLY, **VIRUS** AND **FRIEND** SOMETIMES SHARE THAT ASPECT OF DEFINITION.
BUT WHEN ONE BRINGS ABOUT THAT ASPECT IN THE OTHER, IT CAN CREATE A DRIVE TO FIND ANSWERS.
A FOCUSED SEARCH THAT WILL LEAD TO A BETTER UNDERSTANDING.
AND IF PROPERLY UNDERSTOOD, A VIRUS' POWER TO REDEFINE **FRIEND** CAN BE GREATLY LIMITED.
YET EVEN THOUGH VIRUSES DO NOT LIVE, THEY ARE INDEED ORGANIC. AND ORGANISMS, ON A CELLULAR LEVEL, APPEAR RANDOM IN THEIR STRUCTURE.
THEREFORE, SYMMETRICAL AND MATHEMATICAL ARRANGEMENTS OF CELLS THAT OPERATE IN EASILY RECOGNIZABLE PATTERNS WOULD SUGGEST SOMETHING SYNTHETIC...
ARTIFICIAL.
SOMETHING UNKNOWN TO MODERN SCIENCE.

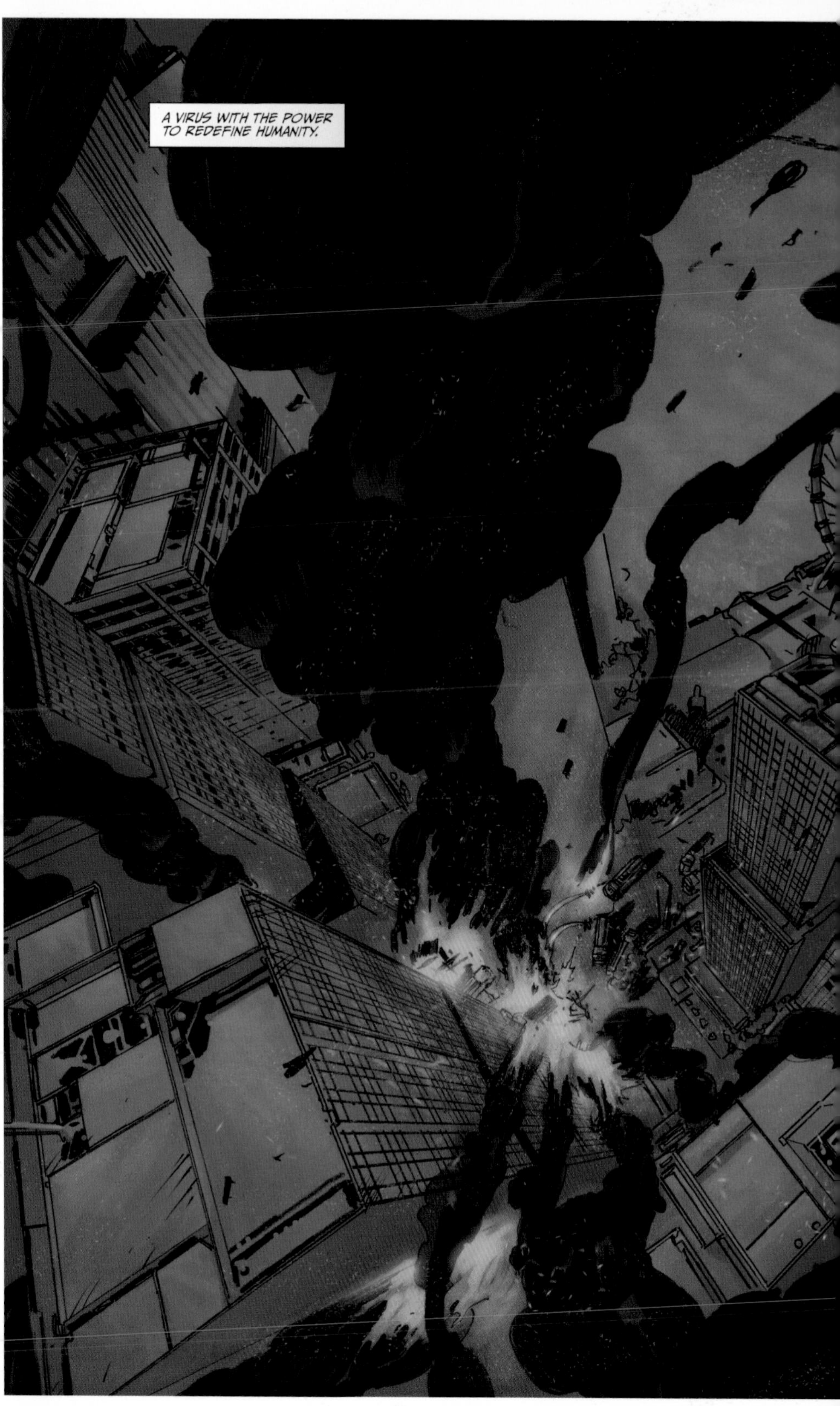
A VIRUS WITH THE POWER
TO REDEFINE HUMANITY.

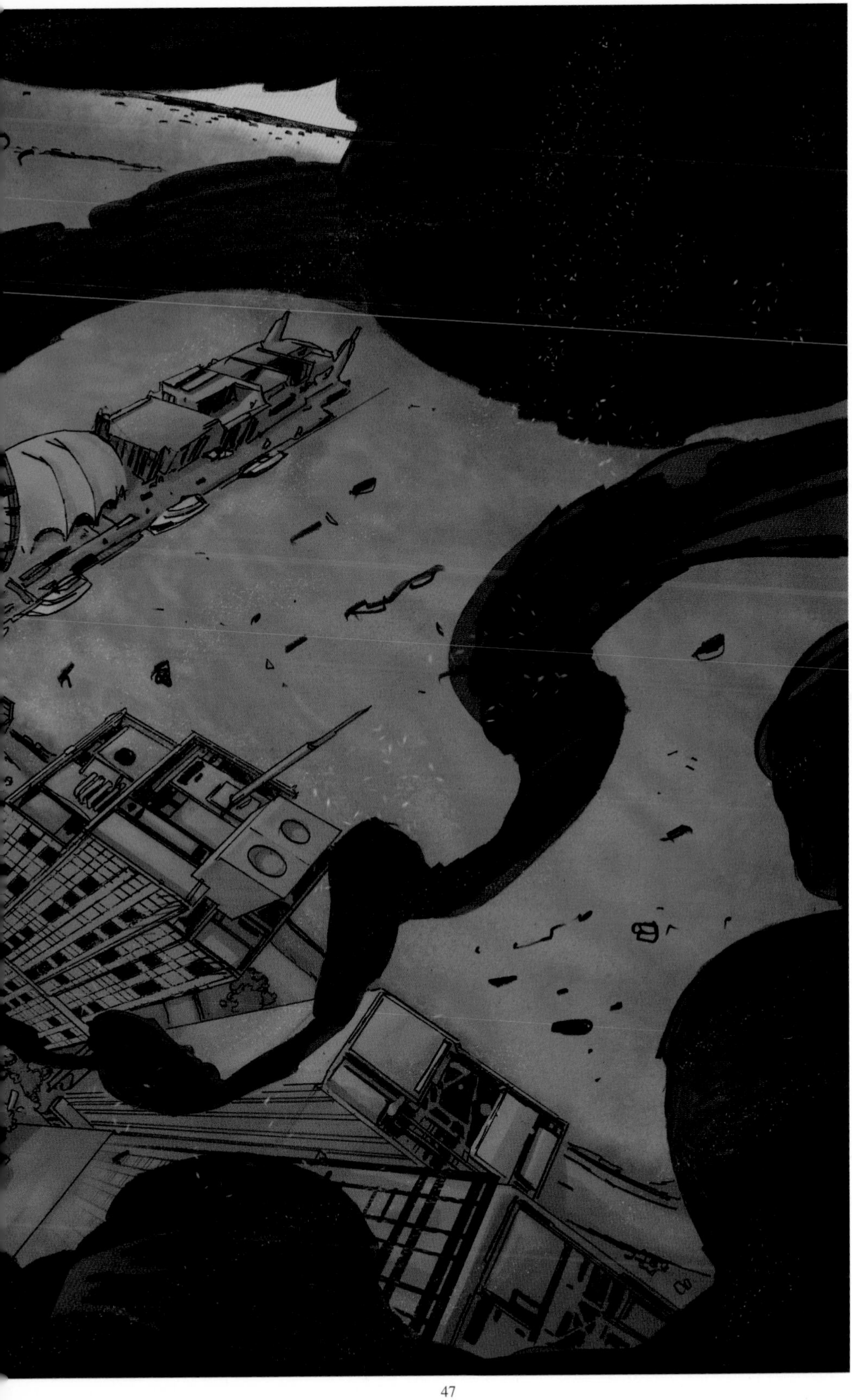

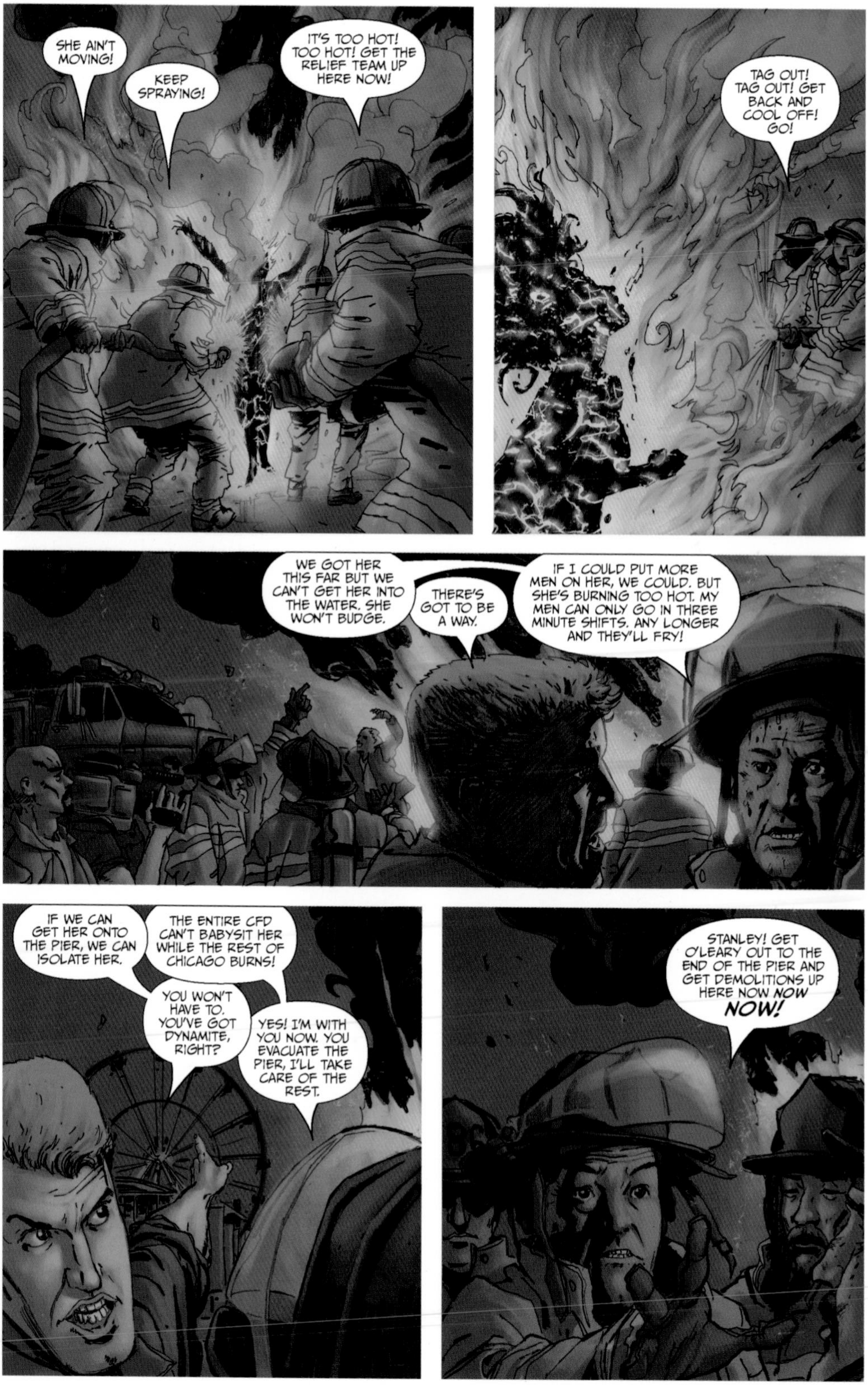

SHE AIN'T MOVING!
KEEP SPRAYING!
IT'S TOO HOT! TOO HOT! GET THE RELIEF TEAM UP HERE NOW!
TAG OUT! TAG OUT! GET BACK AND COOL OFF! GO!
WE GOT HER THIS FAR BUT WE CAN'T GET HER INTO THE WATER. SHE WON'T BUDGE.
THERE'S GOT TO BE A WAY.
IF I COULD PUT MORE MEN ON HER, WE COULD. BUT SHE'S BURNING TOO HOT. MY MEN CAN ONLY GO IN THREE MINUTE SHIFTS. ANY LONGER AND THEY'LL FRY!
IF WE CAN GET HER ONTO THE PIER, WE CAN ISOLATE HER.
THE ENTIRE CFD CAN'T BABYSIT HER WHILE THE REST OF CHICAGO BURNS!
YOU WON'T HAVE TO. YOU'VE GOT DYNAMITE, RIGHT?
YES! I'M WITH YOU NOW. YOU EVACUATE THE PIER, I'LL TAKE CARE OF THE REST.
STANLEY! GET O'LEARY OUT TO THE END OF THE PIER AND GET DEMOLITIONS UP HERE NOW *NOW* ***NOW!***

ON OCTOBER 8, 1871, A FIRE BROKE OUT AT 137 DEKOVEN STREET.

IT RAGED FOR TWO DAYS, DESTROYING FOUR SQUARE MILES OF URBAN LANDSCAPE AND KILLING HUNDREDS OF CHICAGO CITIZENS.

MOVE! MOVE! LET'S GO!

IT HAS SINCE BECOME KNOWN AS THE GREAT CHICAGO FIRE, ONE OF THE GREATEST TRAGEDIES OF 19TH CENTURY AMERICA.

ALL THANKS TO MRS. O'LEARY AND HER COW.

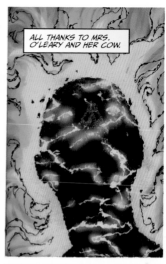

LEGEND TELLS THAT ONE OF HER COWS HAD KICKED OVER A LANTERN SHE HAD LEFT BURNING INSIDE OF HER BARN.

SOON AFTER, MICHAEL AHERN, A REPORTER FOR THE **CHICAGO REPUBLICAN**, WROTE AN ARTICLE BLAMING MRS. O'LEARY FOR STARTING THE DEADLY BLAZE.

MRS. O'LEARY SPENT THE REST OF HER LIFE AS AN OBJECT OF PUBLIC RIDICULE.

BUT IN 1893, MICHAEL AHERN RECANTED HIS ACCUSATION, STATING THAT HE FABRICATED THE STORY OF MRS. O'LEARY AND HER COW BECAUSE IT MADE FOR MORE ENTERTAINING REPORTING.

JUST A CLEVER FICTION DESIGNED TO SELL MORE NEWSPAPERS.

TODAY, NO ONE REMEMBERS THE NAME OF MICHAEL AHERN OR EVEN THE PAPER FOR WHICH HE WROTE. BUT ASK ANYONE IN CHICAGO AND THEY CAN TELL YOU THE LEGEND OF MRS. O'LEARY'S COW.

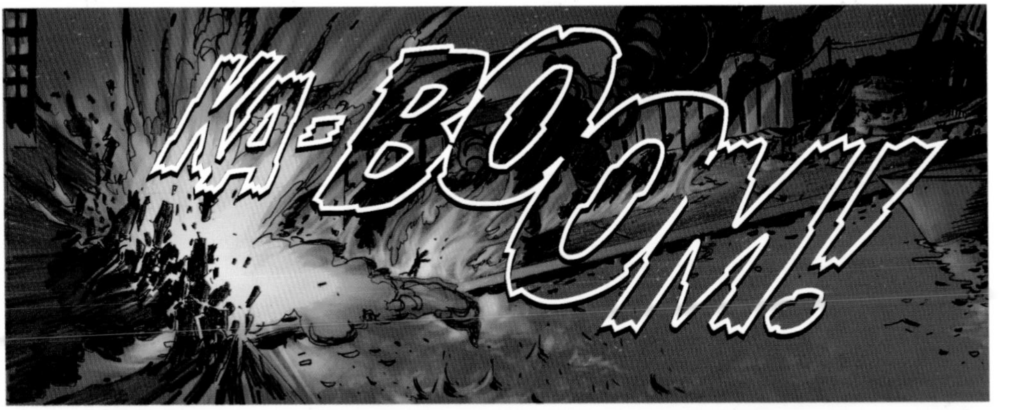
KA-BOOM!

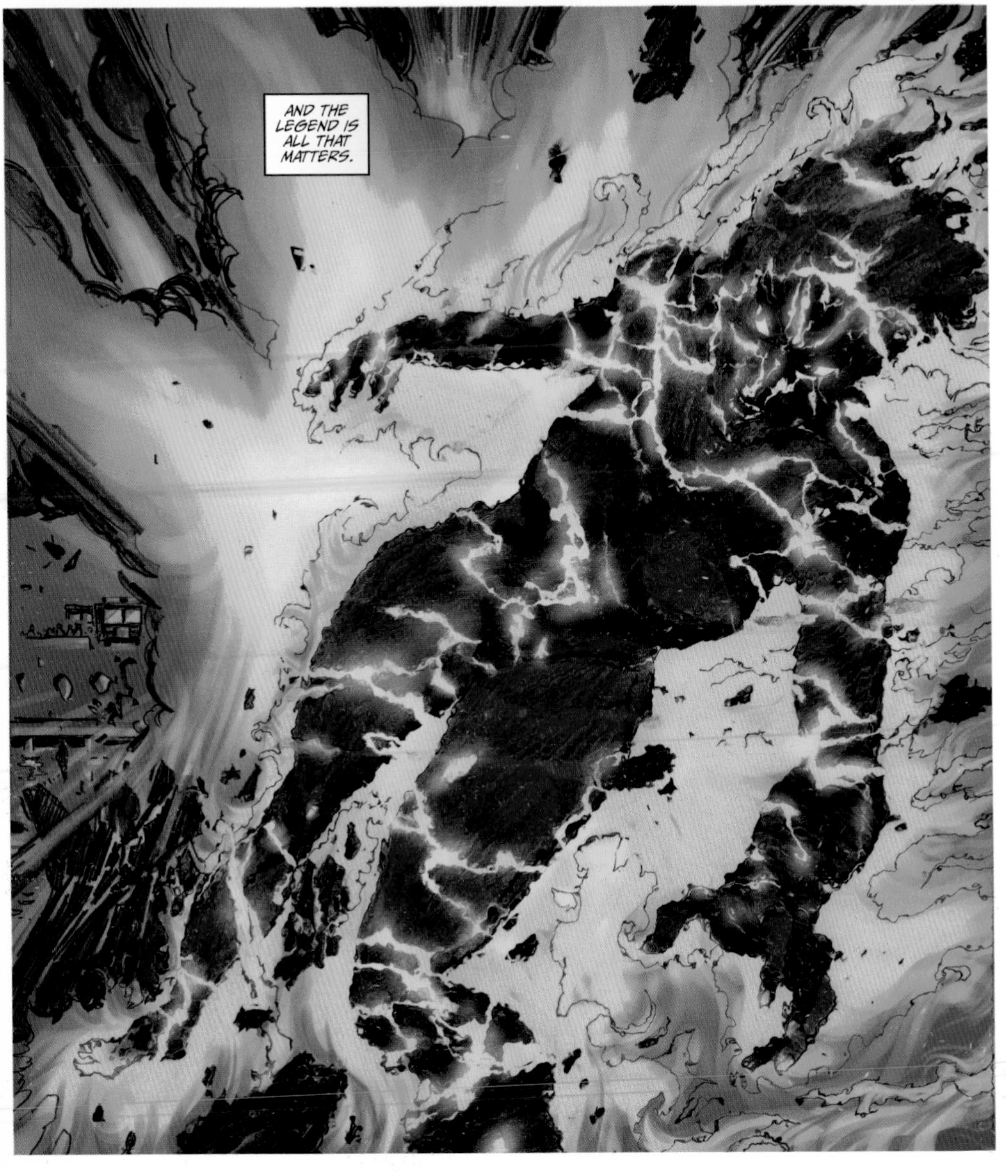
AND THE LEGEND IS ALL THAT MATTERS.

I CAN'T BELIEVE I JUST TURNED NAVY PIER INTO AN ISLAND.

LOOKS LIKE SHE WON'T TRY AND CROSS THE WATER THOUGH. THAT'LL KEEP HER TRAPPED FOR NOW.

THIS IS FOR REAL, ISN'T IT? SOME LADY TORCHED HALF MY CITY JUST BY WALKING THROUGH IT.

AFRAID SO.

ANY IDEA HOW THAT'S POSSIBLE?

NO. BUT MRS. O'LEARY ISN'T THE ONLY IMPOSSIBLE THING IN THE CITY.

SO I HEARD.

I'VE NEVER SEEN A FIRE BURN LIKE THIS. I DON'T KNOW IF I'LL BE ABLE TO CONTAIN IT, EVEN WITHOUT MRS. O'LEARY BREATHING DOWN MY NECK.

WELL, WITH THIS FIRE AND EVERYTHING ELSE GOING ON, WE'RE GOING TO HAVE TO EVACUATE THE CITY.

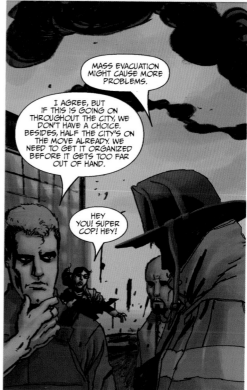

MASS EVACUATION MIGHT CAUSE MORE PROBLEMS.

I AGREE, BUT IF THIS IS GOING ON THROUGHOUT THE CITY, WE DON'T HAVE A CHOICE. BESIDES, HALF THE CITY'S ON THE MOVE ALREADY. WE NEED TO GET IT ORGANIZED BEFORE IT GETS TOO FAR OUT OF HAND.

HEY YOU! SUPER COP! HEY!

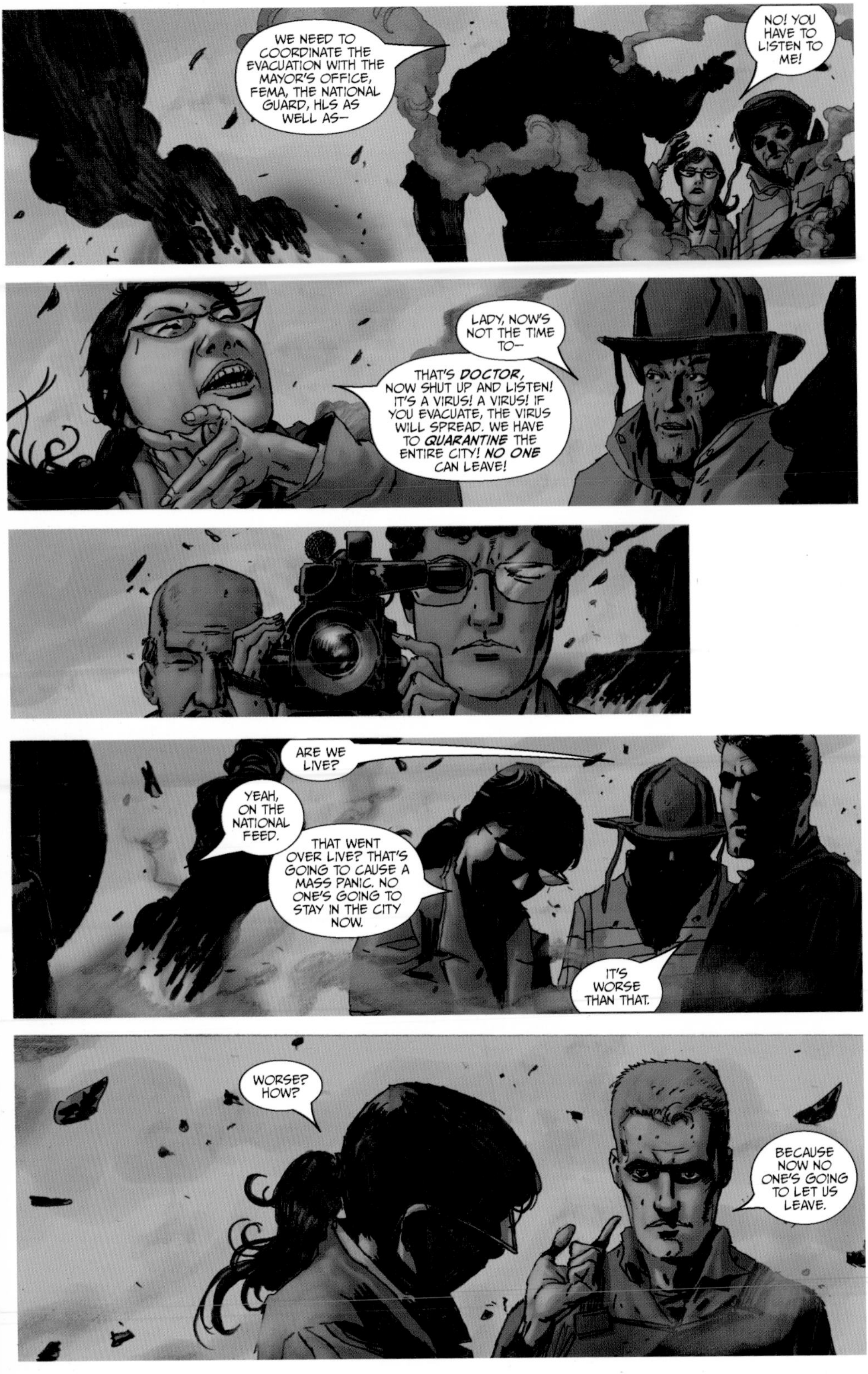
WE NEED TO COORDINATE THE EVACUATION WITH THE MAYOR'S OFFICE, FEMA, THE NATIONAL GUARD, HLS AS WELL AS--
NO! YOU HAVE TO LISTEN TO ME!
LADY, NOW'S NOT THE TIME TO--
THAT'S *DOCTOR*, NOW SHUT UP AND LISTEN! IT'S A VIRUS! A VIRUS! IF YOU EVACUATE, THE VIRUS WILL SPREAD. WE HAVE TO *QUARANTINE* THE ENTIRE CITY! *NO ONE* CAN LEAVE!
ARE WE LIVE?
YEAH, ON THE NATIONAL FEED.
THAT WENT OVER LIVE? THAT'S GOING TO CAUSE A MASS PANIC. NO ONE'S GOING TO STAY IN THE CITY NOW.
IT'S WORSE THAN THAT.
WORSE? HOW?
BECAUSE NOW NO ONE'S GOING TO LET US LEAVE.

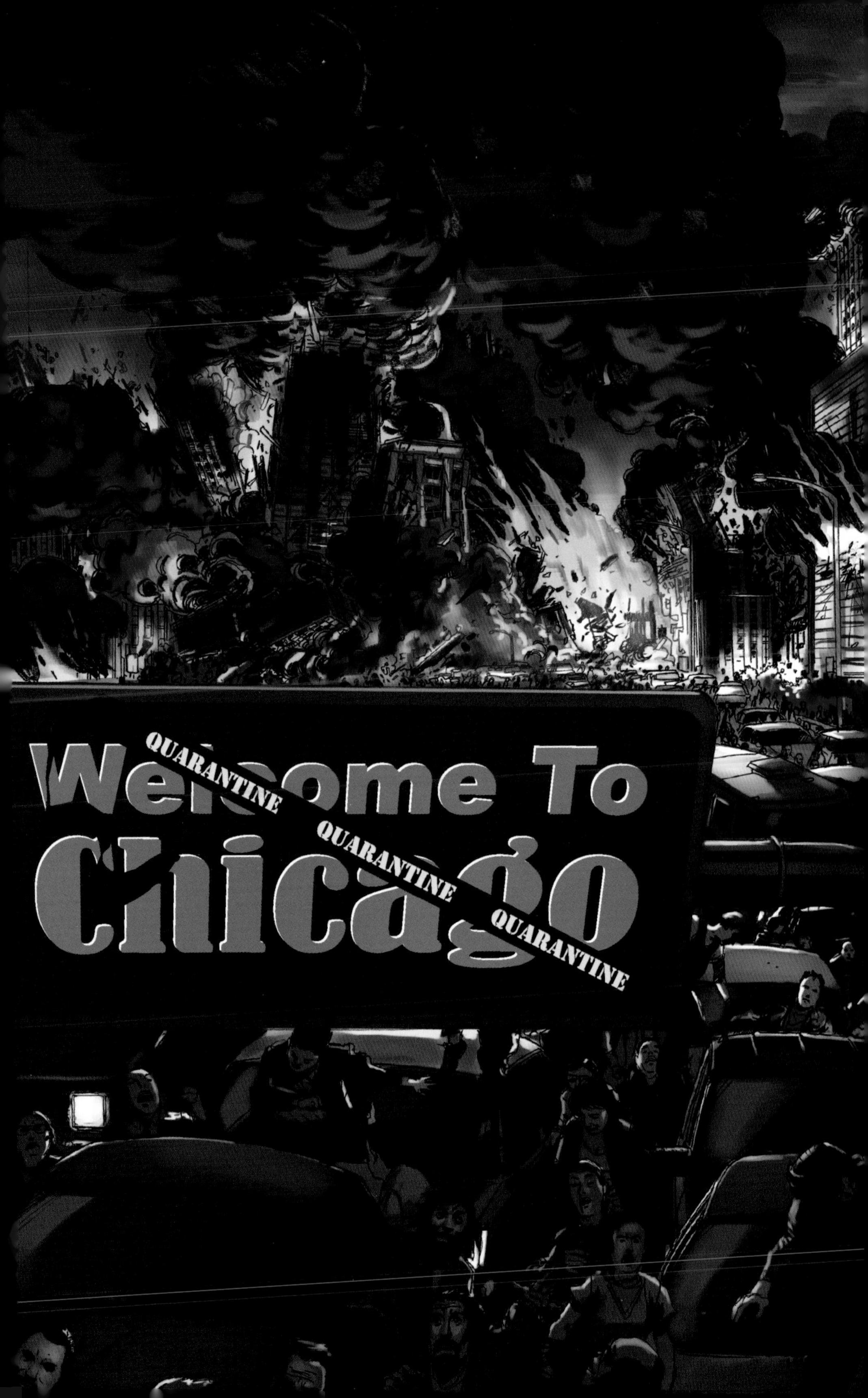
Welcome To Chicago
QUARANTINE
QUARANTINE
QUARANTINE

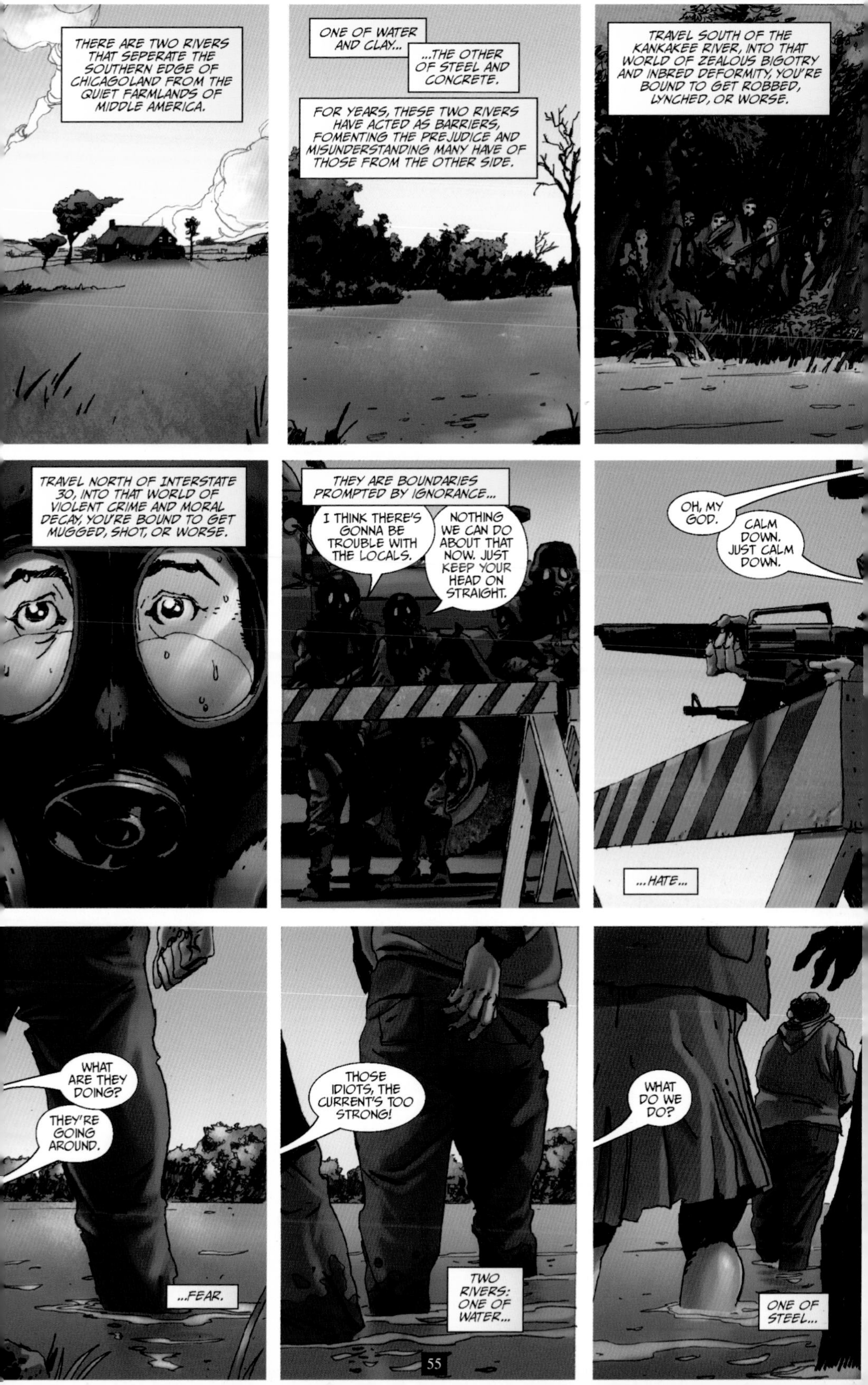
THERE ARE TWO RIVERS THAT SEPERATE THE SOUTHERN EDGE OF CHICAGOLAND FROM THE QUIET FARMLANDS OF MIDDLE AMERICA.
ONE OF WATER AND CLAY...
...THE OTHER OF STEEL AND CONCRETE.
FOR YEARS, THESE TWO RIVERS HAVE ACTED AS BARRIERS, FOMENTING THE PREJUDICE AND MISUNDERSTANDING MANY HAVE OF THOSE FROM THE OTHER SIDE.
TRAVEL SOUTH OF THE KANKAKEE RIVER, INTO THAT WORLD OF ZEALOUS BIGOTRY AND INBRED DEFORMITY, YOU'RE BOUND TO GET ROBBED, LYNCHED, OR WORSE.
TRAVEL NORTH OF INTERSTATE 30, INTO THAT WORLD OF VIOLENT CRIME AND MORAL DECAY, YOU'RE BOUND TO GET MUGGED, SHOT, OR WORSE.
THEY ARE BOUNDARIES PROMPTED BY IGNORANCE...
I THINK THERE'S GONNA BE TROUBLE WITH THE LOCALS.
NOTHING WE CAN DO ABOUT THAT NOW. JUST KEEP YOUR HEAD ON STRAIGHT.
OH, MY GOD.
CALM DOWN. JUST CALM DOWN.
...HATE...
WHAT ARE THEY DOING?
THEY'RE GOING AROUND.
...FEAR.
THOSE IDIOTS, THE CURRENT'S TOO STRONG!
TWO RIVERS: ONE OF WATER...
WHAT DO WE DO?
ONE OF STEEL...

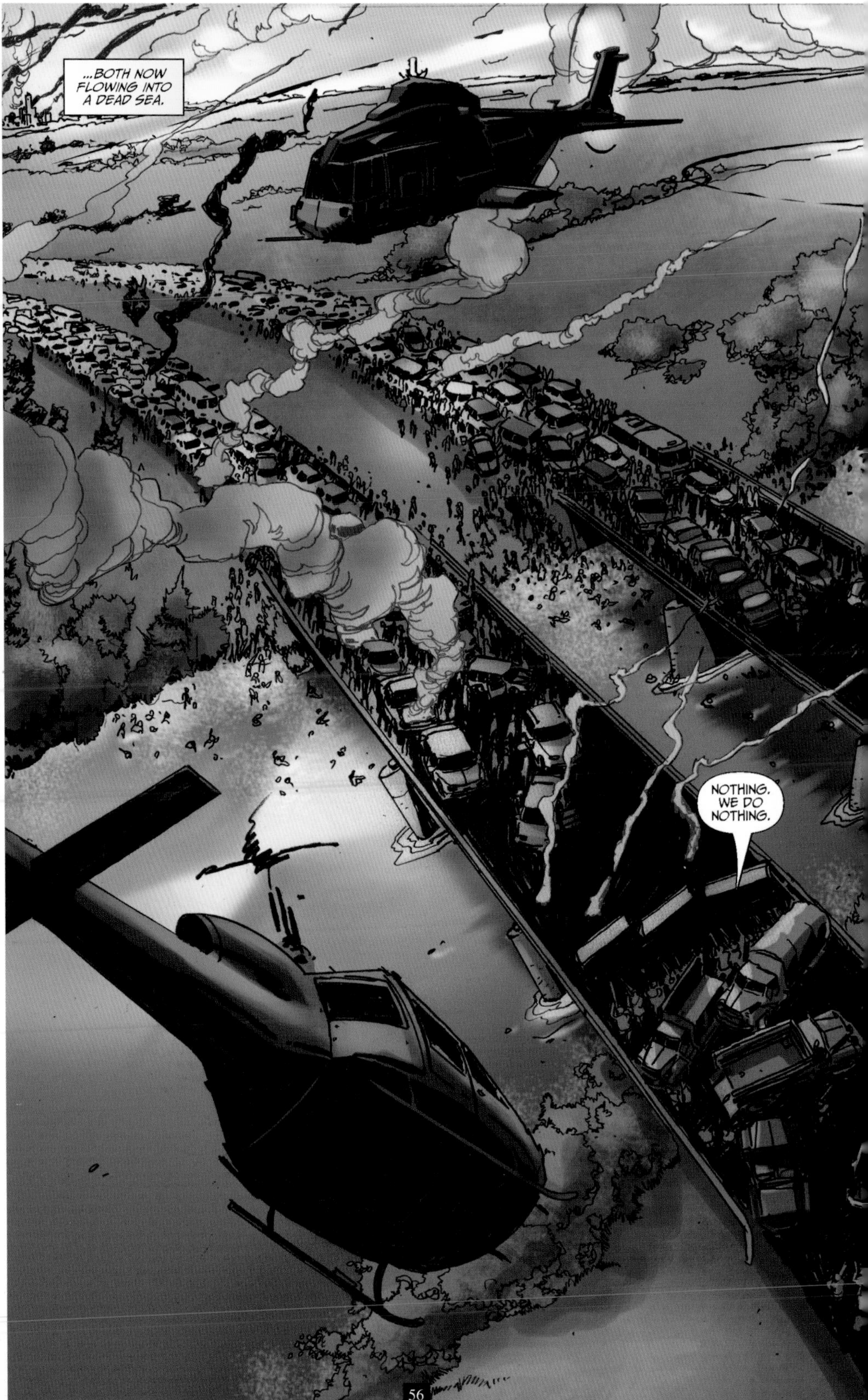
...BOTH NOW FLOWING INTO A DEAD SEA.
NOTHING. WE DO NOTHING.

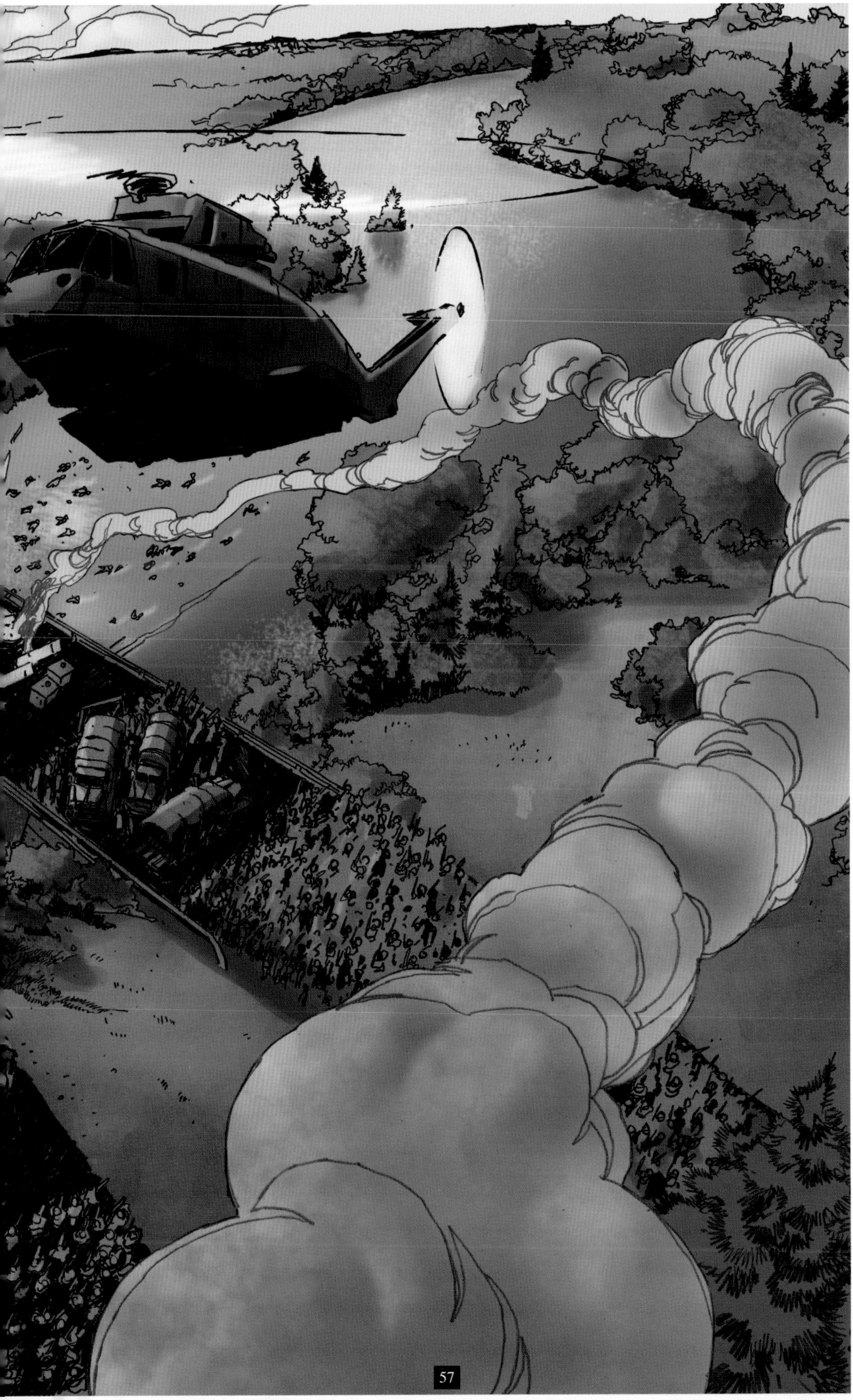

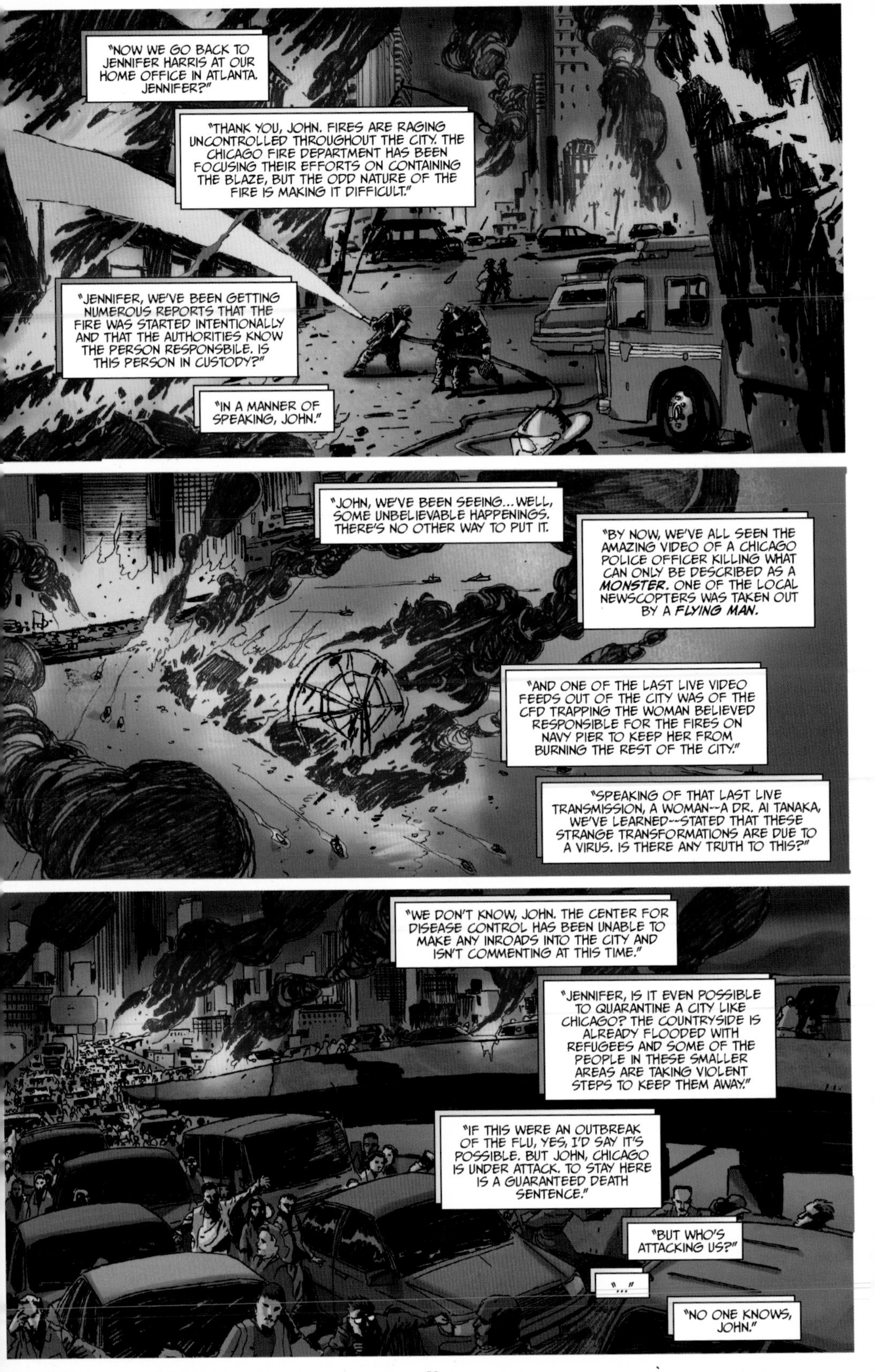
"NOW WE GO BACK TO JENNIFER HARRIS AT OUR HOME OFFICE IN ATLANTA. JENNIFER?"
"THANK YOU, JOHN. FIRES ARE RAGING UNCONTROLLED THROUGHOUT THE CITY. THE CHICAGO FIRE DEPARTMENT HAS BEEN FOCUSING THEIR EFFORTS ON CONTAINING THE BLAZE, BUT THE ODD NATURE OF THE FIRE IS MAKING IT DIFFICULT."
"JENNIFER, WE'VE BEEN GETTING NUMEROUS REPORTS THAT THE FIRE WAS STARTED INTENTIONALLY AND THAT THE AUTHORITIES KNOW THE PERSON RESPONSBILE. IS THIS PERSON IN CUSTODY?"
"IN A MANNER OF SPEAKING, JOHN."
"JOHN, WE'VE BEEN SEEING... WELL, SOME UNBELIEVABLE HAPPENINGS. THERE'S NO OTHER WAY TO PUT IT.
"BY NOW, WE'VE ALL SEEN THE AMAZING VIDEO OF A CHICAGO POLICE OFFICER KILLING WHAT CAN ONLY BE DESCRIBED AS A ***MONSTER.*** ONE OF THE LOCAL NEWSCOPTERS WAS TAKEN OUT BY A ***FLYING MAN.***
"AND ONE OF THE LAST LIVE VIDEO FEEDS OUT OF THE CITY WAS OF THE CFD TRAPPING THE WOMAN BELIEVED RESPONSIBLE FOR THE FIRES ON NAVY PIER TO KEEP HER FROM BURNING THE REST OF THE CITY."
"SPEAKING OF THAT LAST LIVE TRANSMISSION, A WOMAN--A DR. AI TANAKA, WE'VE LEARNED--STATED THAT THESE STRANGE TRANSFORMATIONS ARE DUE TO A VIRUS. IS THERE ANY TRUTH TO THIS?"
"WE DON'T KNOW, JOHN. THE CENTER FOR DISEASE CONTROL HAS BEEN UNABLE TO MAKE ANY INROADS INTO THE CITY AND ISN'T COMMENTING AT THIS TIME."
"JENNIFER, IS IT EVEN POSSIBLE TO QUARANTINE A CITY LIKE CHICAGO? THE COUNTRYSIDE IS ALREADY FLOODED WITH REFUGEES AND SOME OF THE PEOPLE IN THESE SMALLER AREAS ARE TAKING VIOLENT STEPS TO KEEP THEM AWAY."
"IF THIS WERE AN OUTBREAK OF THE FLU, YES, I'D SAY IT'S POSSIBLE. BUT JOHN, CHICAGO IS UNDER ATTACK. TO STAY HERE IS A GUARANTEED DEATH SENTENCE."
"BUT WHO'S ATTACKING US?"
"..."
"NO ONE KNOWS, JOHN."

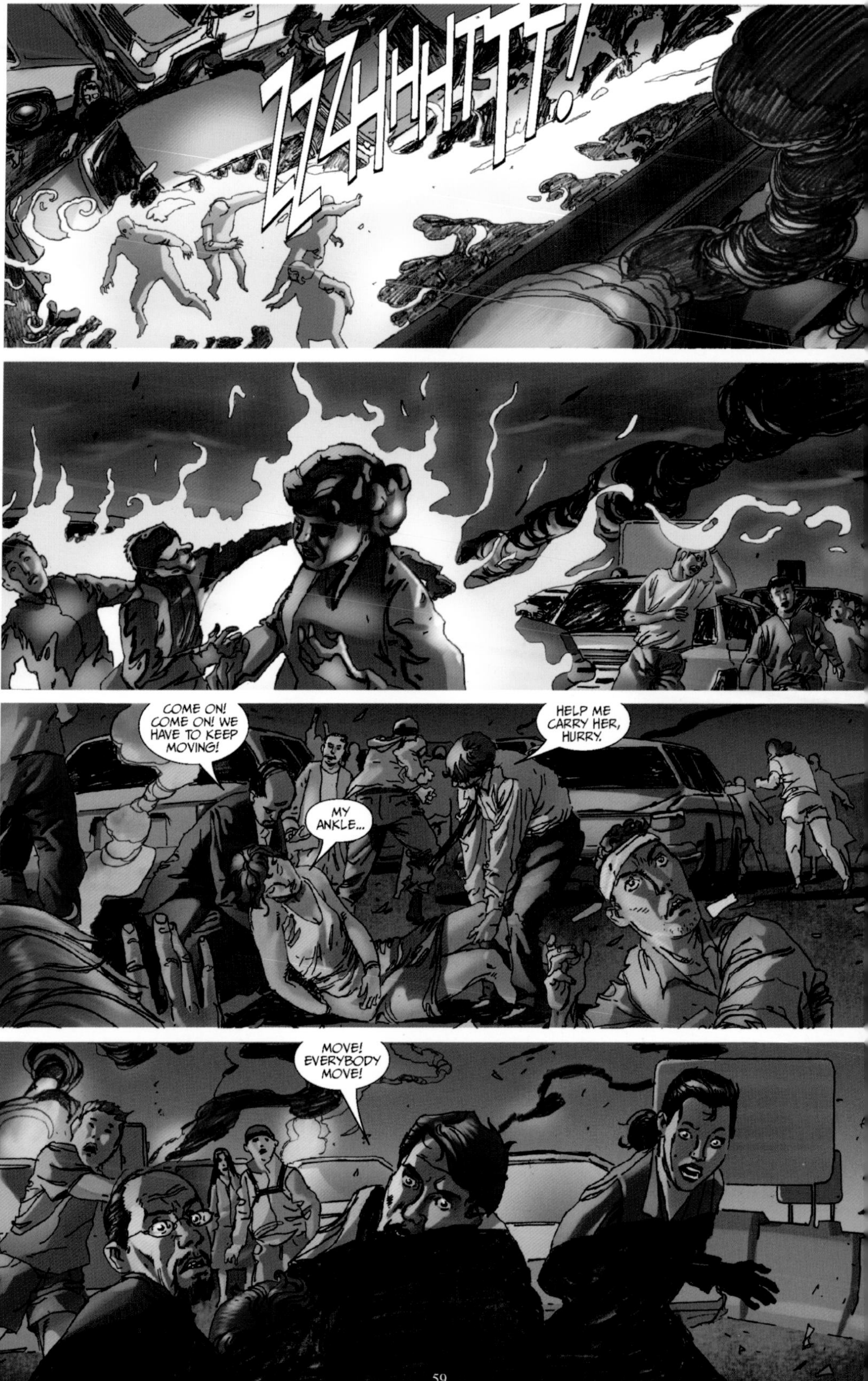
ZZZHHHTTT!
COME ON! COME ON! WE HAVE TO KEEP MOVING!
HELP ME CARRY HER, HURRY.
MY ANKLE...
MOVE! EVERYBODY MOVE!

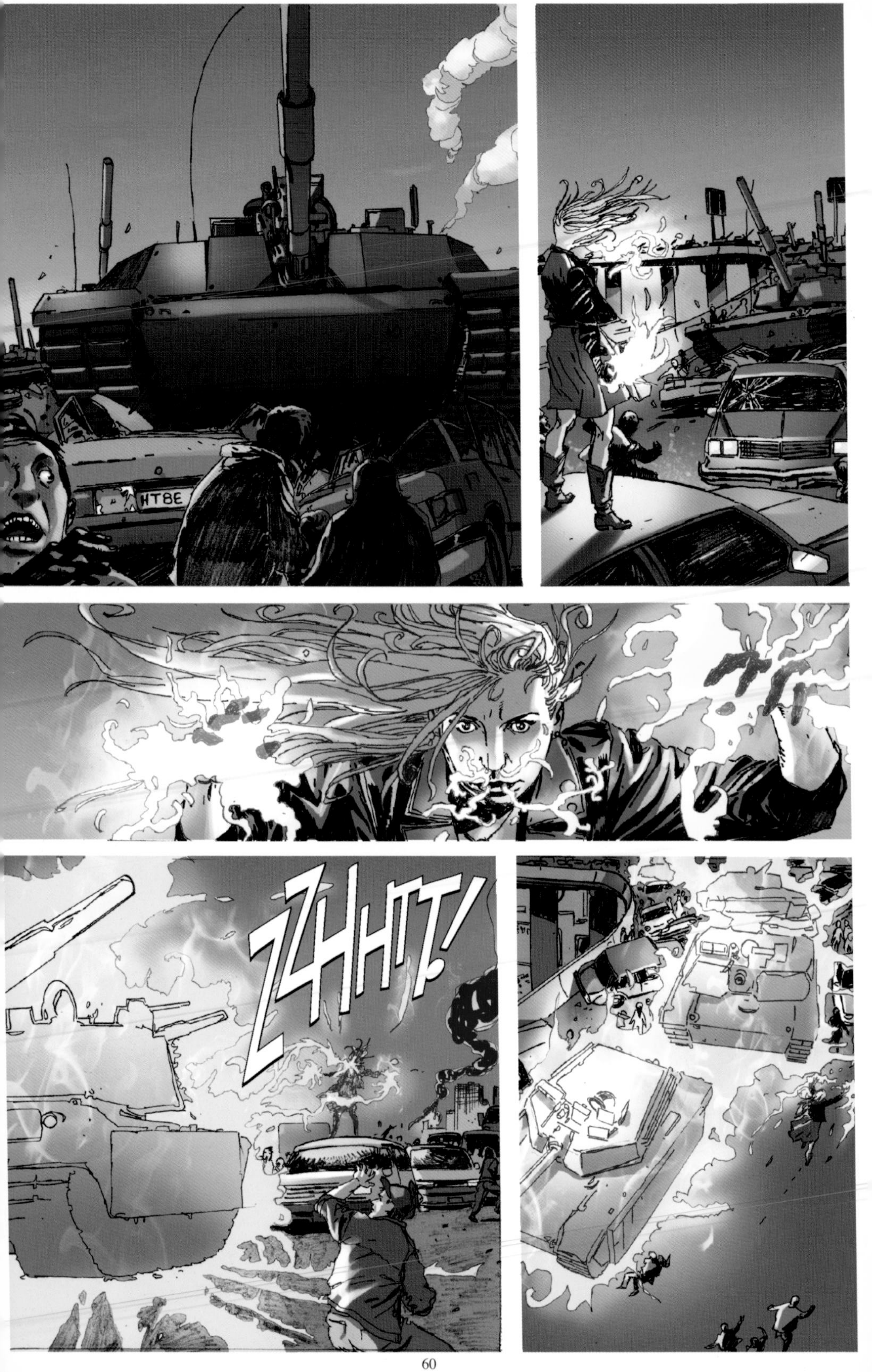
HT8E
ZZHHT!

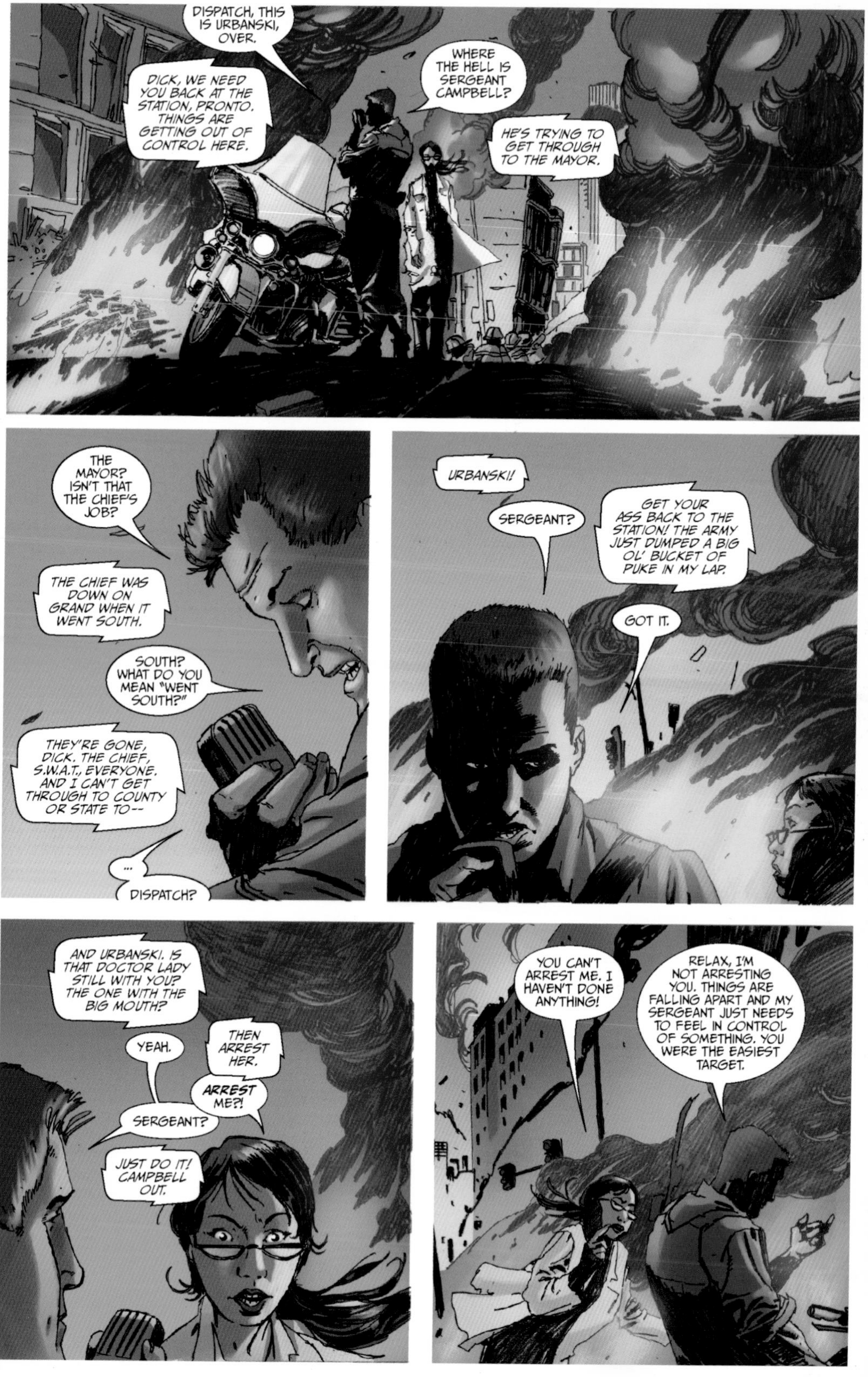
DISPATCH, THIS IS URBANSKI, OVER.
DICK, WE NEED YOU BACK AT THE STATION, PRONTO. THINGS ARE GETTING OUT OF CONTROL HERE.
WHERE THE HELL IS SERGEANT CAMPBELL?
HE'S TRYING TO GET THROUGH TO THE MAYOR.
THE MAYOR? ISN'T THAT THE CHIEF'S JOB?
THE CHIEF WAS DOWN ON GRAND WHEN IT WENT SOUTH.
SOUTH? WHAT DO YOU MEAN "WENT SOUTH?"
THEY'RE GONE, DICK. THE CHIEF, S.W.A.T., EVERYONE. AND I CAN'T GET THROUGH TO COUNTY OR STATE TO--
...
DISPATCH?
URBANSKI!
SERGEANT?
GET YOUR ASS BACK TO THE STATION! THE ARMY JUST DUMPED A BIG OL' BUCKET OF PUKE IN MY LAP.
GOT IT.
AND URBANSKI. IS THAT DOCTOR LADY STILL WITH YOU? THE ONE WITH THE BIG MOUTH?
YEAH.
THEN ARREST HER.
ARREST ME?!
SERGEANT?
JUST DO IT! CAMPBELL OUT.
YOU CAN'T ARREST ME. I HAVEN'T DONE ANYTHING!
RELAX, I'M NOT ARRESTING YOU. THINGS ARE FALLING APART AND MY SERGEANT JUST NEEDS TO FEEL IN CONTROL OF SOMETHING. YOU WERE THE EASIEST TARGET.

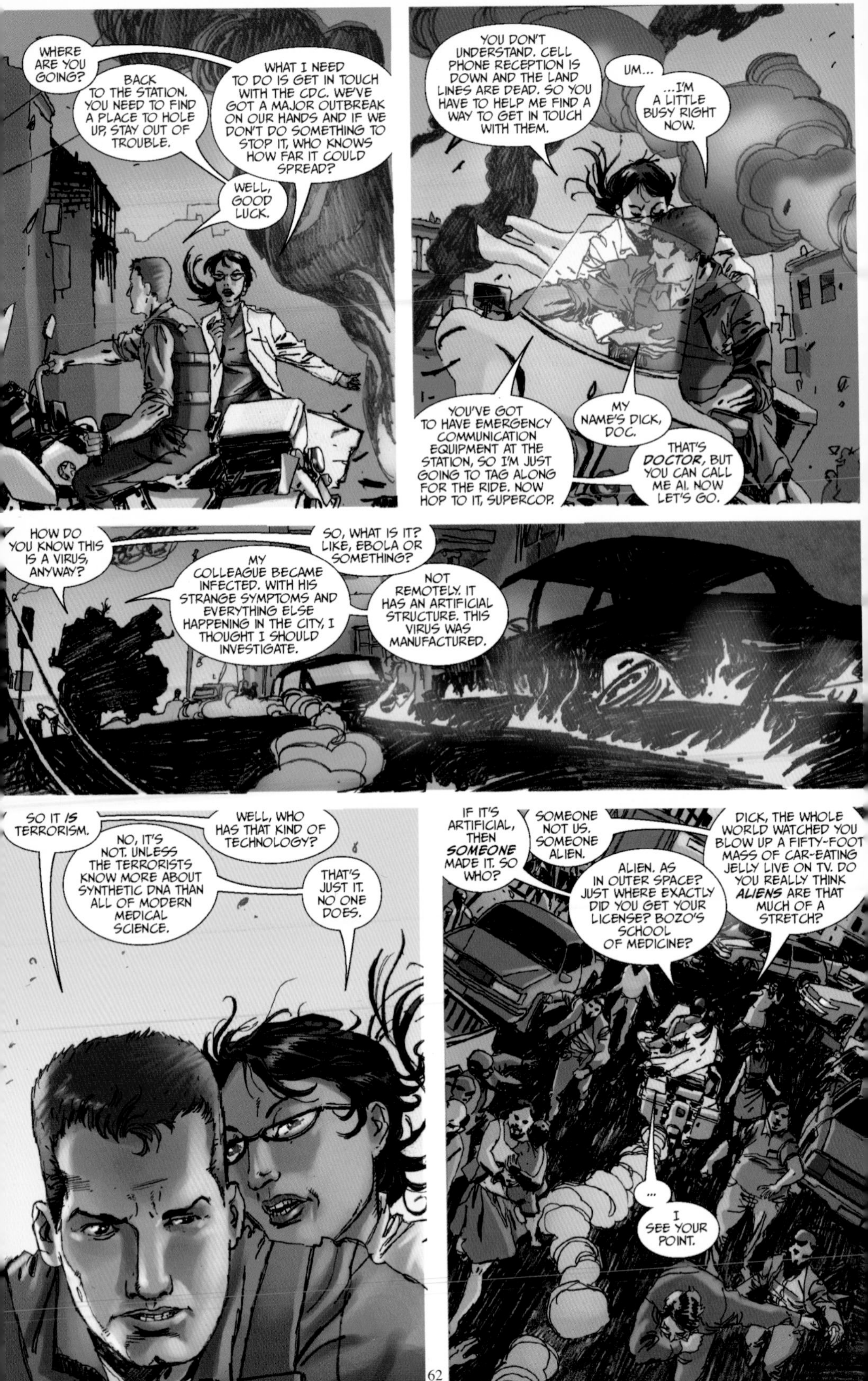
WHERE ARE YOU GOING?
BACK TO THE STATION. YOU NEED TO FIND A PLACE TO HOLE UP, STAY OUT OF TROUBLE.
WHAT I NEED TO DO IS GET IN TOUCH WITH THE CDC. WE'VE GOT A MAJOR OUTBREAK ON OUR HANDS AND IF WE DON'T DO SOMETHING TO STOP IT, WHO KNOWS HOW FAR IT COULD SPREAD?
WELL, GOOD LUCK.
YOU DON'T UNDERSTAND. CELL PHONE RECEPTION IS DOWN AND THE LAND LINES ARE DEAD. SO YOU HAVE TO HELP ME FIND A WAY TO GET IN TOUCH WITH THEM.
UM...
...I'M A LITTLE BUSY RIGHT NOW.
YOU'VE GOT TO HAVE EMERGENCY COMMUNICATION EQUIPMENT AT THE STATION, SO I'M JUST GOING TO TAG ALONG FOR THE RIDE. NOW HOP TO IT, SUPERCOP.
MY NAME'S DICK, DOC.
THAT'S DOCTOR, BUT YOU CAN CALL ME AI. NOW LET'S GO.
HOW DO YOU KNOW THIS IS A VIRUS, ANYWAY?
MY COLLEAGUE BECAME INFECTED. WITH HIS STRANGE SYMPTOMS AND EVERYTHING ELSE HAPPENING IN THE CITY, I THOUGHT I SHOULD INVESTIGATE.
SO, WHAT IS IT? LIKE, EBOLA OR SOMETHING?
NOT REMOTELY. IT HAS AN ARTIFICIAL STRUCTURE. THIS VIRUS WAS MANUFACTURED.
SO IT IS TERRORISM.
NO, IT'S NOT. UNLESS THE TERRORISTS KNOW MORE ABOUT SYNTHETIC DNA THAN ALL OF MODERN MEDICAL SCIENCE.
WELL, WHO HAS THAT KIND OF TECHNOLOGY?
THAT'S JUST IT. NO ONE DOES.
IF IT'S ARTIFICIAL, THEN SOMEONE MADE IT. SO WHO?
SOMEONE NOT US. SOMEONE ALIEN.
ALIEN. AS IN OUTER SPACE? JUST WHERE EXACTLY DID YOU GET YOUR LICENSE? BOZO'S SCHOOL OF MEDICINE?
DICK, THE WHOLE WORLD WATCHED YOU BLOW UP A FIFTY-FOOT MASS OF CAR-EATING JELLY LIVE ON TV. DO YOU REALLY THINK ALIENS ARE THAT MUCH OF A STRETCH?
...
I SEE YOUR POINT.

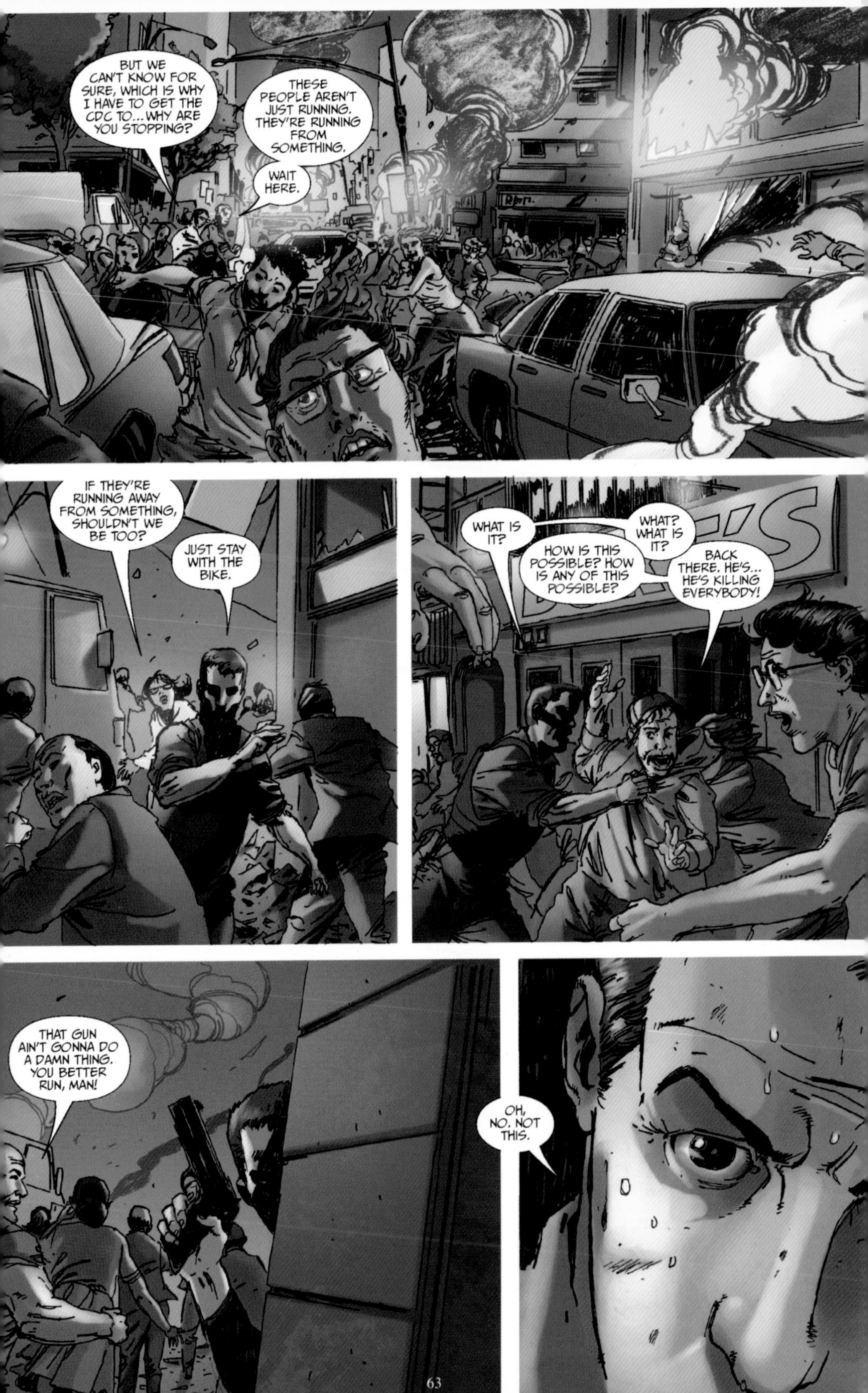
BUT WE CAN'T KNOW FOR SURE, WHICH IS WHY I HAVE TO GET THE CDC TO... WHY ARE YOU STOPPING?
THESE PEOPLE AREN'T JUST RUNNING. THEY'RE RUNNING FROM SOMETHING.
WAIT HERE.
IF THEY'RE RUNNING AWAY FROM SOMETHING, SHOULDN'T WE BE TOO?
JUST STAY WITH THE BIKE.
WHAT IS IT?
WHAT? WHAT IS IT?
HOW IS THIS POSSIBLE? HOW IS ANY OF THIS POSSIBLE?
BACK THERE. HE'S... HE'S KILLING EVERYBODY!
THAT GUN AIN'T GONNA DO A DAMN THING. YOU BETTER RUN, MAN!
OH, NO. NOT THIS.

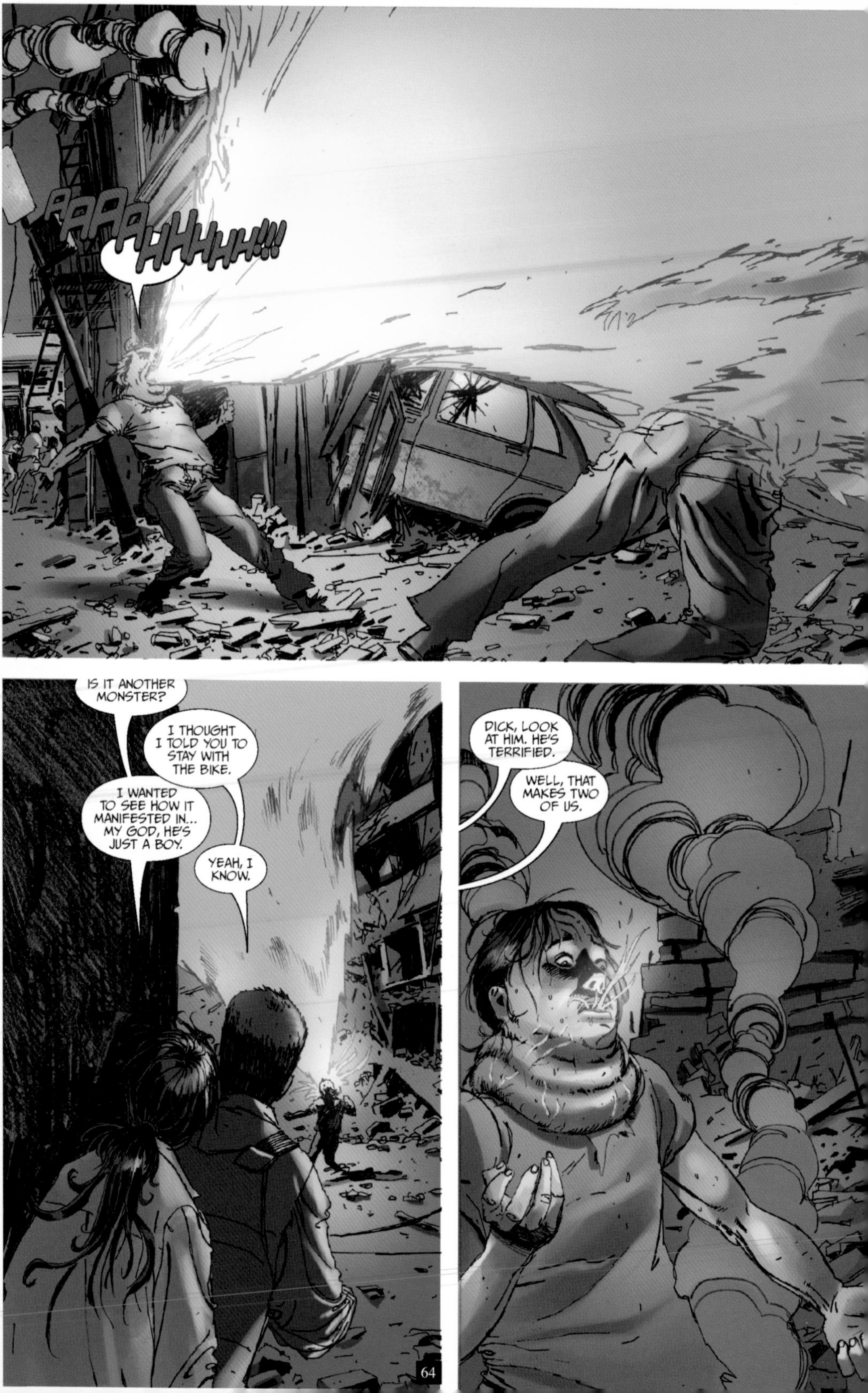
AAAAHHHHHH!!!
IS IT ANOTHER MONSTER?
I THOUGHT I TOLD YOU TO STAY WITH THE BIKE.
I WANTED TO SEE HOW IT MANIFESTED IN... MY GOD, HE'S JUST A BOY.
YEAH, I KNOW.
DICK, LOOK AT HIM. HE'S TERRIFIED.
WELL, THAT MAKES TWO OF US.

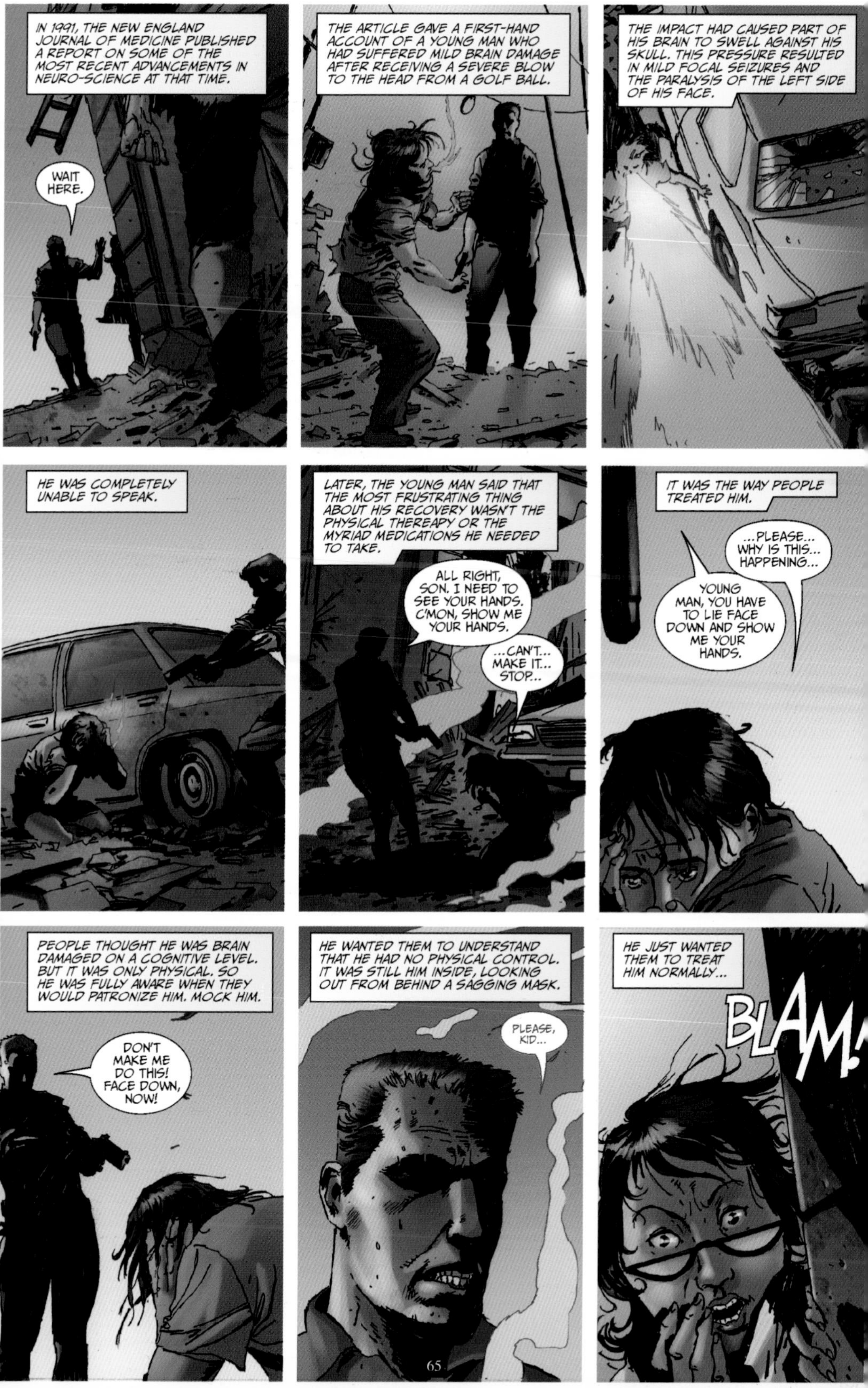
IN 1991, THE NEW ENGLAND JOURNAL OF MEDICINE PUBLISHED A REPORT ON SOME OF THE MOST RECENT ADVANCEMENTS IN NEURO-SCIENCE AT THAT TIME.
WAIT HERE.
THE ARTICLE GAVE A FIRST-HAND ACCOUNT OF A YOUNG MAN WHO HAD SUFFERED MILD BRAIN DAMAGE AFTER RECEIVING A SEVERE BLOW TO THE HEAD FROM A GOLF BALL.
THE IMPACT HAD CAUSED PART OF HIS BRAIN TO SWELL AGAINST HIS SKULL. THIS PRESSURE RESULTED IN MILD FOCAL SEIZURES AND THE PARALYSIS OF THE LEFT SIDE OF HIS FACE.
HE WAS COMPLETELY UNABLE TO SPEAK.
LATER, THE YOUNG MAN SAID THAT THE MOST FRUSTRATING THING ABOUT HIS RECOVERY WASN'T THE PHYSICAL THEREAPY OR THE MYRIAD MEDICATIONS HE NEEDED TO TAKE.
ALL RIGHT, SON. I NEED TO SEE YOUR HANDS. C'MON, SHOW ME YOUR HANDS.
...CAN'T... MAKE IT... STOP...
IT WAS THE WAY PEOPLE TREATED HIM.
...PLEASE... WHY IS THIS... HAPPENING...
YOUNG MAN, YOU HAVE TO LIE FACE DOWN AND SHOW ME YOUR HANDS.
PEOPLE THOUGHT HE WAS BRAIN DAMAGED ON A COGNITIVE LEVEL. BUT IT WAS ONLY PHYSICAL. SO HE WAS FULLY AWARE WHEN THEY WOULD PATRONIZE HIM. MOCK HIM.
DON'T MAKE ME DO THIS! FACE DOWN, NOW!
HE WANTED THEM TO UNDERSTAND THAT HE HAD NO PHYSICAL CONTROL. IT WAS STILL HIM INSIDE, LOOKING OUT FROM BEHIND A SAGGING MASK.
PLEASE, KID...
HE JUST WANTED THEM TO TREAT HIM NORMALLY...
BLAM!

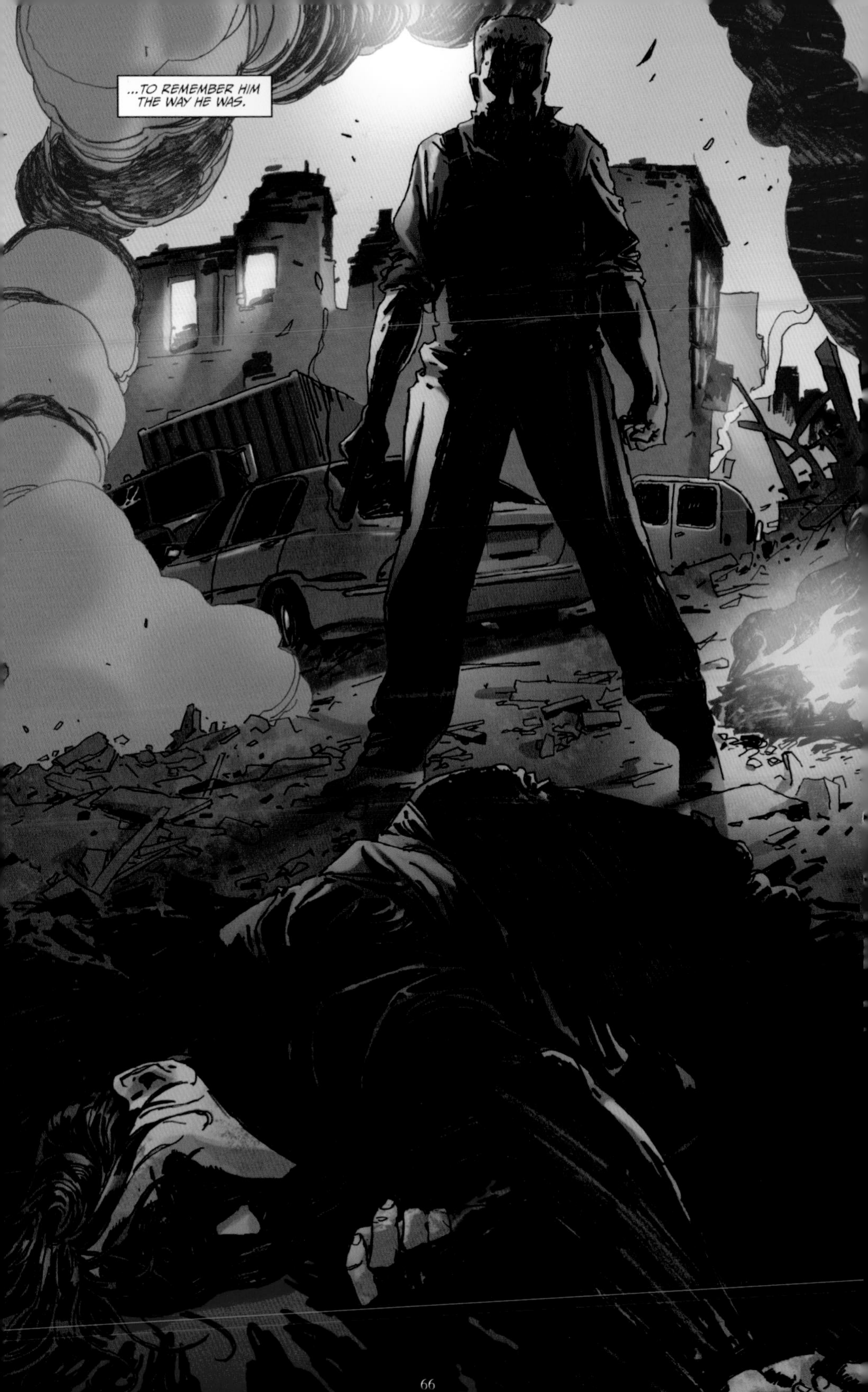
...TO REMEMBER HIM THE WAY HE WAS.

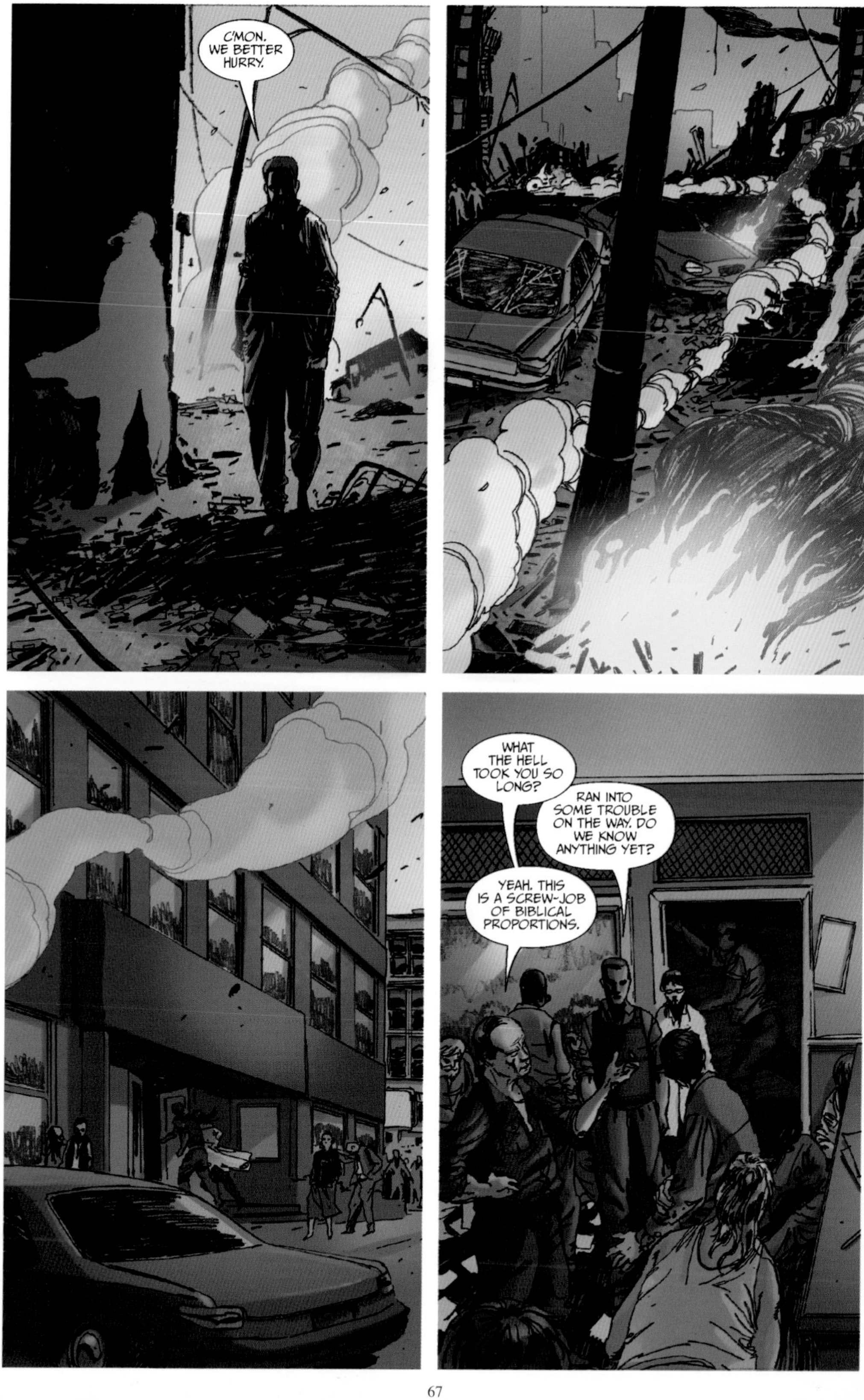
C'MON. WE BETTER HURRY.
WHAT THE HELL TOOK YOU SO LONG?
RAN INTO SOME TROUBLE ON THE WAY. DO WE KNOW ANYTHING YET?
YEAH. THIS IS A SCREW-JOB OF BIBLICAL PROPORTIONS.

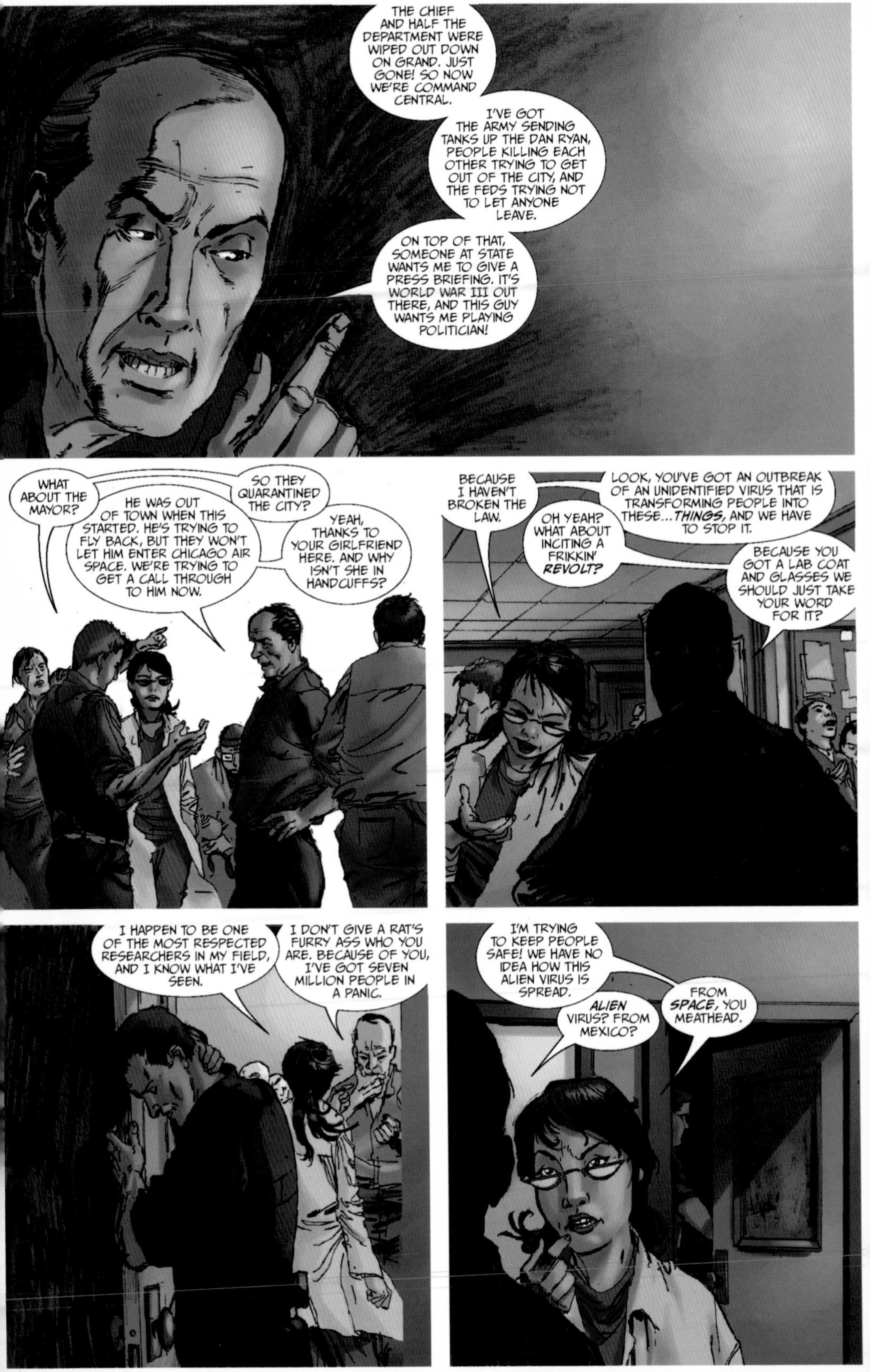
THE CHIEF AND HALF THE DEPARTMENT WERE WIPED OUT DOWN ON GRAND. JUST GONE! SO NOW WE'RE COMMAND CENTRAL.
I'VE GOT THE ARMY SENDING TANKS UP THE DAN RYAN, PEOPLE KILLING EACH OTHER TRYING TO GET OUT OF THE CITY, AND THE FEDS TRYING NOT TO LET ANYONE LEAVE.
ON TOP OF THAT, SOMEONE AT STATE WANTS ME TO GIVE A PRESS BRIEFING. IT'S WORLD WAR III OUT THERE, AND THIS GUY WANTS ME PLAYING POLITICIAN!
WHAT ABOUT THE MAYOR?
HE WAS OUT OF TOWN WHEN THIS STARTED. HE'S TRYING TO FLY BACK, BUT THEY WON'T LET HIM ENTER CHICAGO AIR SPACE. WE'RE TRYING TO GET A CALL THROUGH TO HIM NOW.
SO THEY QUARANTINED THE CITY?
YEAH, THANKS TO YOUR GIRLFRIEND HERE. AND WHY ISN'T SHE IN HANDCUFFS?
BECAUSE I HAVEN'T BROKEN THE LAW.
OH YEAH? WHAT ABOUT INCITING A FRIKKIN' *REVOLT?*
LOOK, YOU'VE GOT AN OUTBREAK OF AN UNIDENTIFIED VIRUS THAT IS TRANSFORMING PEOPLE INTO THESE... *THINGS*, AND WE HAVE TO STOP IT.
BECAUSE YOU GOT A LAB COAT AND GLASSES WE SHOULD JUST TAKE YOUR WORD FOR IT?
I HAPPEN TO BE ONE OF THE MOST RESPECTED RESEARCHERS IN MY FIELD, AND I KNOW WHAT I'VE SEEN.
I DON'T GIVE A RAT'S FURRY ASS WHO YOU ARE. BECAUSE OF YOU, I'VE GOT SEVEN MILLION PEOPLE IN A PANIC.
I'M TRYING TO KEEP PEOPLE SAFE! WE HAVE NO IDEA HOW THIS ALIEN VIRUS IS SPREAD.
ALIEN VIRUS? FROM MEXICO?
FROM *SPACE*, YOU MEATHEAD.

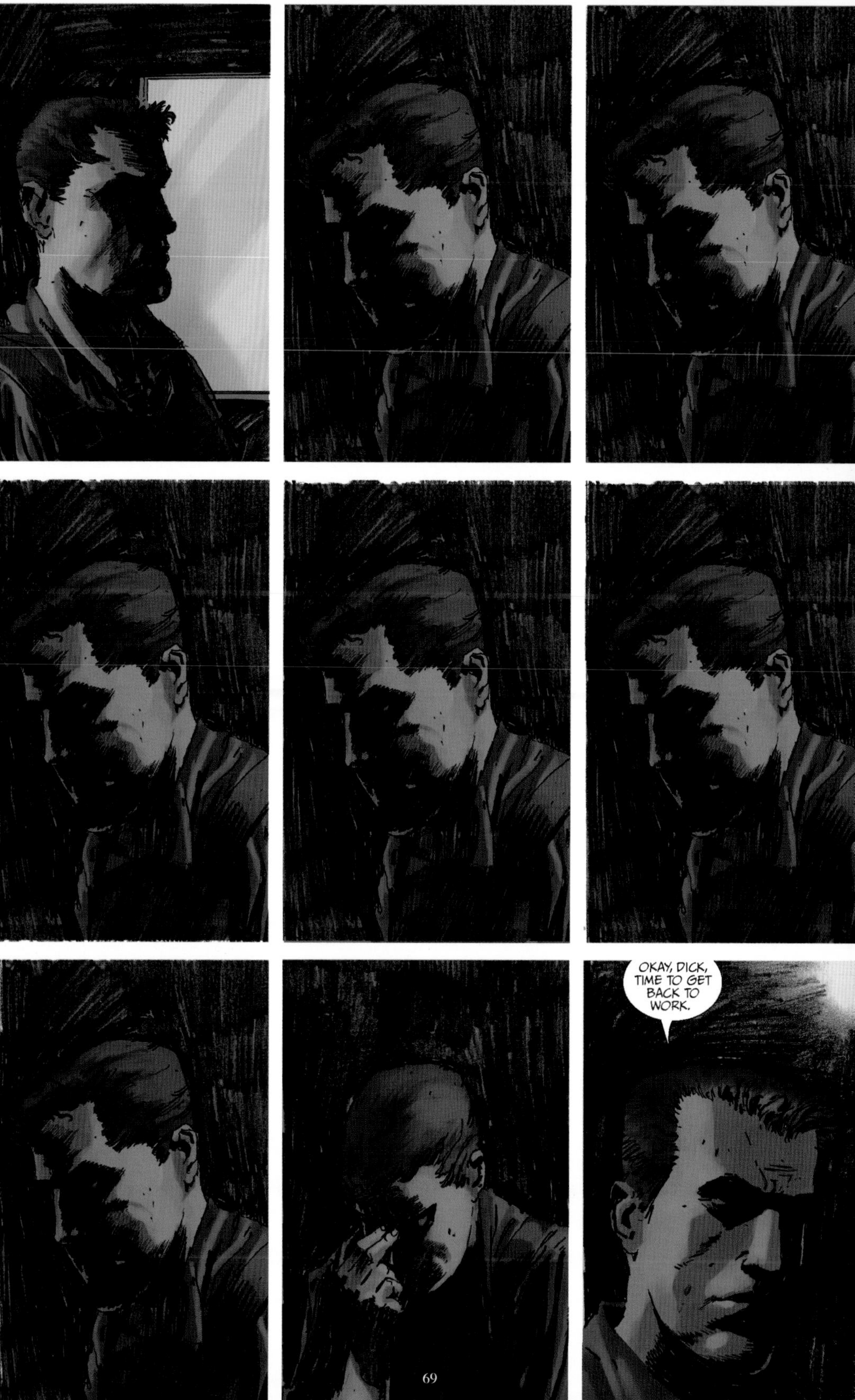
OKAY, DICK, TIME TO GET BACK TO WORK.

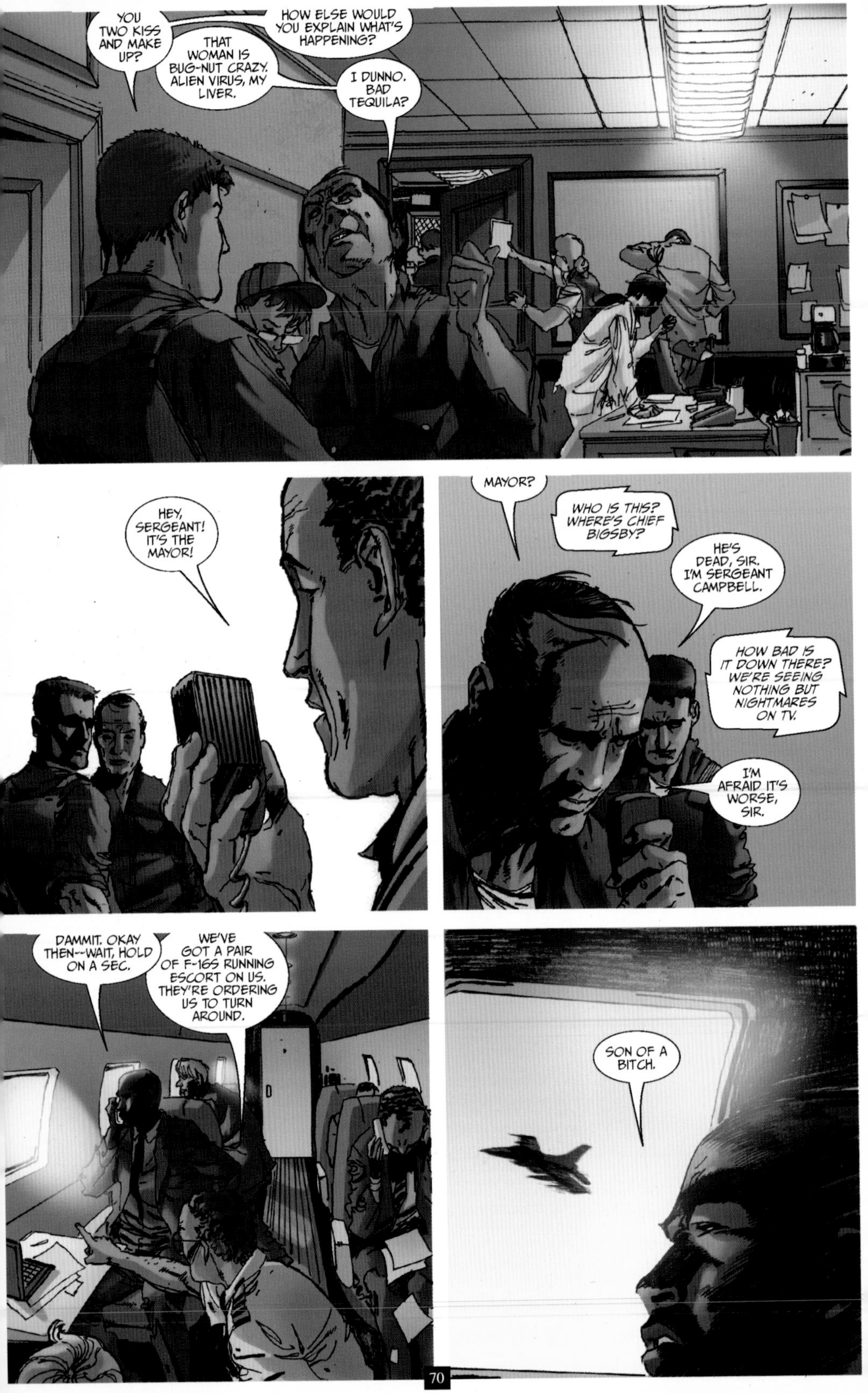

YOU TWO KISS AND MAKE UP?
HOW ELSE WOULD YOU EXPLAIN WHAT'S HAPPENING?
THAT WOMAN IS BUG-NUT CRAZY. ALIEN VIRUS, MY LIVER.
I DUNNO. BAD TEQUILA?
HEY, SERGEANT! IT'S THE MAYOR!
MAYOR?
WHO IS THIS? WHERE'S CHIEF BIGSBY?
HE'S DEAD, SIR. I'M SERGEANT CAMPBELL.
HOW BAD IS IT DOWN THERE? WE'RE SEEING NOTHING BUT NIGHTMARES ON TV.
I'M AFRAID IT'S WORSE, SIR.
DAMMIT. OKAY THEN--WAIT, HOLD ON A SEC.
WE'VE GOT A PAIR OF F-16S RUNNING ESCORT ON US. THEY'RE ORDERING US TO TURN AROUND.
SON OF A BITCH.

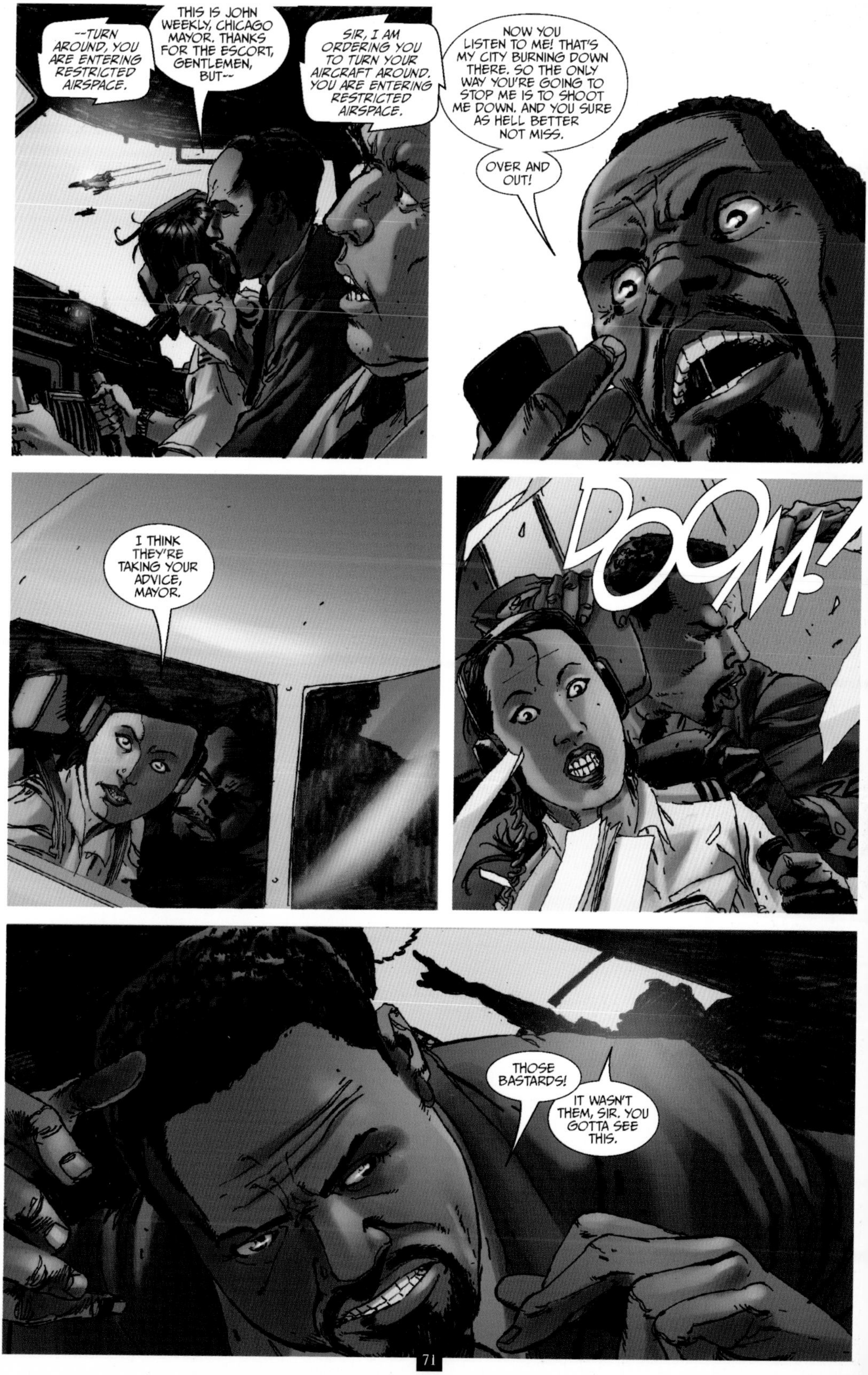
--TURN AROUND, YOU ARE ENTERING RESTRICTED AIRSPACE.
THIS IS JOHN WEEKLY, CHICAGO MAYOR. THANKS FOR THE ESCORT, GENTLEMEN, BUT--
SIR, I AM ORDERING YOU TO TURN YOUR AIRCRAFT AROUND. YOU ARE ENTERING RESTRICTED AIRSPACE.
NOW YOU LISTEN TO ME! THAT'S MY CITY BURNING DOWN THERE. SO THE ONLY WAY YOU'RE GOING TO STOP ME IS TO SHOOT ME DOWN. AND YOU SURE AS HELL BETTER NOT MISS.
OVER AND OUT!
I THINK THEY'RE TAKING YOUR ADVICE, MAYOR.
DOOM!
THOSE BASTARDS!
IT WASN'T THEM, SIR. YOU GOTTA SEE THIS.

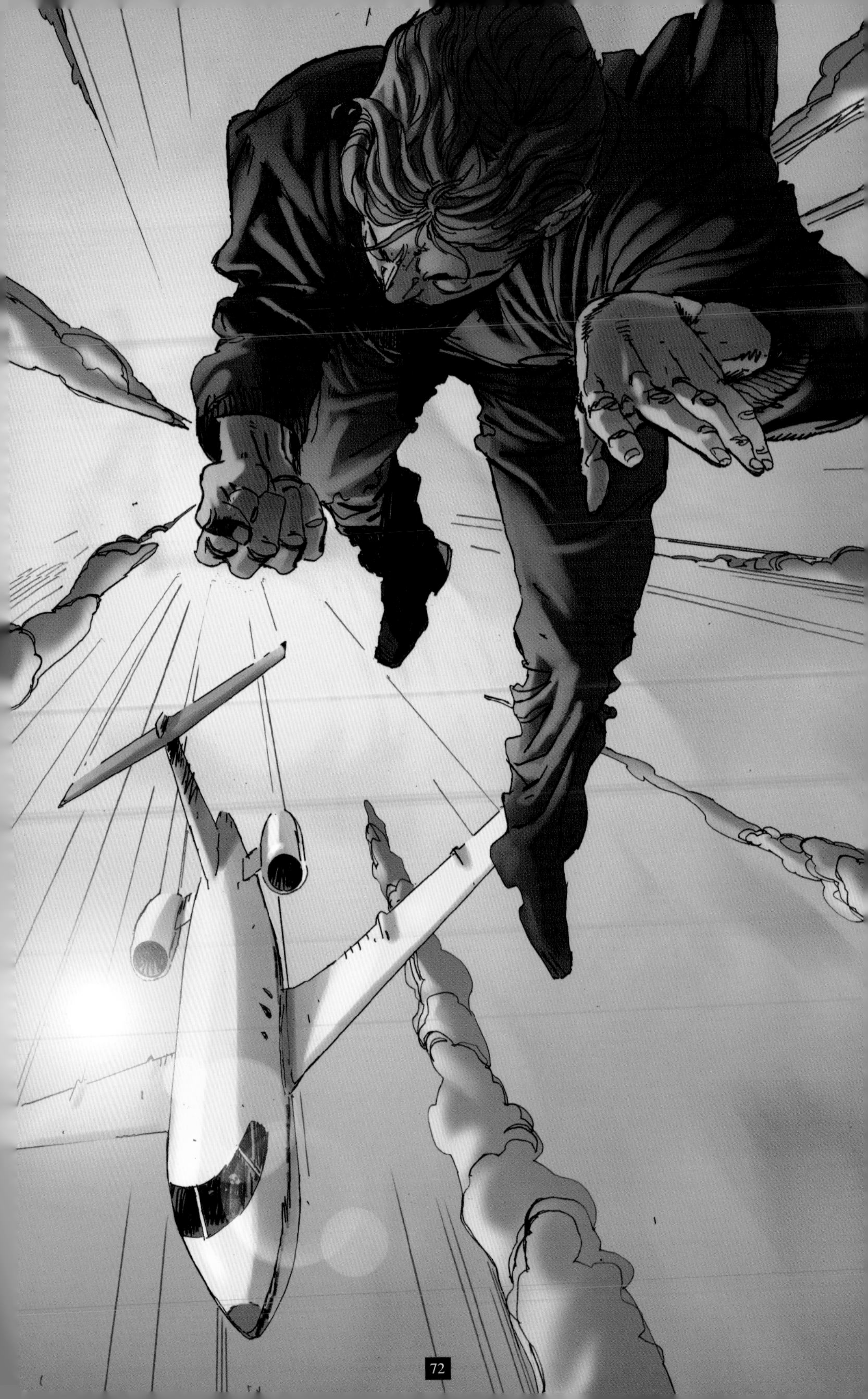

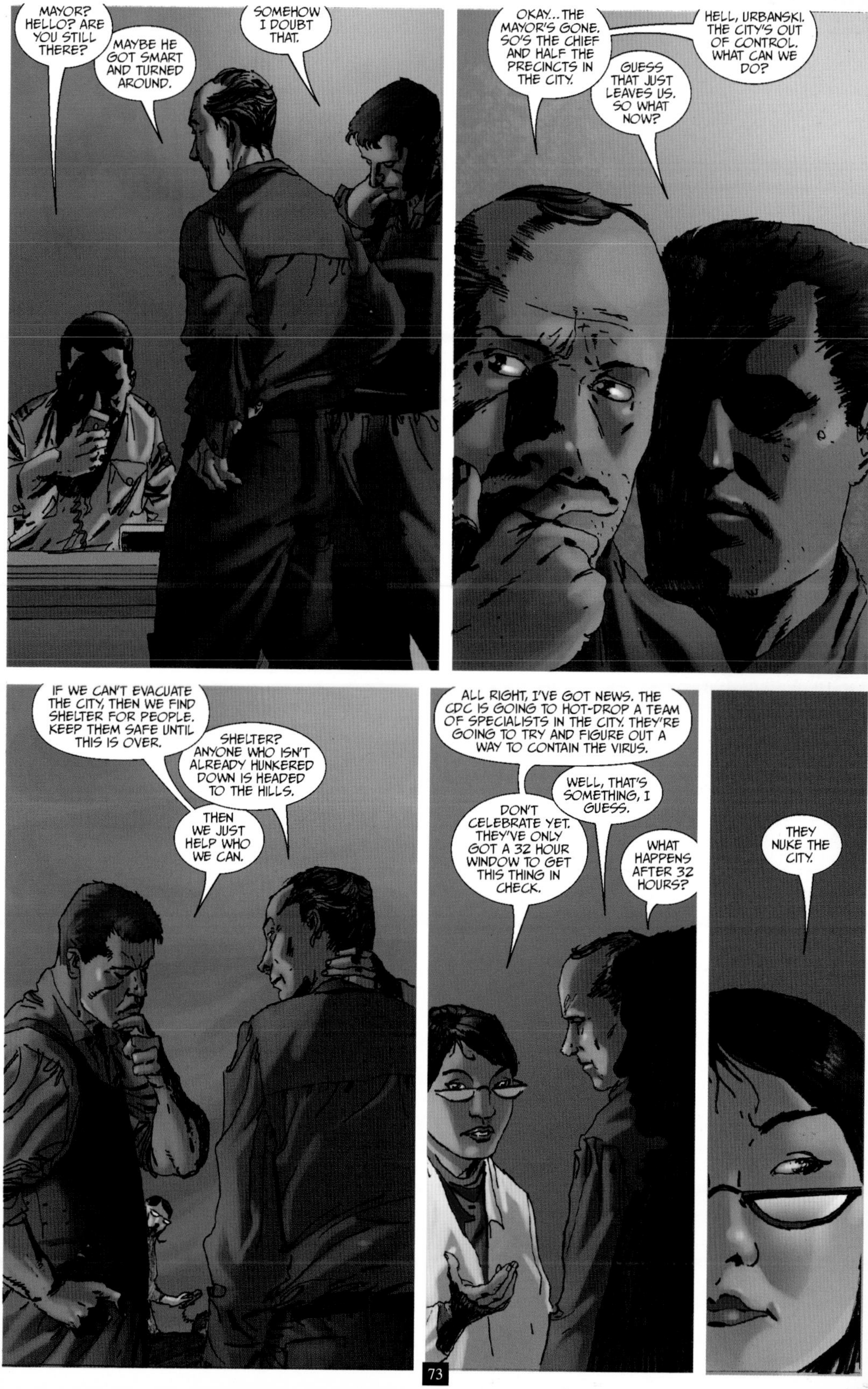
MAYOR? HELLO? ARE YOU STILL THERE?
MAYBE HE GOT SMART AND TURNED AROUND.
SOMEHOW I DOUBT THAT.
OKAY... THE MAYOR'S GONE. SO'S THE CHIEF AND HALF THE PRECINCTS IN THE CITY.
HELL, URBANSKI. THE CITY'S OUT OF CONTROL. WHAT CAN WE DO?
GUESS THAT JUST LEAVES US. SO WHAT NOW?
IF WE CAN'T EVACUATE THE CITY, THEN WE FIND SHELTER FOR PEOPLE. KEEP THEM SAFE UNTIL THIS IS OVER.
SHELTER? ANYONE WHO ISN'T ALREADY HUNKERED DOWN IS HEADED TO THE HILLS.
THEN WE JUST HELP WHO WE CAN.
ALL RIGHT, I'VE GOT NEWS. THE CDC IS GOING TO HOT-DROP A TEAM OF SPECIALISTS IN THE CITY. THEY'RE GOING TO TRY AND FIGURE OUT A WAY TO CONTAIN THE VIRUS.
WELL, THAT'S SOMETHING, I GUESS.
DON'T CELEBRATE YET. THEY'VE ONLY GOT A 32 HOUR WINDOW TO GET THIS THING IN CHECK.
WHAT HAPPENS AFTER 32 HOURS?
THEY NUKE THE CITY.

NUKE CHICAGO? ARE YOU ON CRACK, LADY?

THIS ISN'T THE FLU WE'RE TALKING ABOUT! THEY CAN'T LET IT OUT OF THE CITY. THIS WHOLE COUNTRY WILL DIE IF THEY DO.

AI, ARE YOU SURE? THAT'S A PRETTY RADICAL SOLUTION.

HE DROWNED?

MY CONTACT AT THE CDC CONFIRMED IT. A CHILD IN CAL CITY WAS SNEEZING 2000 VOLTS OF ELECTRICITY UNTIL HE FELL INTO A POOL.

NO, HE ELECTROCUTED HIMSELF. THEY EXAMINED HIS BODY AND FOUND THE SAME THING I DID. AN ARTIFICIAL VIRUS.

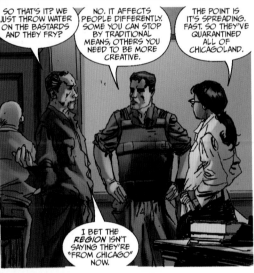

SO THAT'S IT? WE JUST THROW WATER ON THE BASTARDS AND THEY FRY?

NO. IT AFFECTS PEOPLE DIFFERENTLY. SOME YOU CAN STOP BY TRADITIONAL MEANS, OTHERS YOU NEED TO BE MORE CREATIVE.

THE POINT IS IT'S SPREADING. FAST. SO THEY'VE QUARANTINED ALL OF CHICAGOLAND.

I BET THE *REGION* ISN'T SAYING THEY'RE "FROM CHICAGO" NOW.

WHAT ABOUT PROTECTION? DID THEY SAY HOW WE CAN KEEP IT FROM SPREADING?

THEY DON'T KNOW HOW IT'S TRANSMITTED YET. BUT BEFORE THEY CAN STUDY IT FURTHER, THEY HAVE TO GET INTO THE CITY.

FEMA ISN'T COOPERATING WITH THEM AND THE MILITARY'S TOO BUSY, SO THEY'VE ASKED FOR A POLICE ESCORT ONCE THEY'RE HERE.

POLICE ESCORT?

YOU SPECIFICALLY. YOU'RE BECOMING A BIT OF A CELEBRITY.

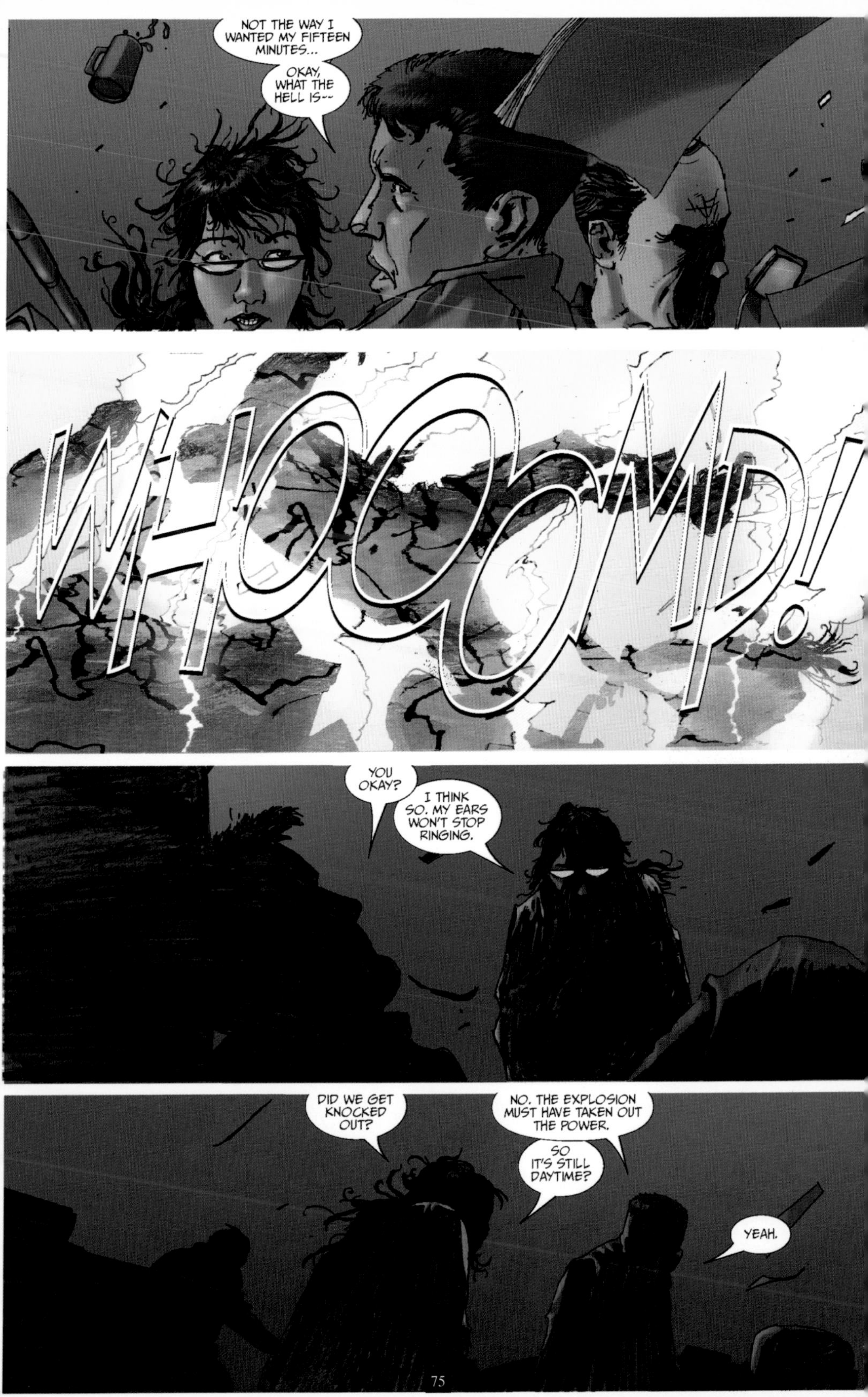
NOT THE WAY I WANTED MY FIFTEEN MINUTES...
OKAY, WHAT THE HELL IS--
WHOOOMP!
YOU OKAY?
I THINK SO. MY EARS WON'T STOP RINGING.
DID WE GET KNOCKED OUT?
NO. THE EXPLOSION MUST HAVE TAKEN OUT THE POWER.
SO IT'S STILL DAYTIME?
YEAH.

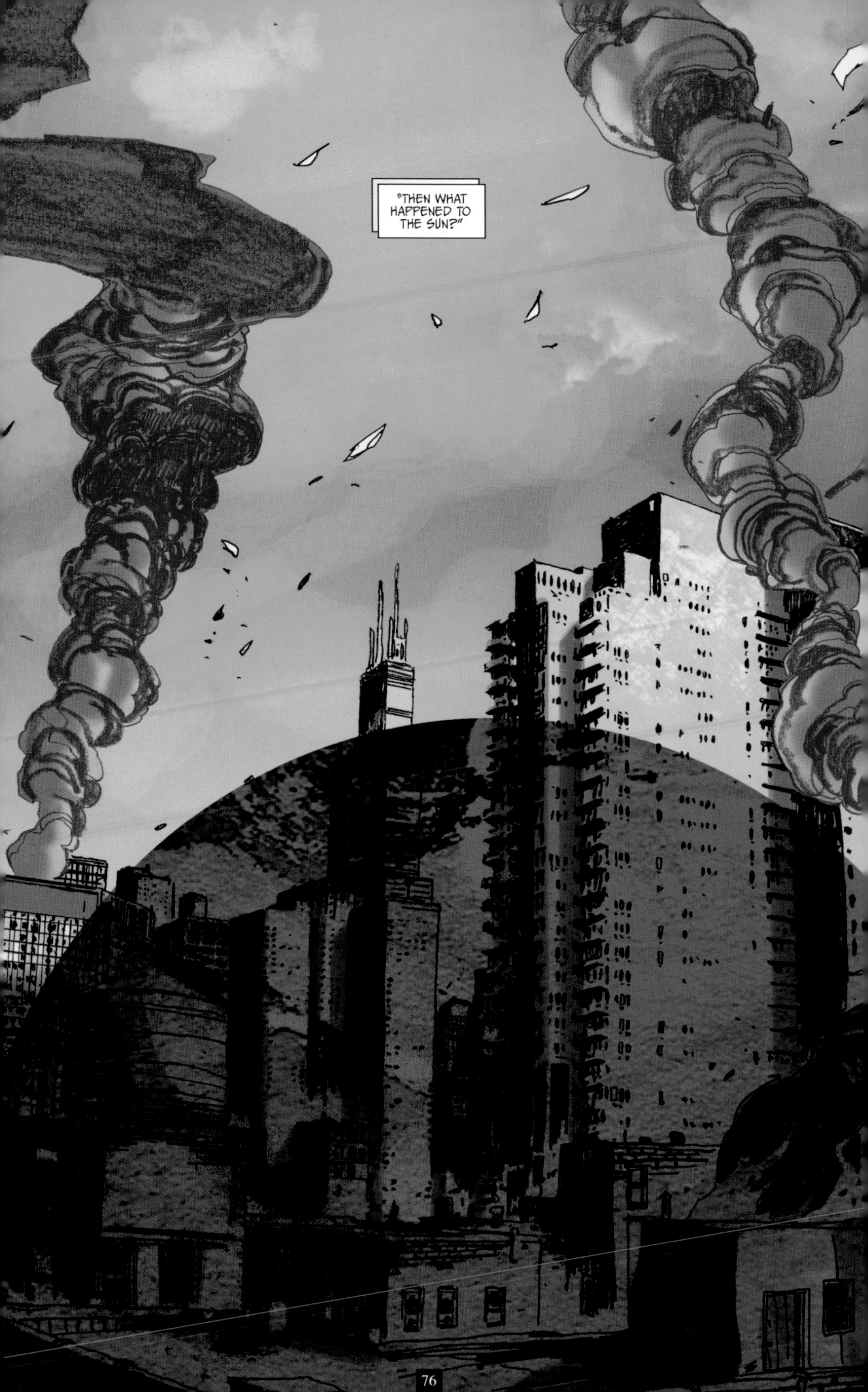
"THEN WHAT HAPPENED TO THE SUN?"

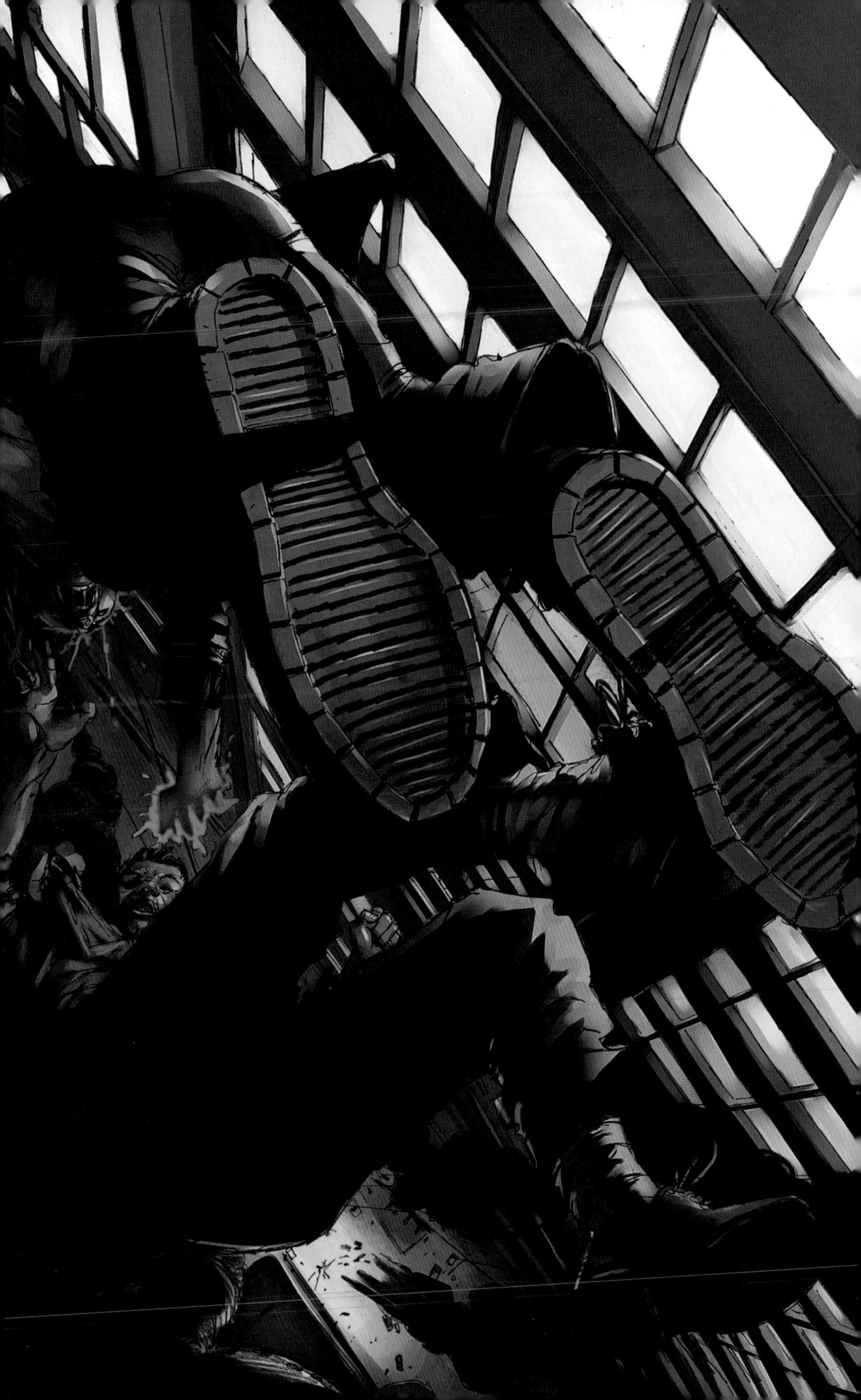

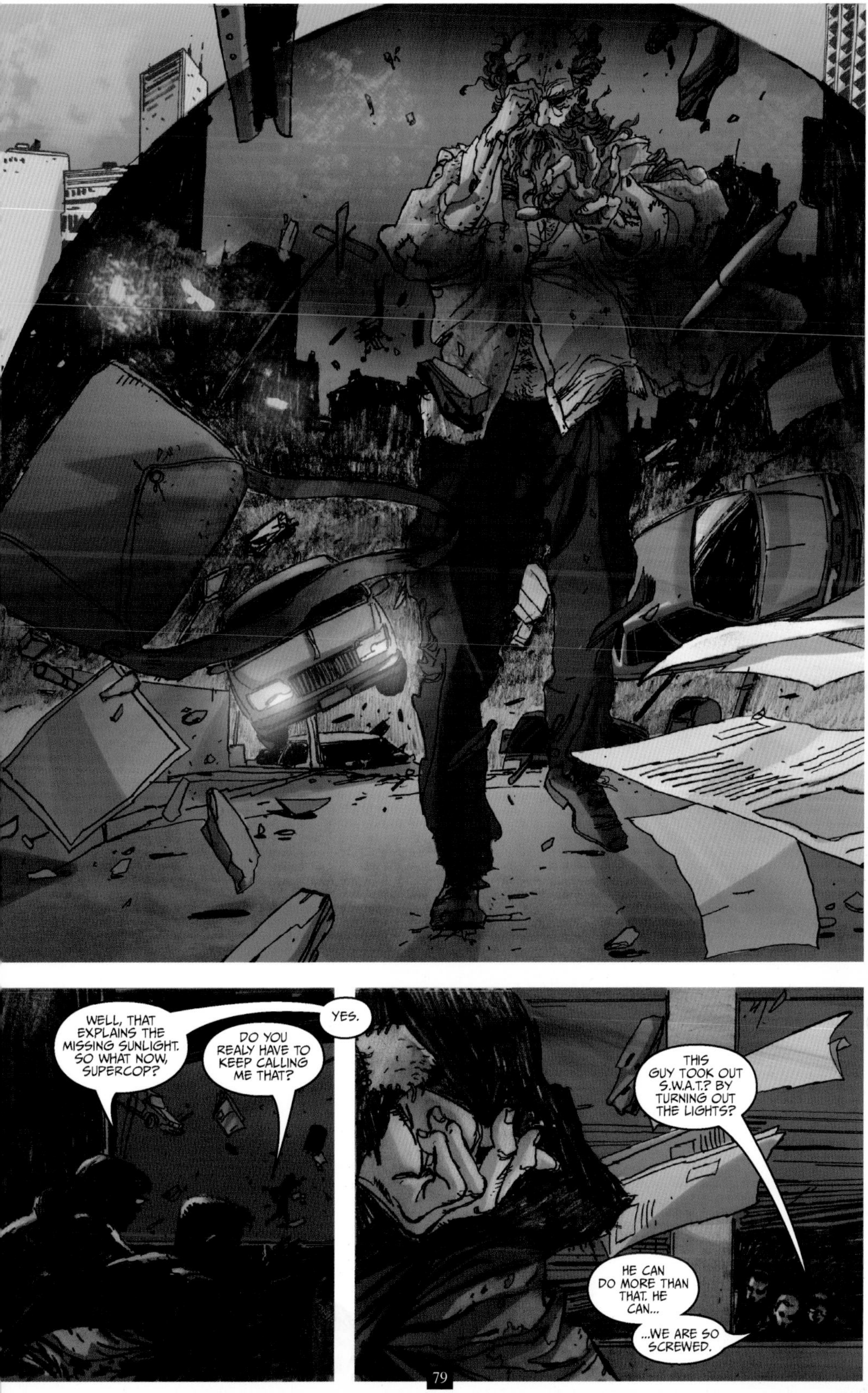
WELL, THAT EXPLAINS THE MISSING SUNLIGHT. SO WHAT NOW, SUPERCOP?
DO YOU REALY HAVE TO KEEP CALLING ME THAT?
YES.
THIS GUY TOOK OUT S.W.A.T.? BY TURNING OUT THE LIGHTS?
HE CAN DO MORE THAN THAT. HE CAN...
...WE ARE SO SCREWED.

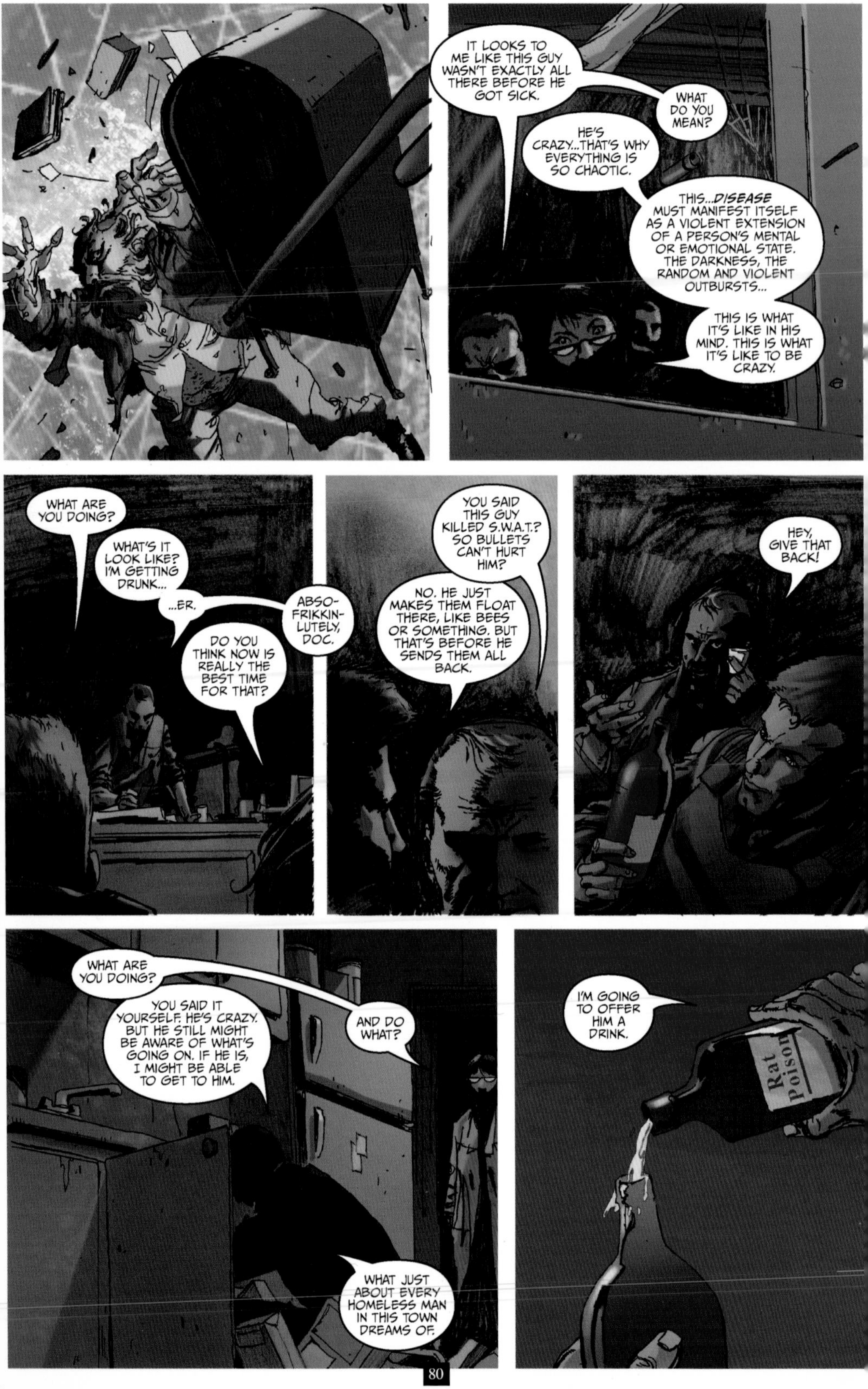
IT LOOKS TO ME LIKE THIS GUY WASN'T EXACTLY ALL THERE BEFORE HE GOT SICK.
WHAT DO YOU MEAN?
HE'S CRAZY...THAT'S WHY EVERYTHING IS SO CHAOTIC.
THIS...*DISEASE* MUST MANIFEST ITSELF AS A VIOLENT EXTENSION OF A PERSON'S MENTAL OR EMOTIONAL STATE. THE DARKNESS, THE RANDOM AND VIOLENT OUTBURSTS...
THIS IS WHAT IT'S LIKE IN HIS MIND. THIS IS WHAT IT'S LIKE TO BE CRAZY.
WHAT ARE YOU DOING?
WHAT'S IT LOOK LIKE? I'M GETTING DRUNK...
...ER.
ABSO-FRIKKIN-LUTELY, DOC.
DO YOU THINK NOW IS REALLY THE BEST TIME FOR THAT?
YOU SAID THIS GUY KILLED S.W.A.T.? SO BULLETS CAN'T HURT HIM?
NO. HE JUST MAKES THEM FLOAT THERE, LIKE BEES OR SOMETHING. BUT THAT'S BEFORE HE SENDS THEM ALL BACK.
HEY, GIVE THAT BACK!
WHAT ARE YOU DOING?
YOU SAID IT YOURSELF. HE'S CRAZY. BUT HE STILL MIGHT BE AWARE OF WHAT'S GOING ON. IF HE IS, I MIGHT BE ABLE TO GET TO HIM.
AND DO WHAT?
WHAT JUST ABOUT EVERY HOMELESS MAN IN THIS TOWN DREAMS OF.
I'M GOING TO OFFER HIM A DRINK.
Rat Poison

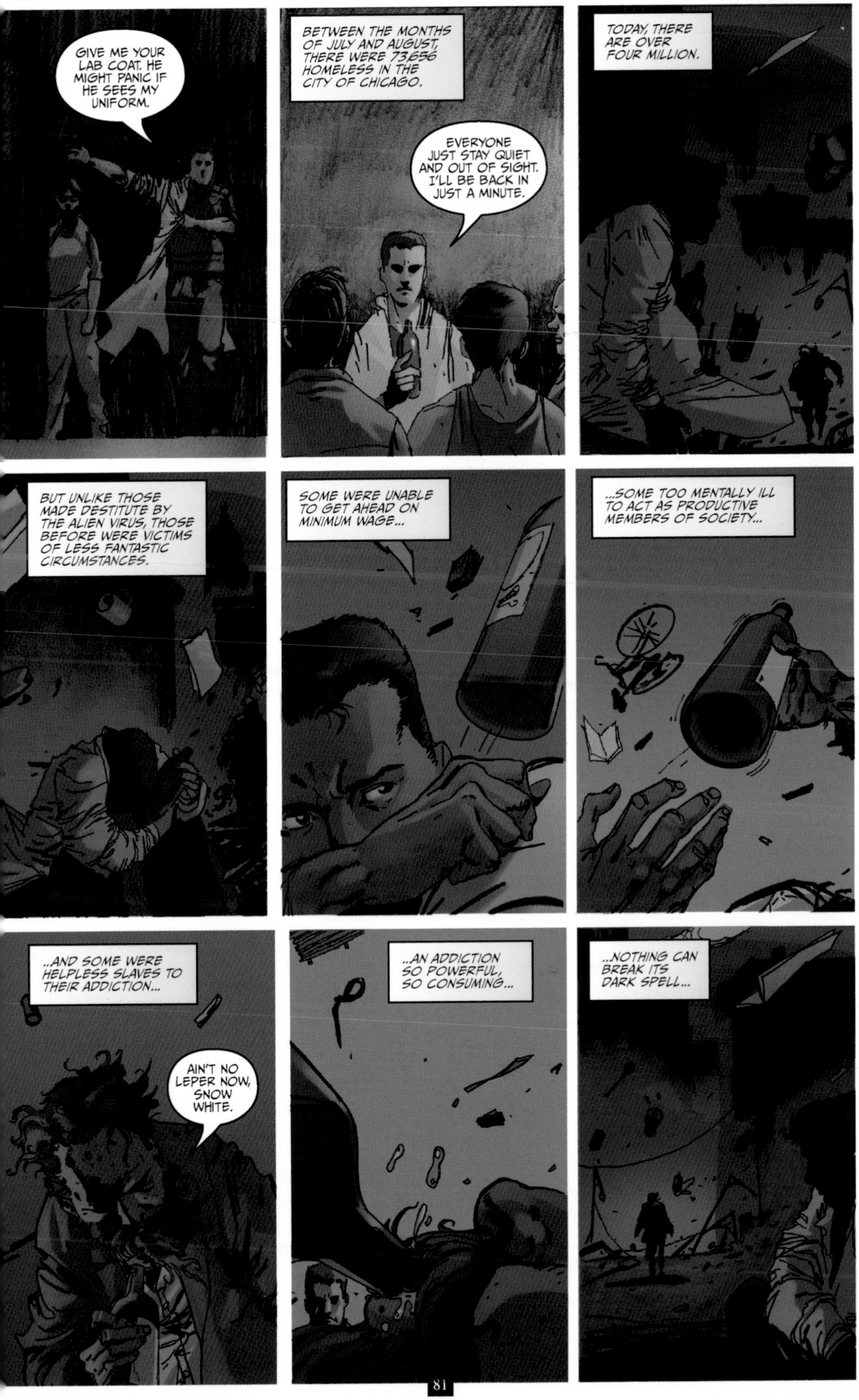
GIVE ME YOUR LAB COAT. HE MIGHT PANIC IF HE SEES MY UNIFORM.
BETWEEN THE MONTHS OF JULY AND AUGUST, THERE WERE 73,656 HOMELESS IN THE CITY OF CHICAGO.
EVERYONE JUST STAY QUIET AND OUT OF SIGHT. I'LL BE BACK IN JUST A MINUTE.
TODAY, THERE ARE OVER FOUR MILLION.
BUT UNLIKE THOSE MADE DESTITUTE BY THE ALIEN VIRUS, THOSE BEFORE WERE VICTIMS OF LESS FANTASTIC CIRCUMSTANCES.
SOME WERE UNABLE TO GET AHEAD ON MINIMUM WAGE...
...SOME TOO MENTALLY ILL TO ACT AS PRODUCTIVE MEMBERS OF SOCIETY...
...AND SOME WERE HELPLESS SLAVES TO THEIR ADDICTION...
AIN'T NO LEPER NOW, SNOW WHITE.
...AN ADDICTION SO POWERFUL, SO CONSUMING...
...NOTHING CAN BREAK ITS DARK SPELL...

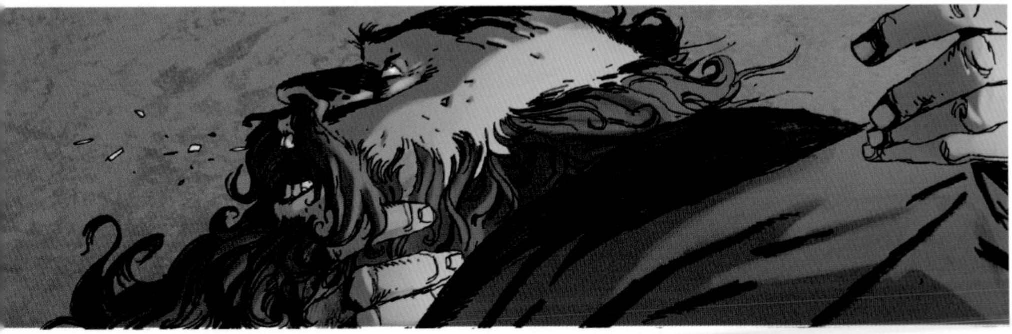

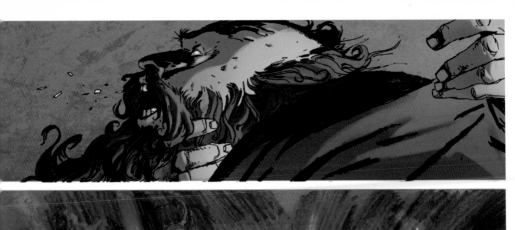

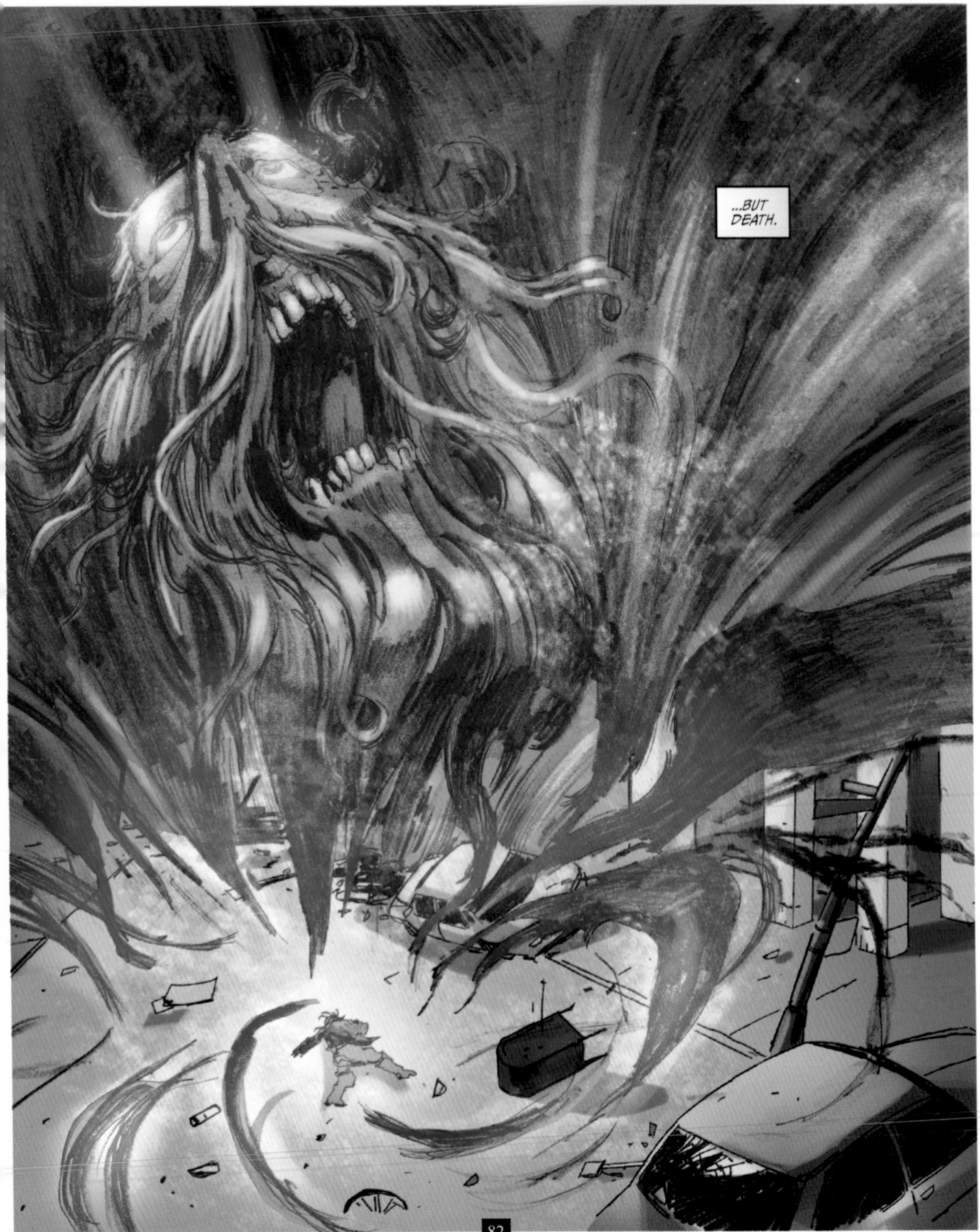
...BUT
DEATH.

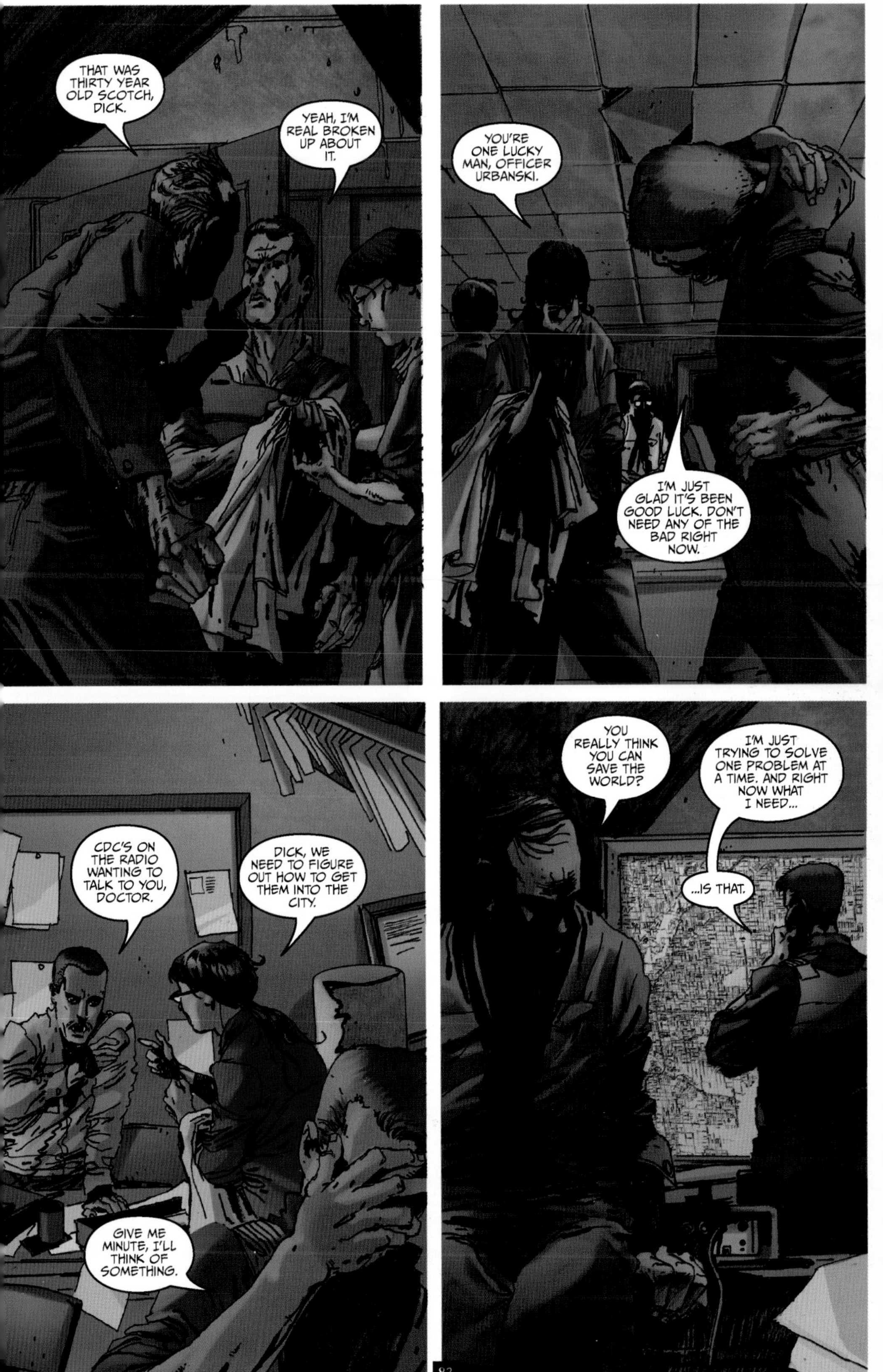

THAT WAS THIRTY YEAR OLD SCOTCH, DICK.
YEAH, I'M REAL BROKEN UP ABOUT IT.
YOU'RE ONE LUCKY MAN, OFFICER URBANSKI.
I'M JUST GLAD IT'S BEEN GOOD LUCK. DON'T NEED ANY OF THE BAD RIGHT NOW.
CDC'S ON THE RADIO WANTING TO TALK TO YOU, DOCTOR.
DICK, WE NEED TO FIGURE OUT HOW TO GET THEM INTO THE CITY.
GIVE ME MINUTE, I'LL THINK OF SOMETHING.
YOU REALLY THINK YOU CAN SAVE THE WORLD?
I'M JUST TRYING TO SOLVE ONE PROBLEM AT A TIME. AND RIGHT NOW WHAT I NEED...
...IS THAT.

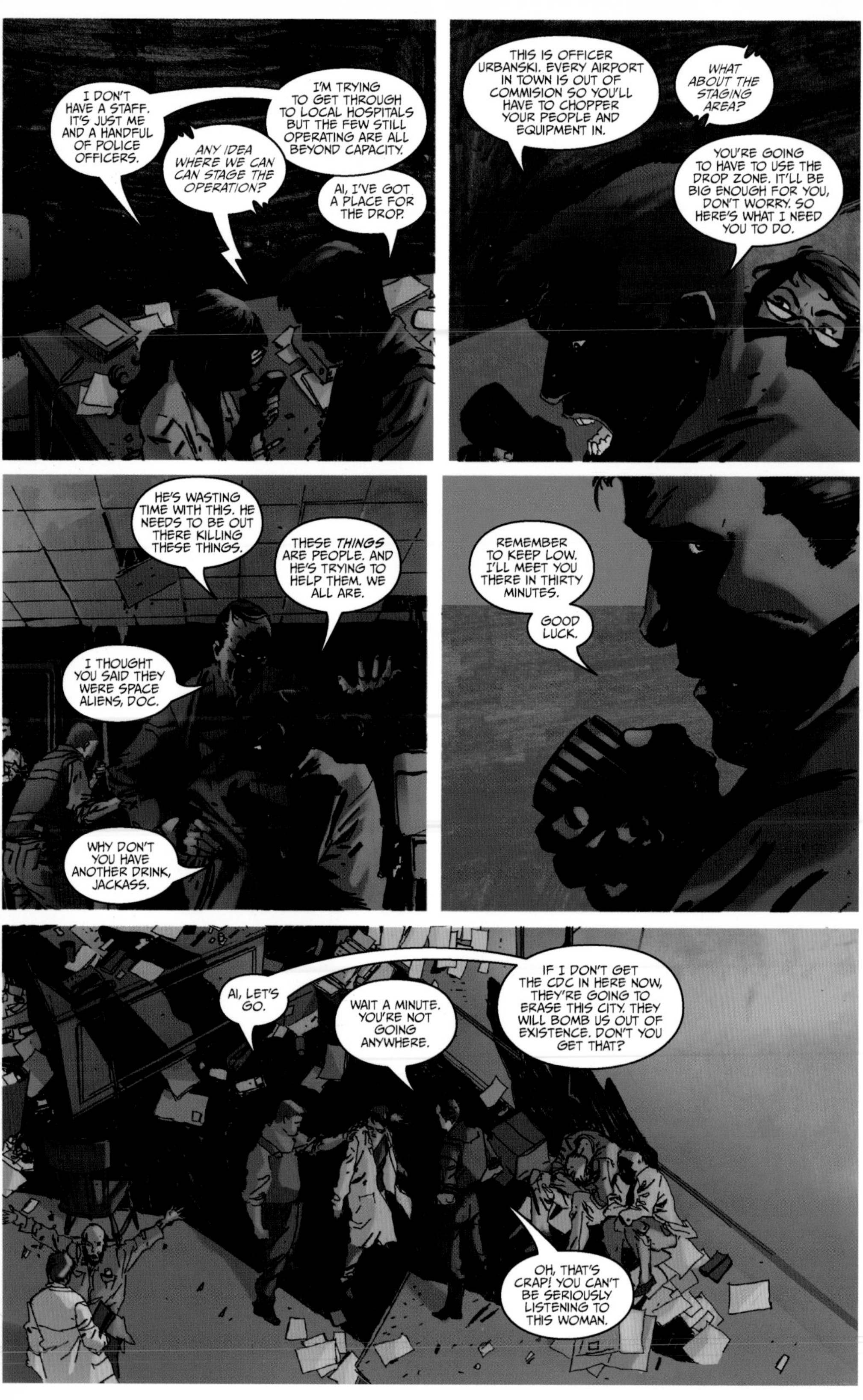

I DON'T HAVE A STAFF. IT'S JUST ME AND A HANDFUL OF POLICE OFFICERS.
I'M TRYING TO GET THROUGH TO LOCAL HOSPITALS BUT THE FEW STILL OPERATING ARE ALL BEYOND CAPACITY.
ANY IDEA WHERE WE CAN CAN STAGE THE OPERATION?
AI, I'VE GOT A PLACE FOR THE DROP.
THIS IS OFFICER URBANSKI. EVERY AIRPORT IN TOWN IS OUT OF COMMISION SO YOU'LL HAVE TO CHOPPER YOUR PEOPLE AND EQUIPMENT IN.
WHAT ABOUT THE STAGING AREA?
YOU'RE GOING TO HAVE TO USE THE DROP ZONE. IT'LL BE BIG ENOUGH FOR YOU, DON'T WORRY. SO HERE'S WHAT I NEED YOU TO DO.
HE'S WASTING TIME WITH THIS. HE NEEDS TO BE OUT THERE KILLING THESE THINGS.
THESE THINGS ARE PEOPLE. AND HE'S TRYING TO HELP THEM. WE ALL ARE.
I THOUGHT YOU SAID THEY WERE SPACE ALIENS, DOC.
WHY DON'T YOU HAVE ANOTHER DRINK, JACKASS.
REMEMBER TO KEEP LOW. I'LL MEET YOU THERE IN THIRTY MINUTES.
GOOD LUCK.
AI, LET'S GO.
WAIT A MINUTE. YOU'RE NOT GOING ANYWHERE.
IF I DON'T GET THE CDC IN HERE NOW, THEY'RE GOING TO ERASE THIS CITY. THEY WILL BOMB US OUT OF EXISTENCE. DON'T YOU GET THAT?
OH, THAT'S CRAP! YOU CAN'T BE SERIOUSLY LISTENING TO THIS WOMAN.

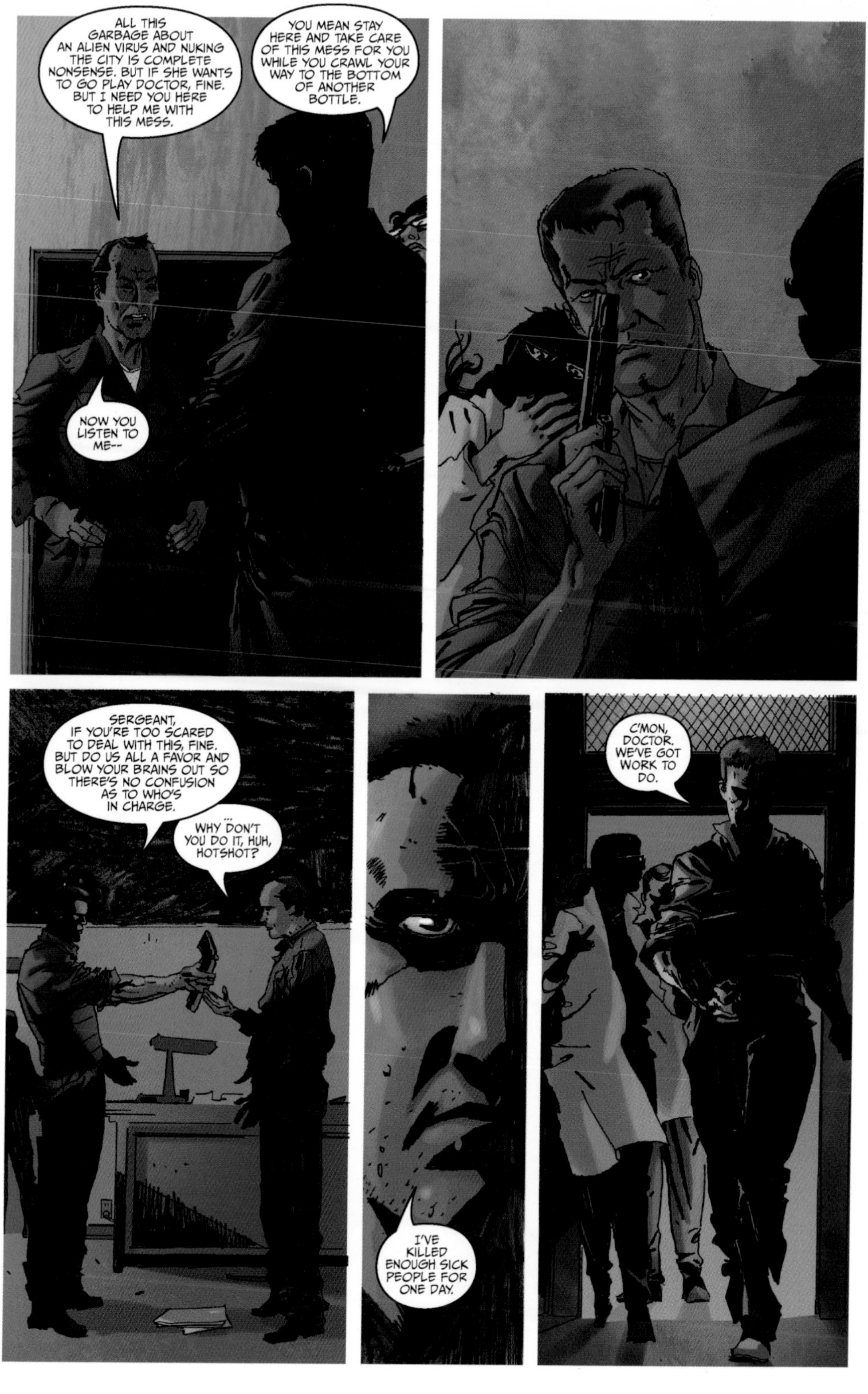
ALL THIS GARBAGE ABOUT AN ALIEN VIRUS AND NUKING THE CITY IS COMPLETE NONSENSE. BUT IF SHE WANTS TO GO PLAY DOCTOR, FINE. BUT I NEED YOU HERE TO HELP ME WITH THIS MESS.
YOU MEAN STAY HERE AND TAKE CARE OF THIS MESS FOR YOU WHILE YOU CRAWL YOUR WAY TO THE BOTTOM OF ANOTHER BOTTLE.
NOW YOU LISTEN TO ME--
SERGEANT, IF YOU'RE TOO SCARED TO DEAL WITH THIS, FINE. BUT DO US ALL A FAVOR AND BLOW YOUR BRAINS OUT SO THERE'S NO CONFUSION AS TO WHO'S IN CHARGE.
... WHY DON'T YOU DO IT, HUH, HOTSHOT?
I'VE KILLED ENOUGH SICK PEOPLE FOR ONE DAY.
C'MON, DOCTOR. WE'VE GOT WORK TO DO.

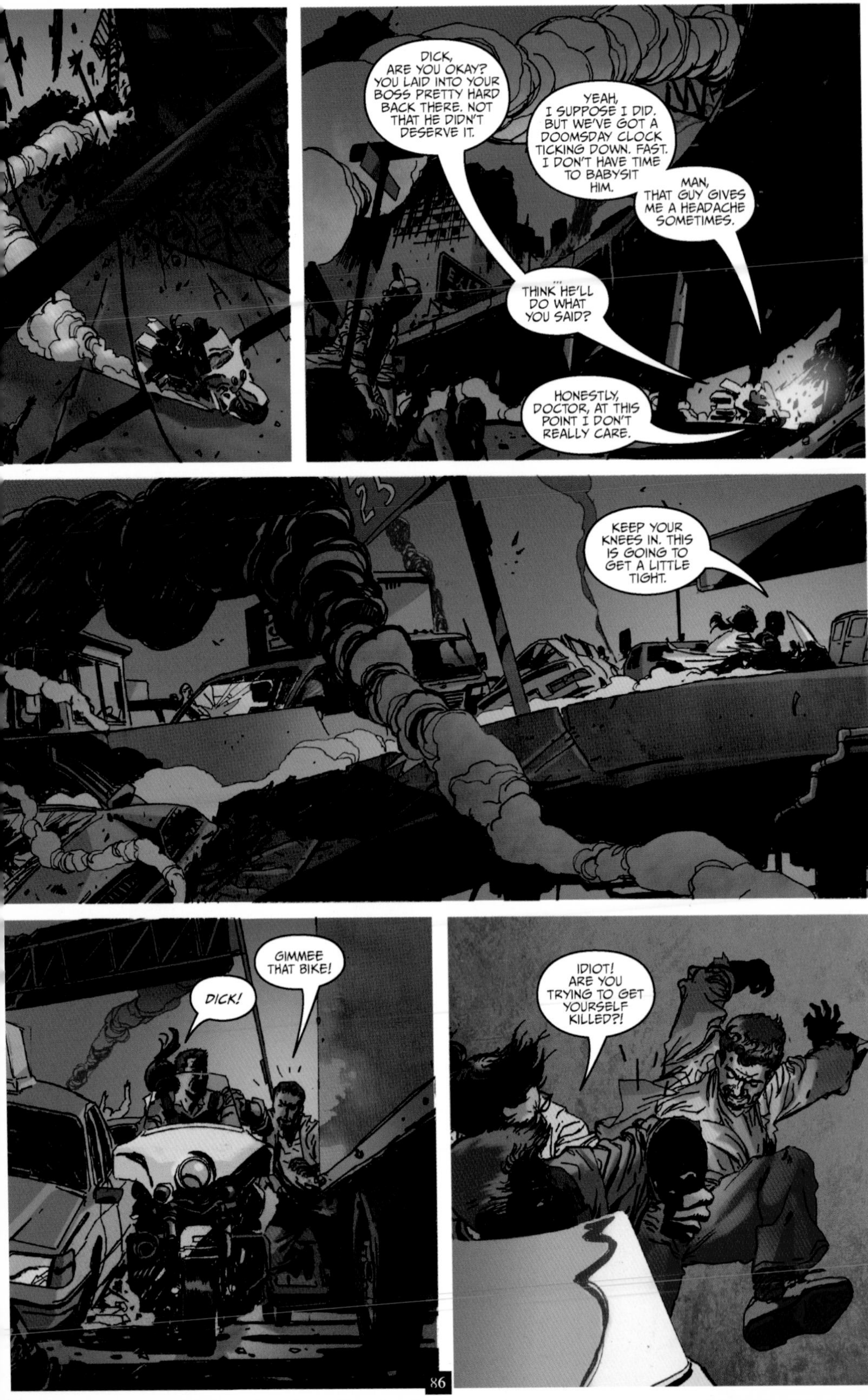
DICK, ARE YOU OKAY? YOU LAID INTO YOUR BOSS PRETTY HARD BACK THERE. NOT THAT HE DIDN'T DESERVE IT.
YEAH, I SUPPOSE I DID. BUT WE'VE GOT A DOOMSDAY CLOCK TICKING DOWN. FAST. I DON'T HAVE TIME TO BABYSIT HIM.
MAN, THAT GUY GIVES ME A HEADACHE SOMETIMES.
... THINK HE'LL DO WHAT YOU SAID?
HONESTLY, DOCTOR, AT THIS POINT I DON'T REALLY CARE.
KEEP YOUR KNEES IN. THIS IS GOING TO GET A LITTLE TIGHT.
DICK!
GIMMEE THAT BIKE!
IDIOT! ARE YOU TRYING TO GET YOURSELF KILLED?!

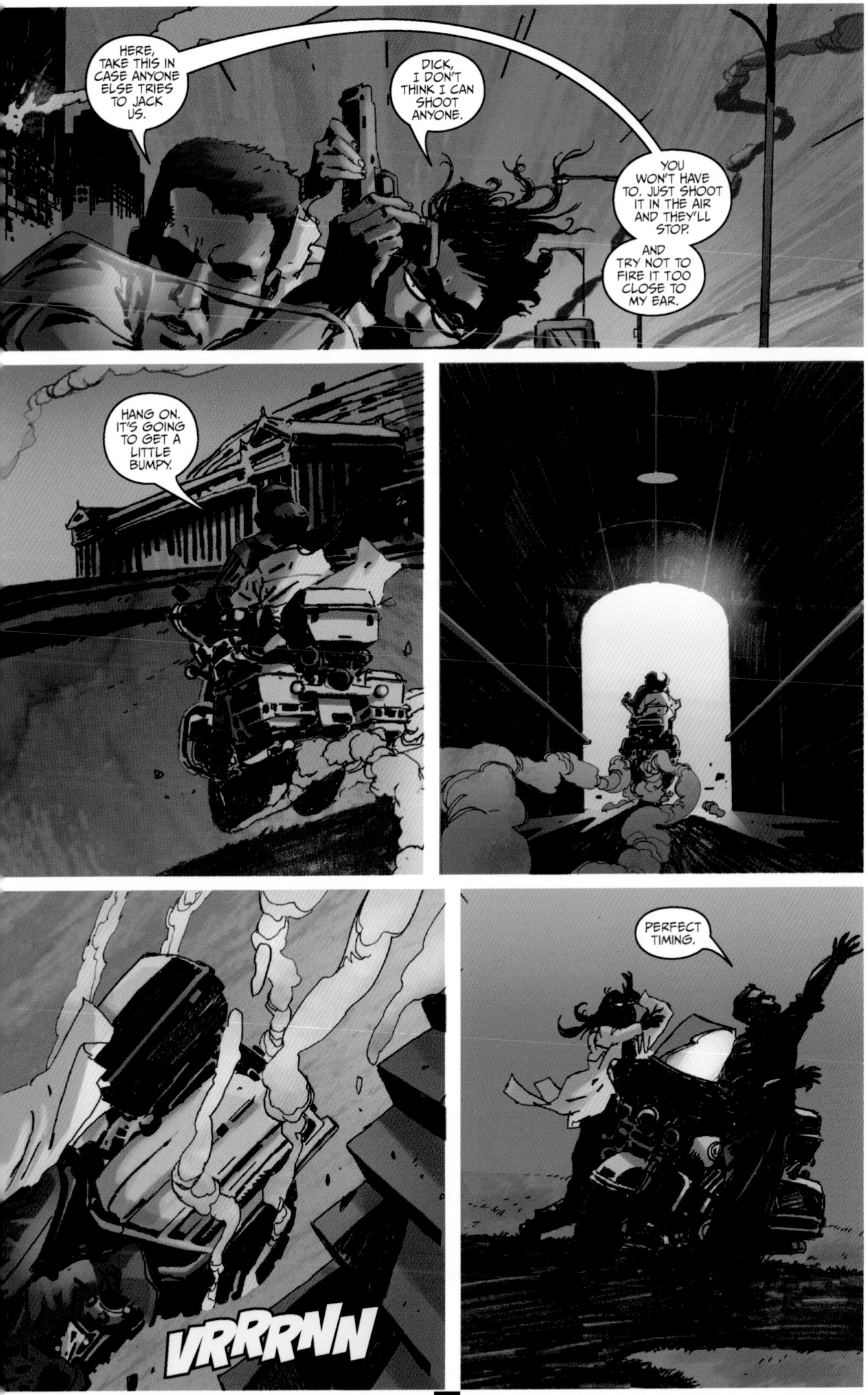
HERE, TAKE THIS IN CASE ANYONE ELSE TRIES TO JACK US.
DICK, I DON'T THINK I CAN SHOOT ANYONE.
YOU WON'T HAVE TO. JUST SHOOT IT IN THE AIR AND THEY'LL STOP.
AND TRY NOT TO FIRE IT TOO CLOSE TO MY EAR.
HANG ON. IT'S GOING TO GET A LITTLE BUMPY.
VRRRNN
PERFECT TIMING.

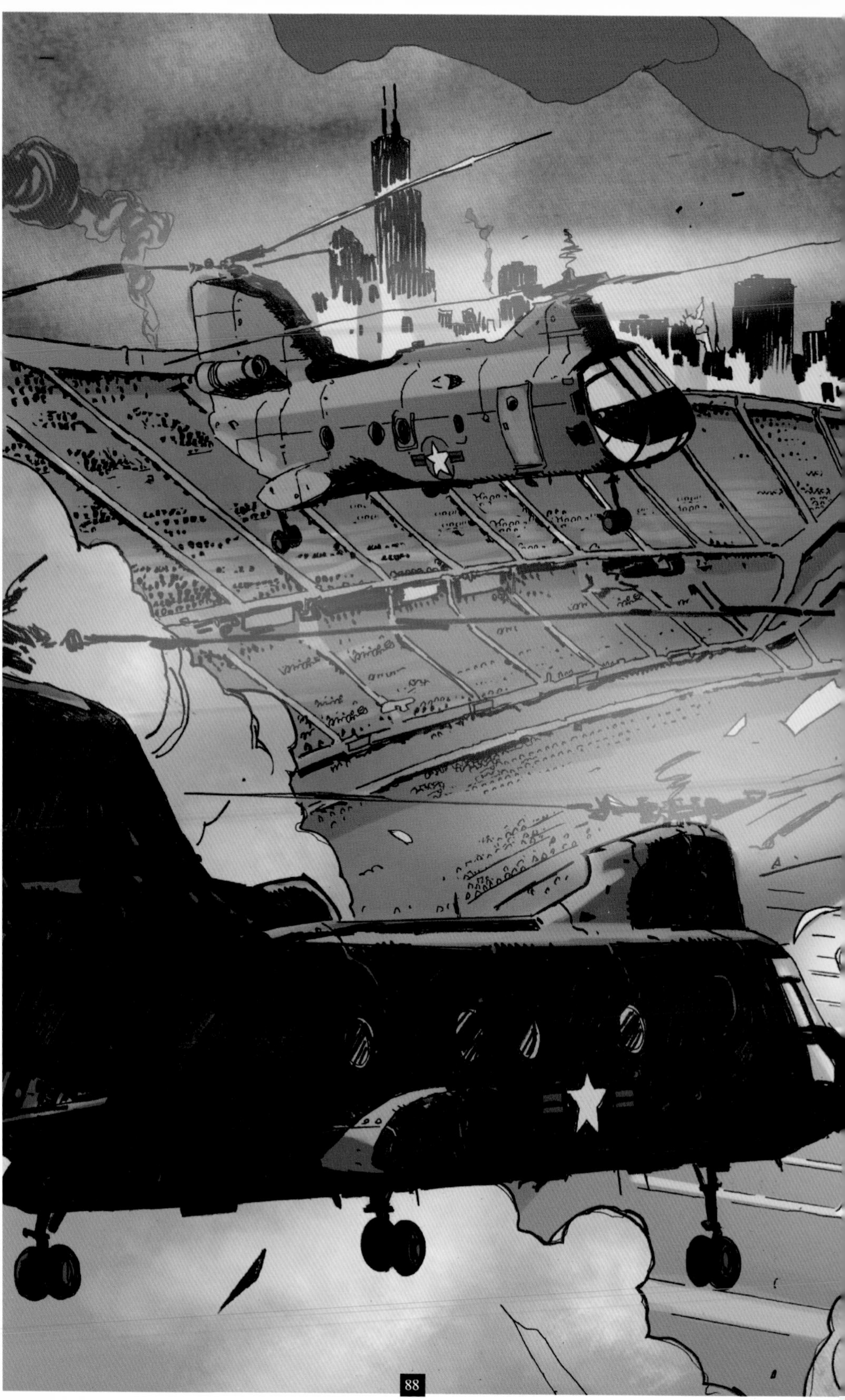

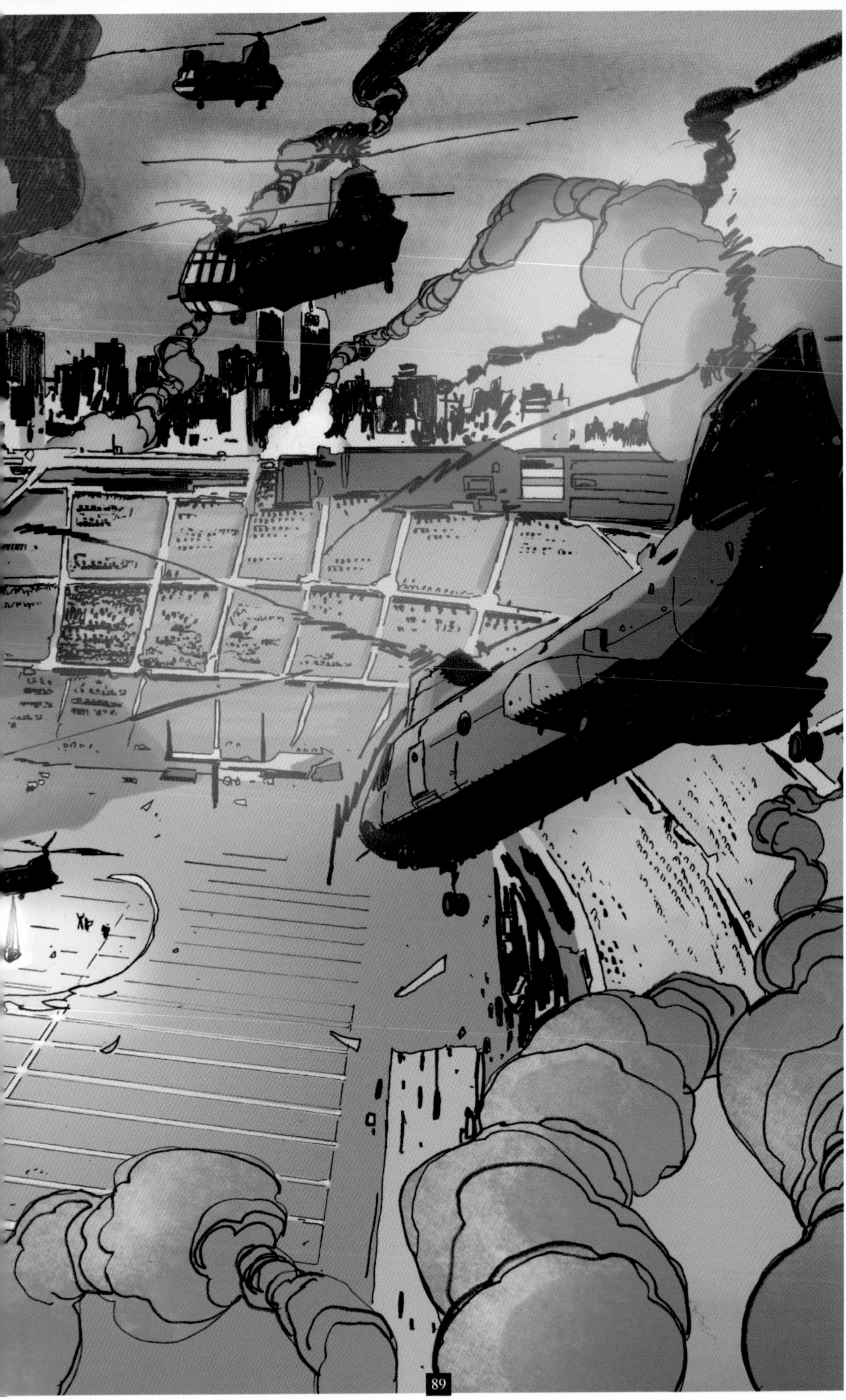

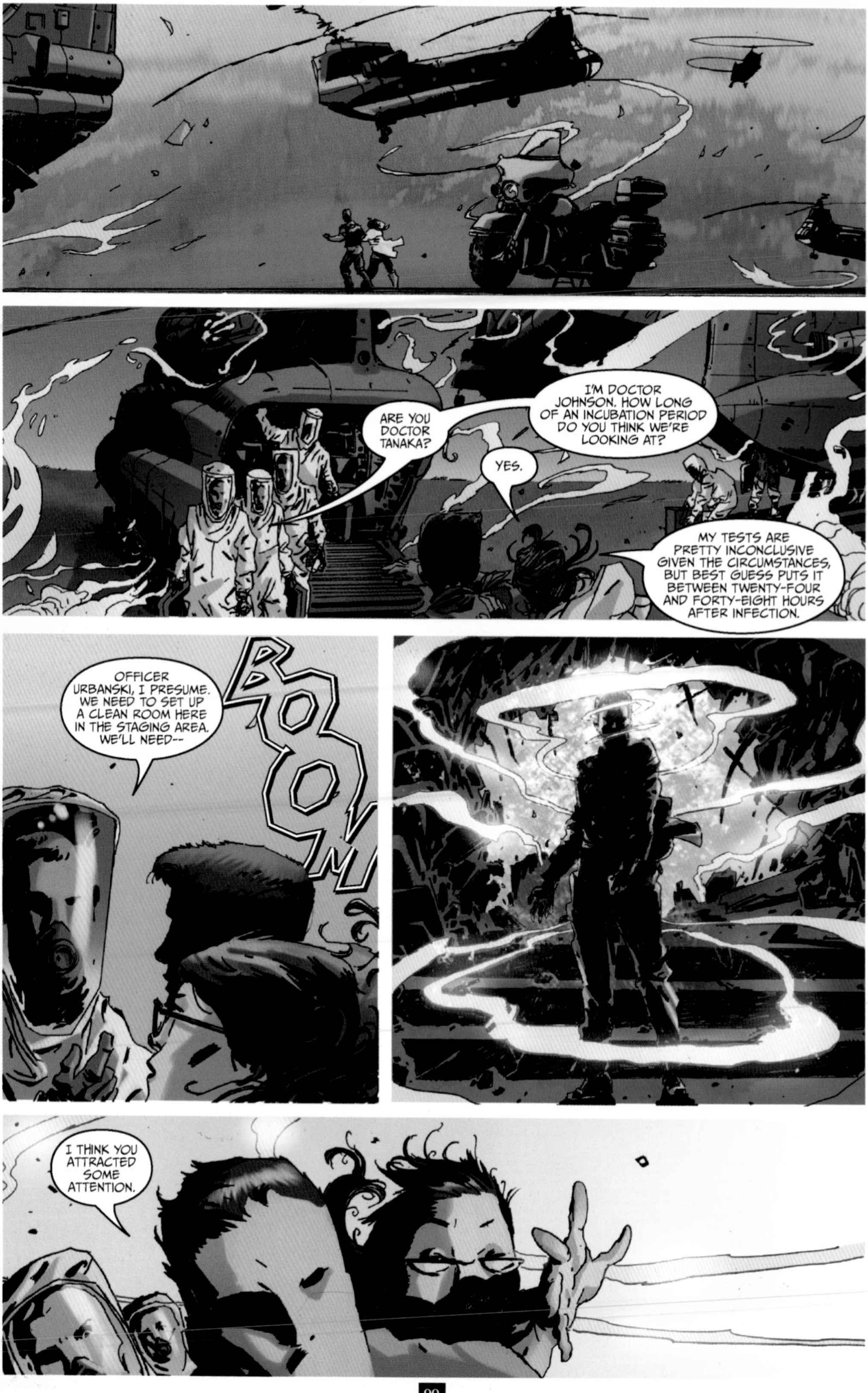
ARE YOU DOCTOR TANAKA?
I'M DOCTOR JOHNSON. HOW LONG OF AN INCUBATION PERIOD DO YOU THINK WE'RE LOOKING AT?
YES.
MY TESTS ARE PRETTY INCONCLUSIVE GIVEN THE CIRCUMSTANCES, BUT BEST GUESS PUTS IT BETWEEN TWENTY-FOUR AND FORTY-EIGHT HOURS AFTER INFECTION.
OFFICER URBANSKI, I PRESUME. WE NEED TO SET UP A CLEAN ROOM HERE IN THE STAGING AREA. WE'LL NEED--
BOOM
I THINK YOU ATTRACTED SOME ATTENTION.

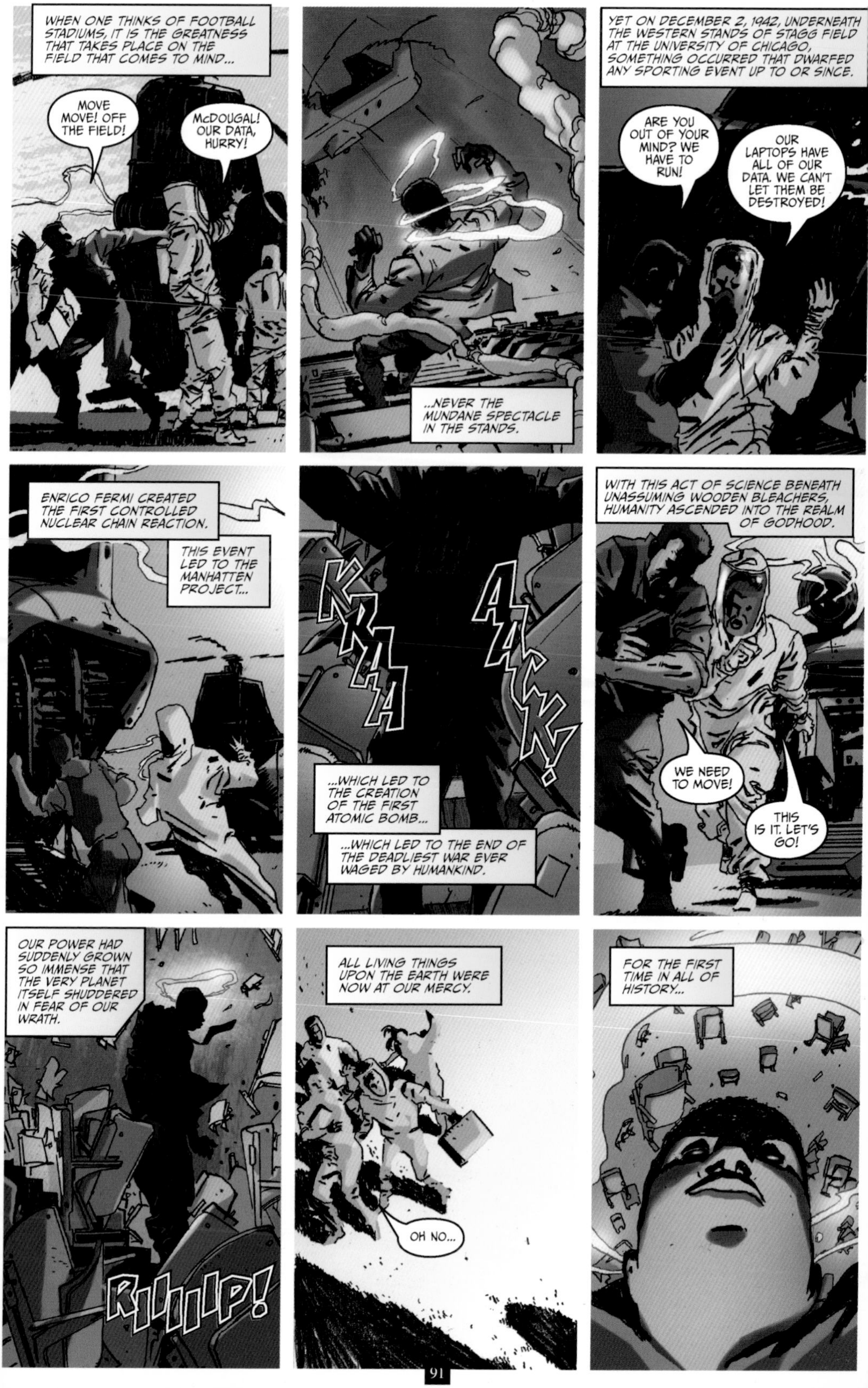
WHEN ONE THINKS OF FOOTBALL STADIUMS, IT IS THE GREATNESS THAT TAKES PLACE ON THE FIELD THAT COMES TO MIND...
MOVE MOVE! OFF THE FIELD!
McDOUGAL! OUR DATA, HURRY!
...NEVER THE MUNDANE SPECTACLE IN THE STANDS.
YET ON DECEMBER 2, 1942, UNDERNEATH THE WESTERN STANDS OF STAGG FIELD AT THE UNIVERSITY OF CHICAGO, SOMETHING OCCURRED THAT DWARFED ANY SPORTING EVENT UP TO OR SINCE.
ARE YOU OUT OF YOUR MIND? WE HAVE TO RUN!
OUR LAPTOPS HAVE ALL OF OUR DATA. WE CAN'T LET THEM BE DESTROYED!
ENRICO FERMI CREATED THE FIRST CONTROLLED NUCLEAR CHAIN REACTION.
THIS EVENT LED TO THE MANHATTEN PROJECT...
KRAAA
AACK!
...WHICH LED TO THE CREATION OF THE FIRST ATOMIC BOMB...
...WHICH LED TO THE END OF THE DEADLIEST WAR EVER WAGED BY HUMANKIND.
WITH THIS ACT OF SCIENCE BENEATH UNASSUMING WOODEN BLEACHERS, HUMANITY ASCENDED INTO THE REALM OF GODHOOD.
WE NEED TO MOVE!
THIS IS IT. LET'S GO!
OUR POWER HAD SUDDENLY GROWN SO IMMENSE THAT THE VERY PLANET ITSELF SHUDDERED IN FEAR OF OUR WRATH.
RIIIIP!
ALL LIVING THINGS UPON THE EARTH WERE NOW AT OUR MERCY.
OH NO...
FOR THE FIRST TIME IN ALL OF HISTORY...

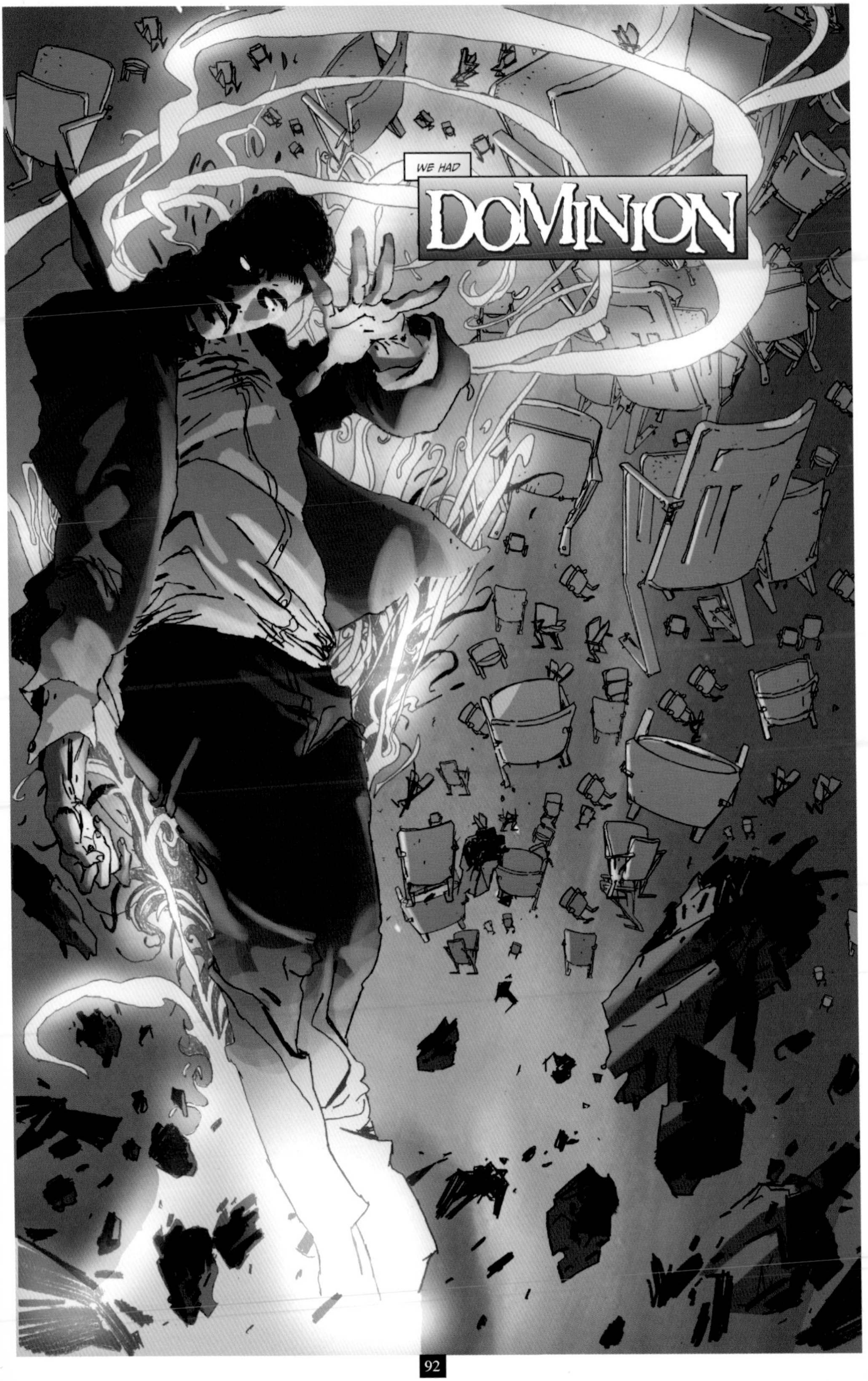
WE HAD
DOMINION

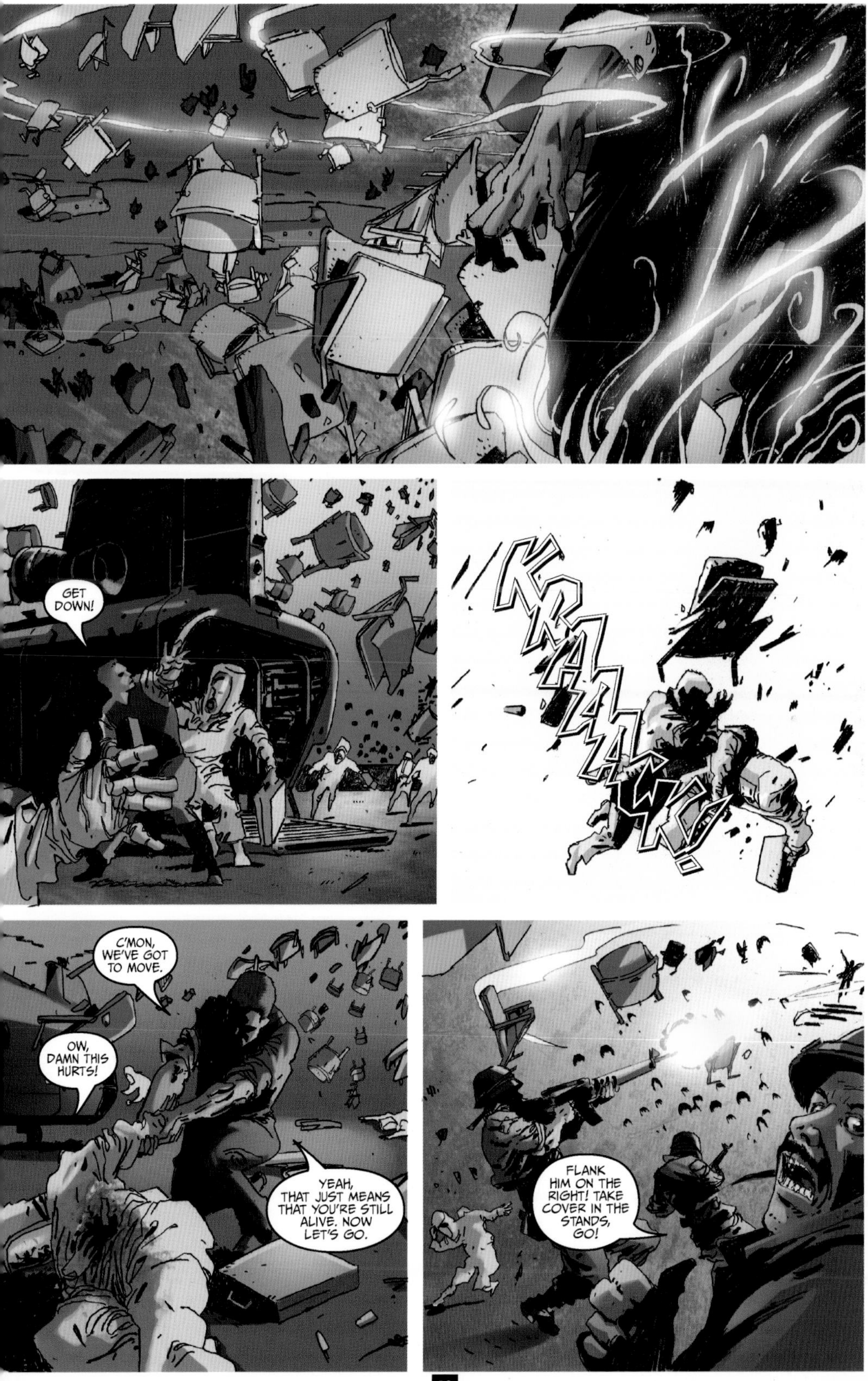

GET DOWN!
KRAAAACK!
C'MON, WE'VE GOT TO MOVE.
OW, DAMN THIS HURTS!
YEAH, THAT JUST MEANS THAT YOU'RE STILL ALIVE. NOW LET'S GO.
FLANK HIM ON THE RIGHT! TAKE COVER IN THE STANDS, GO!

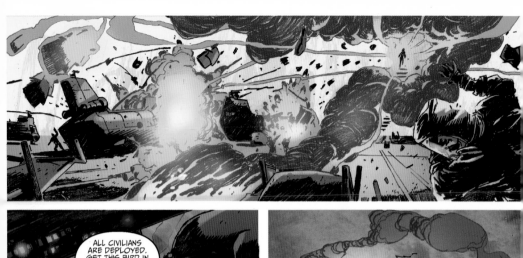

ALL CIVILIANS ARE DEPLOYED. GET THIS BIRD IN THE AIR SO WE CAN BRING THE BIG GUNS OUT.

ON IT!

NOW, WE GOT--

OH CRAP. BANK RIGHT! BANK RIGHT!

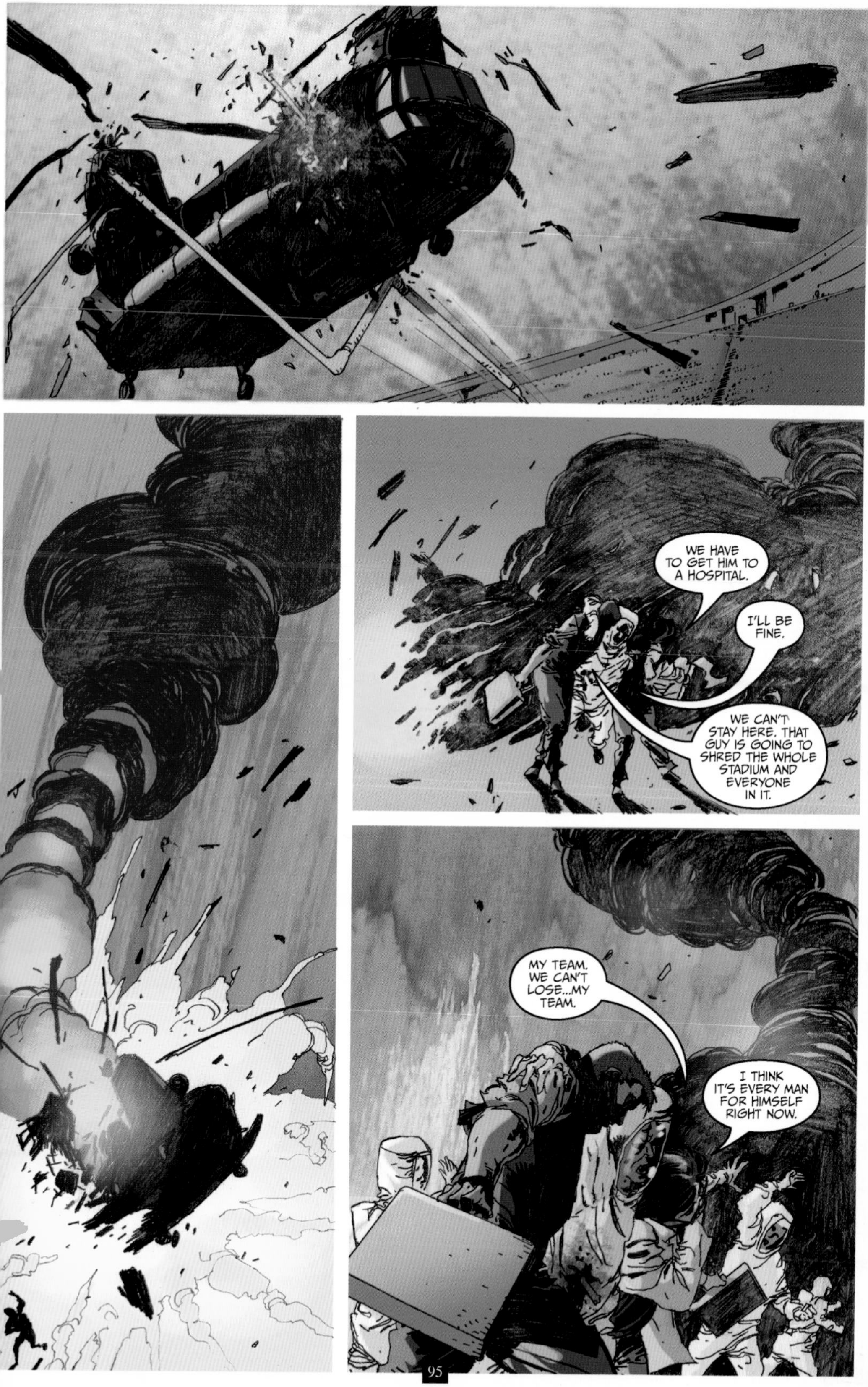
WE HAVE TO GET HIM TO A HOSPITAL.
I'LL BE FINE.
WE CAN'T STAY HERE. THAT GUY IS GOING TO SHRED THE WHOLE STADIUM AND EVERYONE IN IT.
MY TEAM. WE CAN'T LOSE...MY TEAM.
I THINK IT'S EVERY MAN FOR HIMSELF RIGHT NOW.

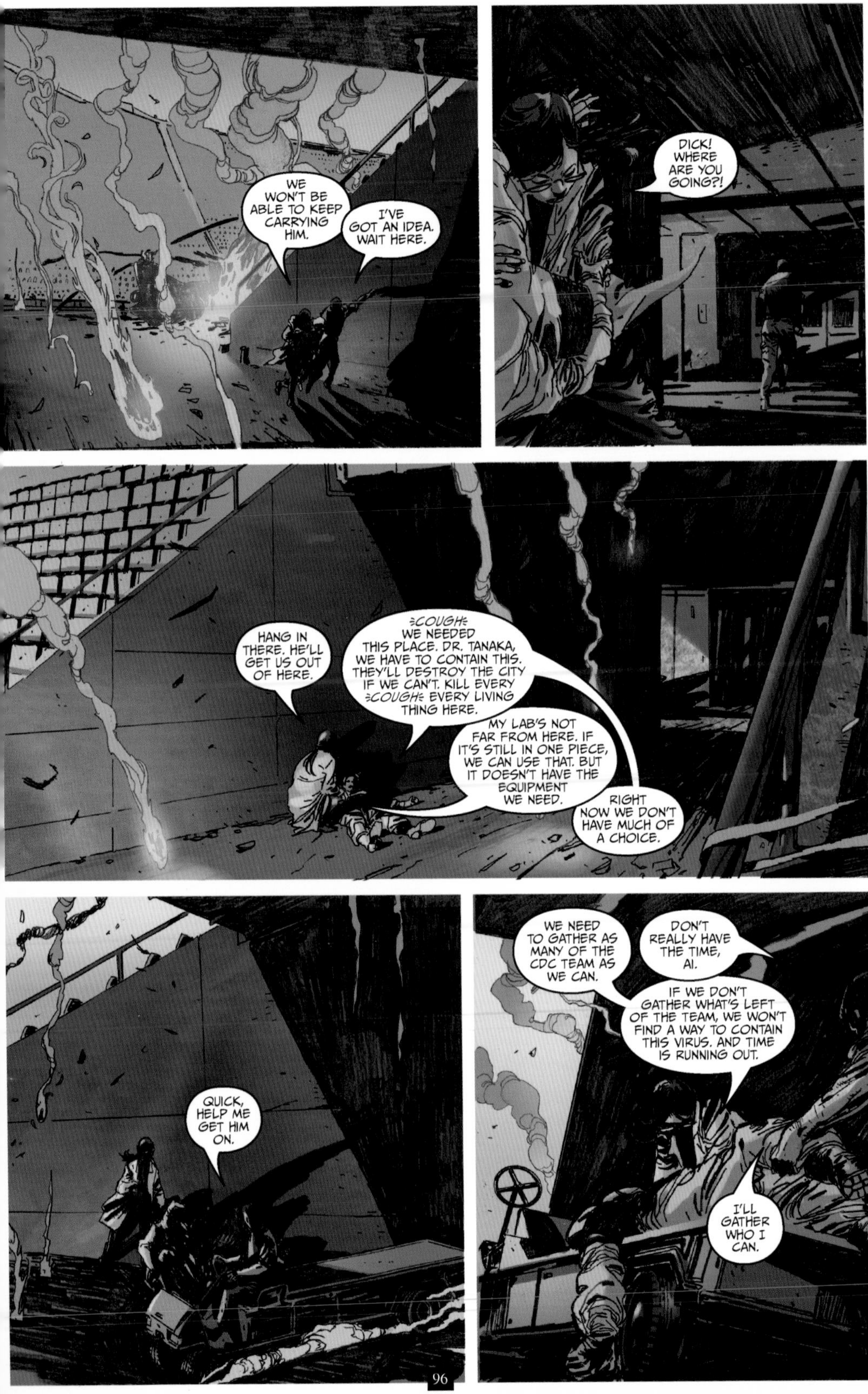

WE WON'T BE ABLE TO KEEP CARRYING HIM.
I'VE GOT AN IDEA. WAIT HERE.
DICK! WHERE ARE YOU GOING?!
HANG IN THERE. HE'LL GET US OUT OF HERE.
=COUGH= WE NEEDED THIS PLACE. DR. TANAKA, WE HAVE TO CONTAIN THIS. THEY'LL DESTROY THE CITY IF WE CAN'T. KILL EVERY =COUGH= EVERY LIVING THING HERE.
MY LAB'S NOT FAR FROM HERE. IF IT'S STILL IN ONE PIECE, WE CAN USE THAT. BUT IT DOESN'T HAVE THE EQUIPMENT WE NEED.
RIGHT NOW WE DON'T HAVE MUCH OF A CHOICE.
QUICK, HELP ME GET HIM ON.
WE NEED TO GATHER AS MANY OF THE CDC TEAM AS WE CAN.
DON'T REALLY HAVE THE TIME, AI.
IF WE DON'T GATHER WHAT'S LEFT OF THE TEAM, WE WON'T FIND A WAY TO CONTAIN THIS VIRUS. AND TIME IS RUNNING OUT.
I'LL GATHER WHO I CAN.

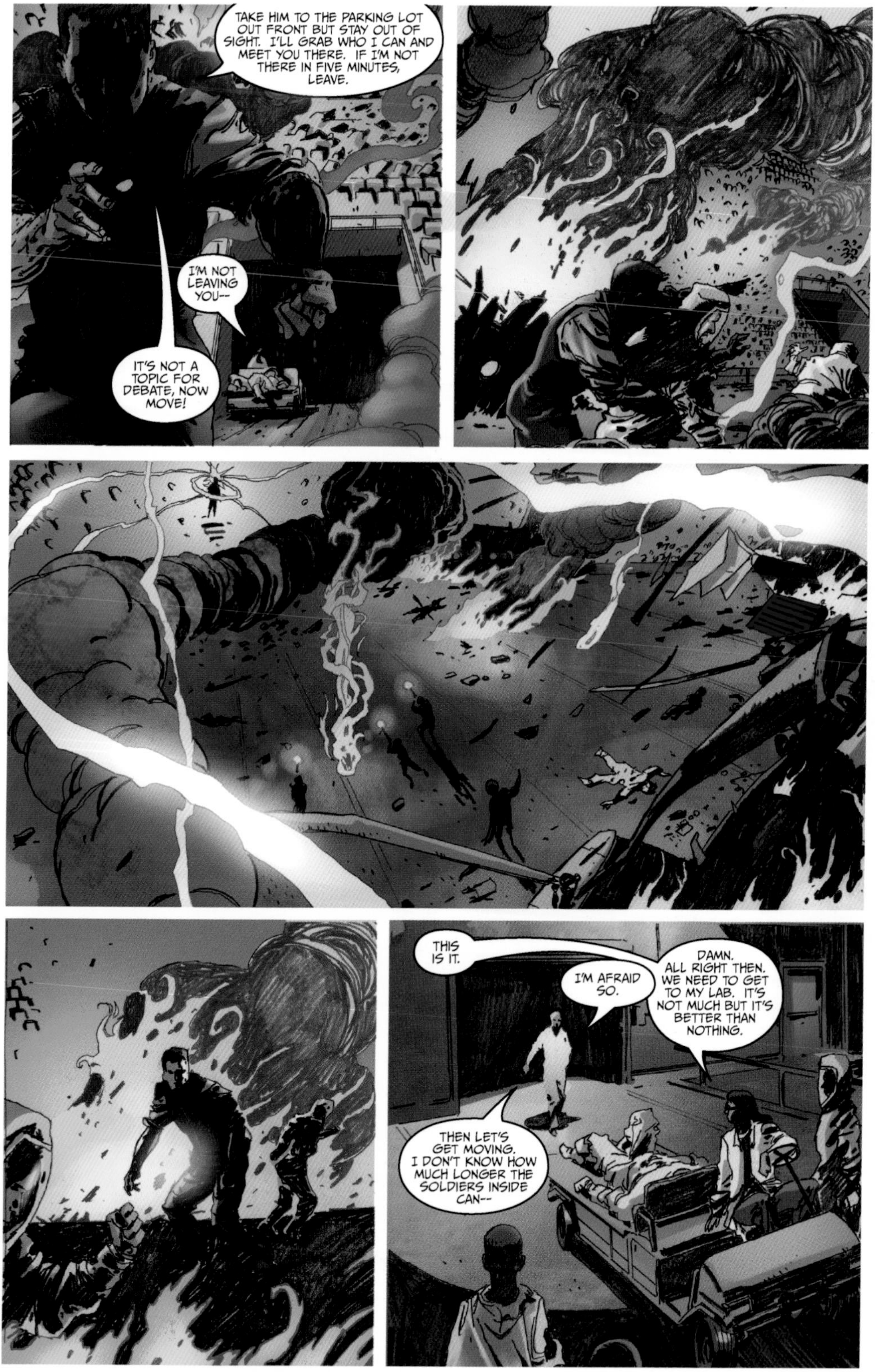
TAKE HIM TO THE PARKING LOT OUT FRONT BUT STAY OUT OF SIGHT. I'LL GRAB WHO I CAN AND MEET YOU THERE. IF I'M NOT THERE IN FIVE MINUTES, LEAVE.
I'M NOT LEAVING YOU--
IT'S NOT A TOPIC FOR DEBATE, NOW MOVE!
THIS IS IT.
I'M AFRAID SO.
DAMN. ALL RIGHT THEN. WE NEED TO GET TO MY LAB. IT'S NOT MUCH BUT IT'S BETTER THAN NOTHING.
THEN LET'S GET MOVING. I DON'T KNOW HOW MUCH LONGER THE SOLDIERS INSIDE CAN--

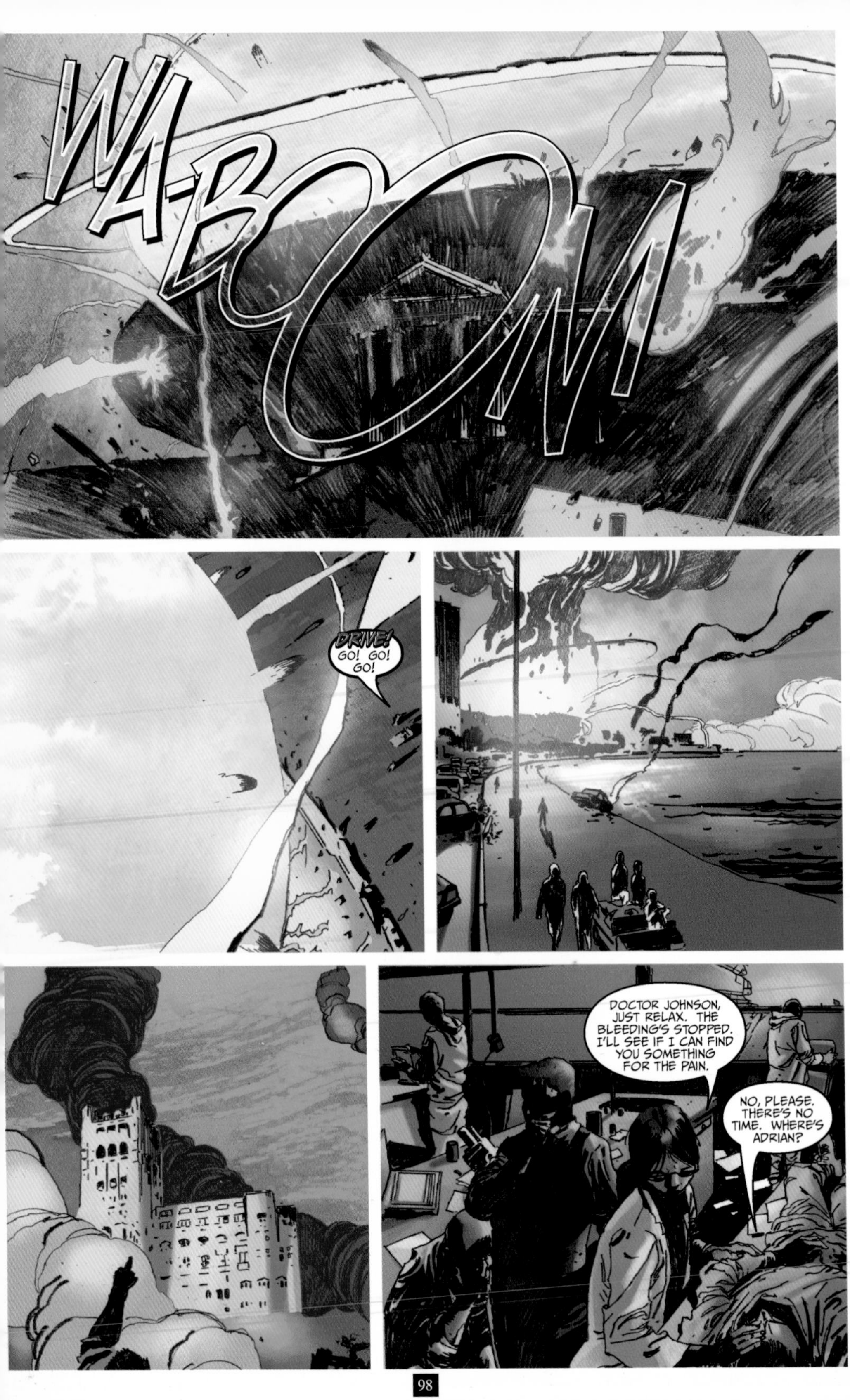
WA-BOOM
DRIVE! GO! GO! GO!
DOCTOR JOHNSON, JUST RELAX. THE BLEEDING'S STOPPED. I'LL SEE IF I CAN FIND YOU SOMETHING FOR THE PAIN.
NO, PLEASE. THERE'S NO TIME. WHERE'S ADRIAN?

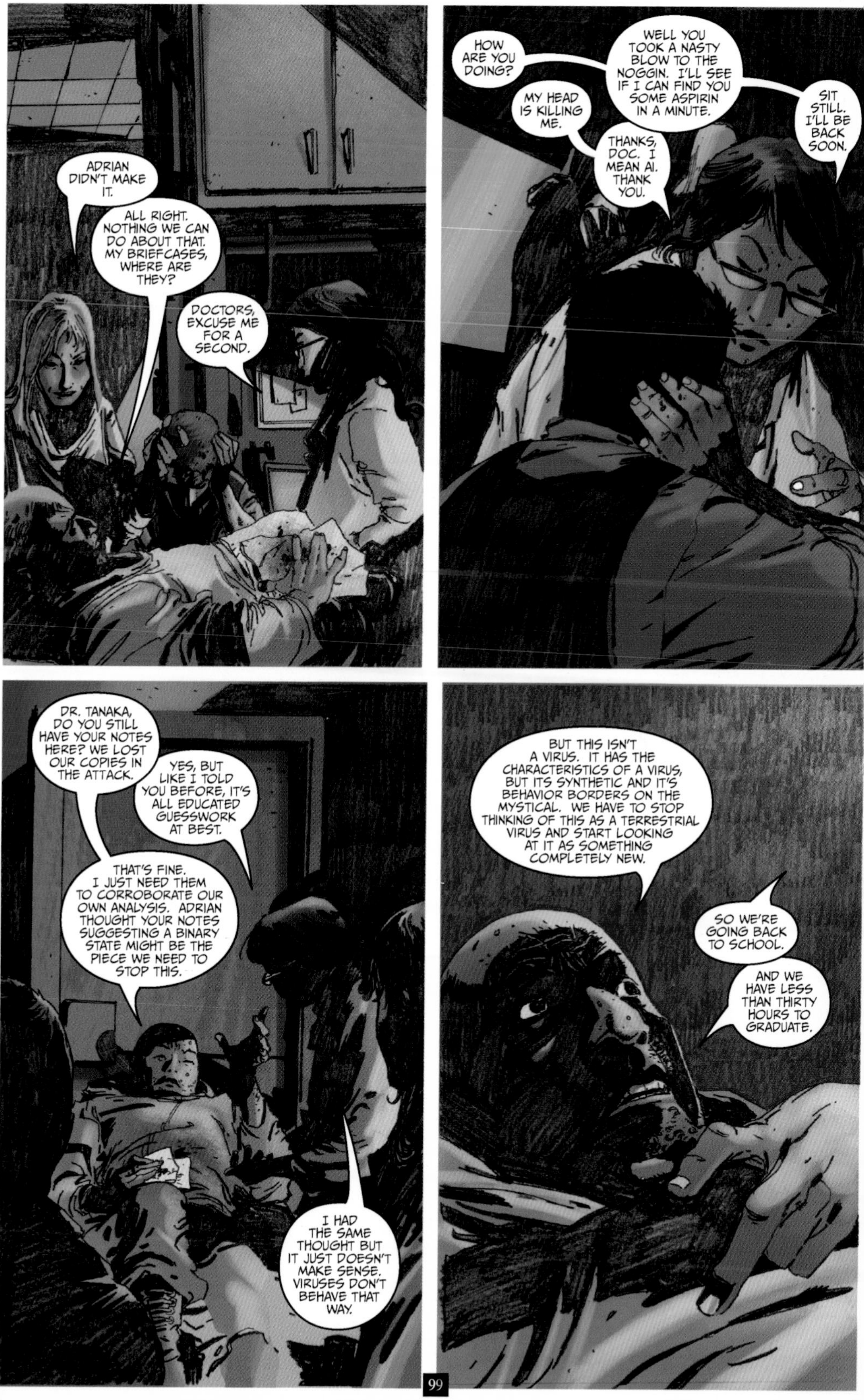
ADRIAN DIDN'T MAKE IT.
ALL RIGHT. NOTHING WE CAN DO ABOUT THAT. MY BRIEFCASES, WHERE ARE THEY?
DOCTORS, EXCUSE ME FOR A SECOND.
HOW ARE YOU DOING?
MY HEAD IS KILLING ME.
WELL YOU TOOK A NASTY BLOW TO THE NOGGIN. I'LL SEE IF I CAN FIND YOU SOME ASPIRIN IN A MINUTE.
THANKS, DOC. I MEAN AI. THANK YOU.
SIT STILL. I'LL BE BACK SOON.
DR. TANAKA, DO YOU STILL HAVE YOUR NOTES HERE? WE LOST OUR COPIES IN THE ATTACK.
YES, BUT LIKE I TOLD YOU BEFORE, IT'S ALL EDUCATED GUESSWORK AT BEST.
THAT'S FINE. I JUST NEED THEM TO CORROBORATE OUR OWN ANALYSIS. ADRIAN THOUGHT YOUR NOTES SUGGESTING A BINARY STATE MIGHT BE THE PIECE WE NEED TO STOP THIS.
I HAD THE SAME THOUGHT BUT IT JUST DOESN'T MAKE SENSE. VIRUSES DON'T BEHAVE THAT WAY.
BUT THIS ISN'T A VIRUS. IT HAS THE CHARACTERISTICS OF A VIRUS, BUT ITS SYNTHETIC AND IT'S BEHAVIOR BORDERS ON THE MYSTICAL. WE HAVE TO STOP THINKING OF THIS AS A TERRESTRIAL VIRUS AND START LOOKING AT IT AS SOMETHING COMPLETELY NEW.
SO WE'RE GOING BACK TO SCHOOL.
AND WE HAVE LESS THAN THIRTY HOURS TO GRADUATE.

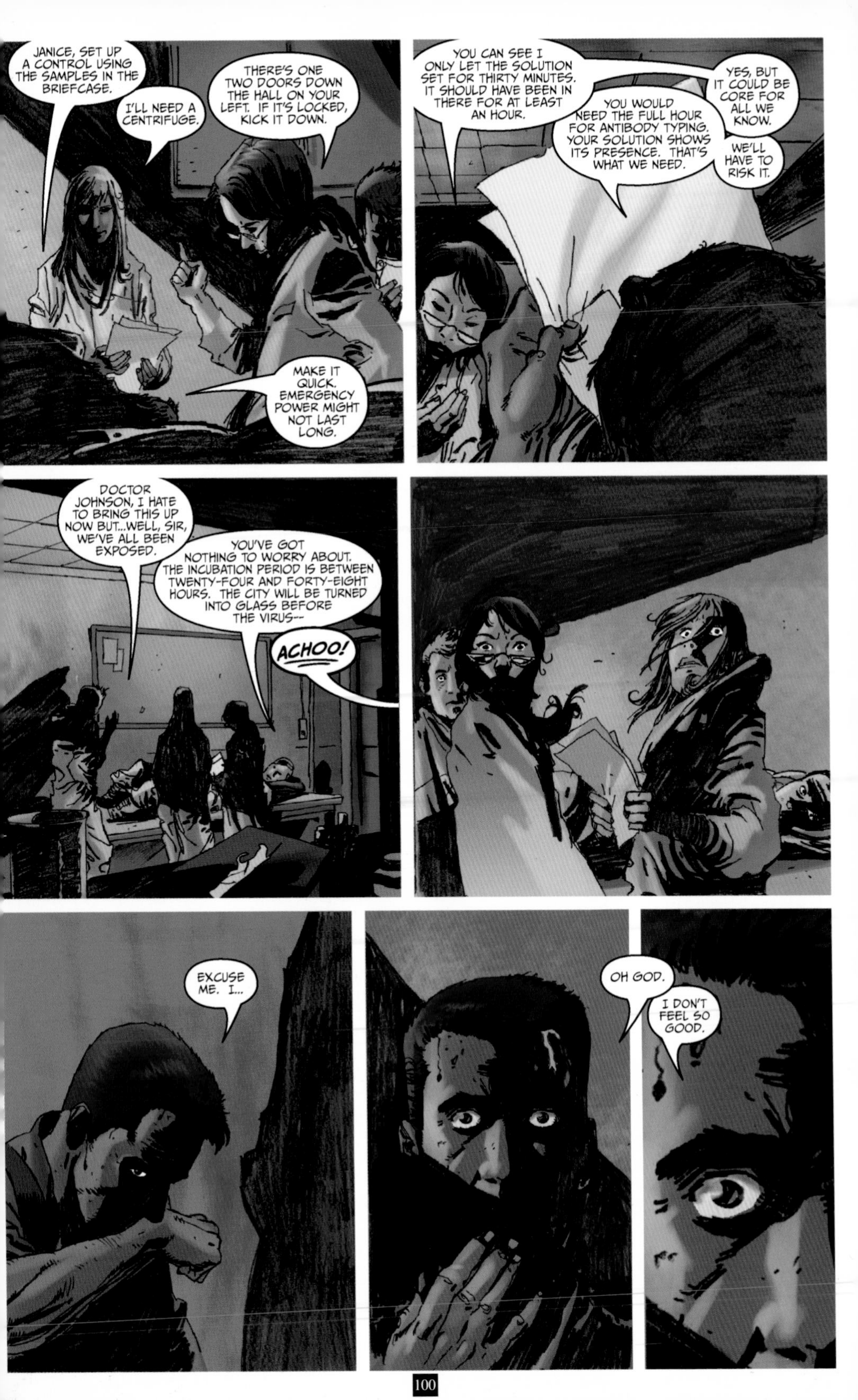

JANICE, SET UP A CONTROL USING THE SAMPLES IN THE BRIEFCASE.
I'LL NEED A CENTRIFUGE.
THERE'S ONE TWO DOORS DOWN THE HALL ON YOUR LEFT. IF IT'S LOCKED, KICK IT DOWN.
MAKE IT QUICK. EMERGENCY POWER MIGHT NOT LAST LONG.
YOU CAN SEE I ONLY LET THE SOLUTION SET FOR THIRTY MINUTES. IT SHOULD HAVE BEEN IN THERE FOR AT LEAST AN HOUR.
YOU WOULD NEED THE FULL HOUR FOR ANTIBODY TYPING. YOUR SOLUTION SHOWS ITS PRESENCE. THAT'S WHAT WE NEED.
YES, BUT IT COULD BE CORE FOR ALL WE KNOW.
WE'LL HAVE TO RISK IT.
DOCTOR JOHNSON, I HATE TO BRING THIS UP NOW BUT...WELL, SIR, WE'VE ALL BEEN EXPOSED.
YOU'VE GOT NOTHING TO WORRY ABOUT. THE INCUBATION PERIOD IS BETWEEN TWENTY-FOUR AND FORTY-EIGHT HOURS. THE CITY WILL BE TURNED INTO GLASS BEFORE THE VIRUS--
ACHOO!
EXCUSE ME. I...
OH GOD.
I DON'T FEEL SO GOOD.

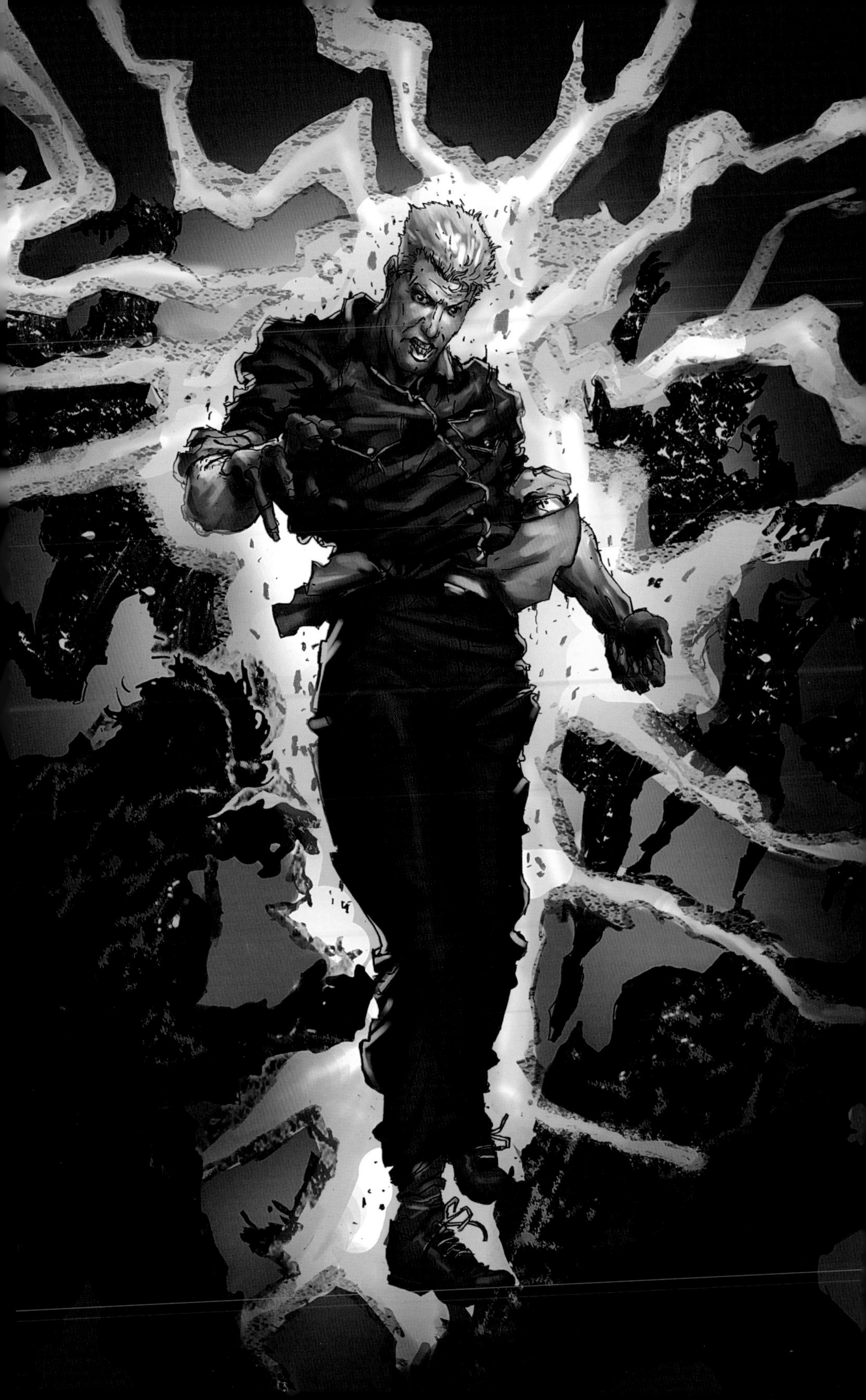

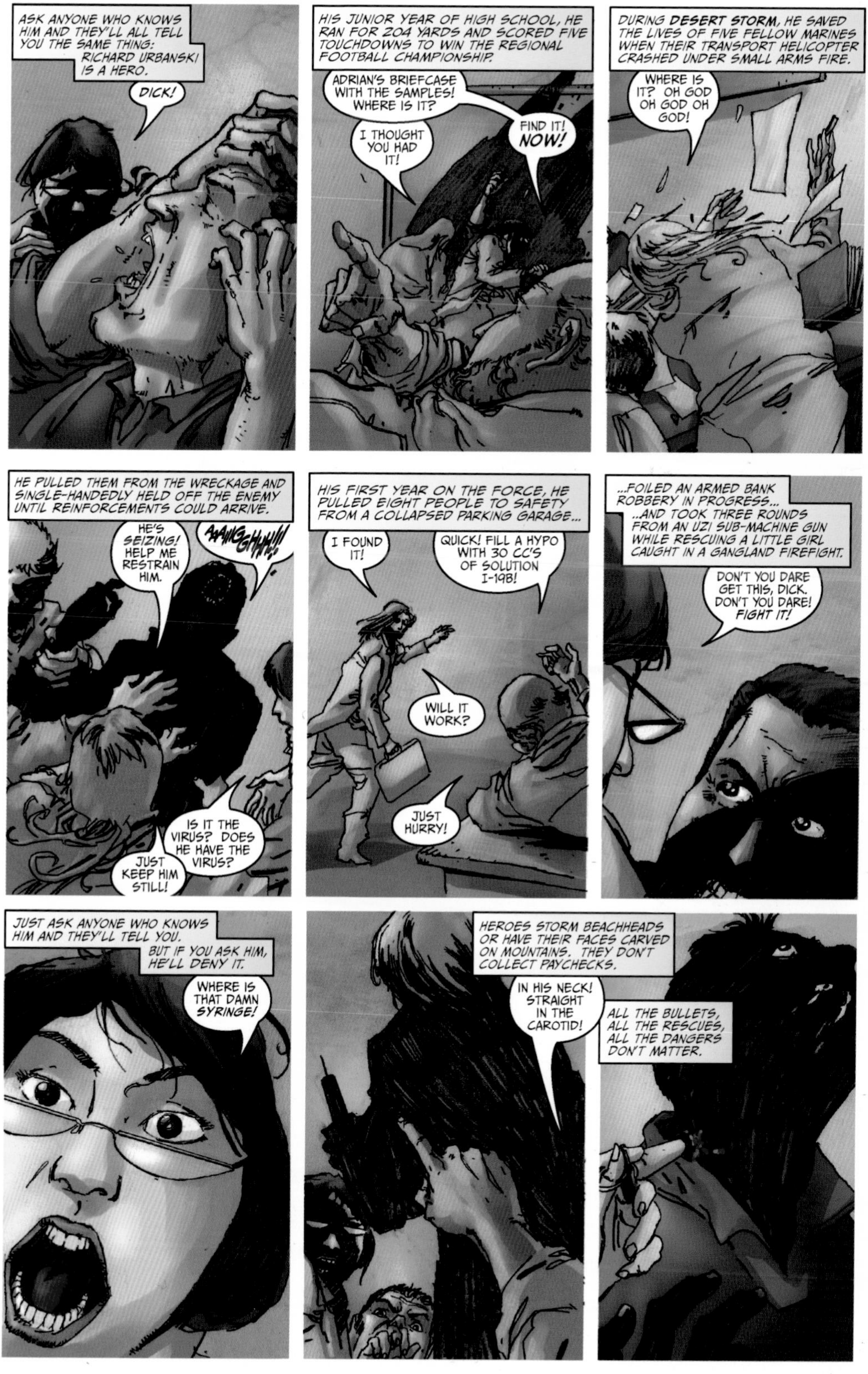
ASK ANYONE WHO KNOWS HIM AND THEY'LL ALL TELL YOU THE SAME THING: RICHARD URBANSKI IS A HERO.
DICK!
HIS JUNIOR YEAR OF HIGH SCHOOL, HE RAN FOR 204 YARDS AND SCORED FIVE TOUCHDOWNS TO WIN THE REGIONAL FOOTBALL CHAMPIONSHIP.
ADRIAN'S BRIEFCASE WITH THE SAMPLES! WHERE IS IT?
I THOUGHT YOU HAD IT!
FIND IT! NOW!
DURING DESERT STORM, HE SAVED THE LIVES OF FIVE FELLOW MARINES WHEN THEIR TRANSPORT HELICOPTER CRASHED UNDER SMALL ARMS FIRE.
WHERE IS IT? OH GOD OH GOD OH GOD!
HE PULLED THEM FROM THE WRECKAGE AND SINGLE-HANDEDLY HELD OFF THE ENEMY UNTIL REINFORCEMENTS COULD ARRIVE.
HE'S SEIZING! HELP ME RESTRAIN HIM.
AAAHGHHH!!
IS IT THE VIRUS? DOES HE HAVE THE VIRUS?
JUST KEEP HIM STILL!
HIS FIRST YEAR ON THE FORCE, HE PULLED EIGHT PEOPLE TO SAFETY FROM A COLLAPSED PARKING GARAGE...
I FOUND IT!
QUICK! FILL A HYPO WITH 30 CC'S OF SOLUTION I-19B!
WILL IT WORK?
JUST HURRY!
...FOILED AN ARMED BANK ROBBERY IN PROGRESS...
...AND TOOK THREE ROUNDS FROM AN UZI SUB-MACHINE GUN WHILE RESCUING A LITTLE GIRL CAUGHT IN A GANGLAND FIREFIGHT.
DON'T YOU DARE GET THIS, DICK. DON'T YOU DARE! FIGHT IT!
JUST ASK ANYONE WHO KNOWS HIM AND THEY'LL TELL YOU.
BUT IF YOU ASK HIM, HE'LL DENY IT.
WHERE IS THAT DAMN SYRINGE!
HEROES STORM BEACHHEADS OR HAVE THEIR FACES CARVED ON MOUNTAINS. THEY DON'T COLLECT PAYCHECKS.
IN HIS NECK! STRAIGHT IN THE CAROTID!
ALL THE BULLETS, ALL THE RESCUES, ALL THE DANGERS DON'T MATTER.

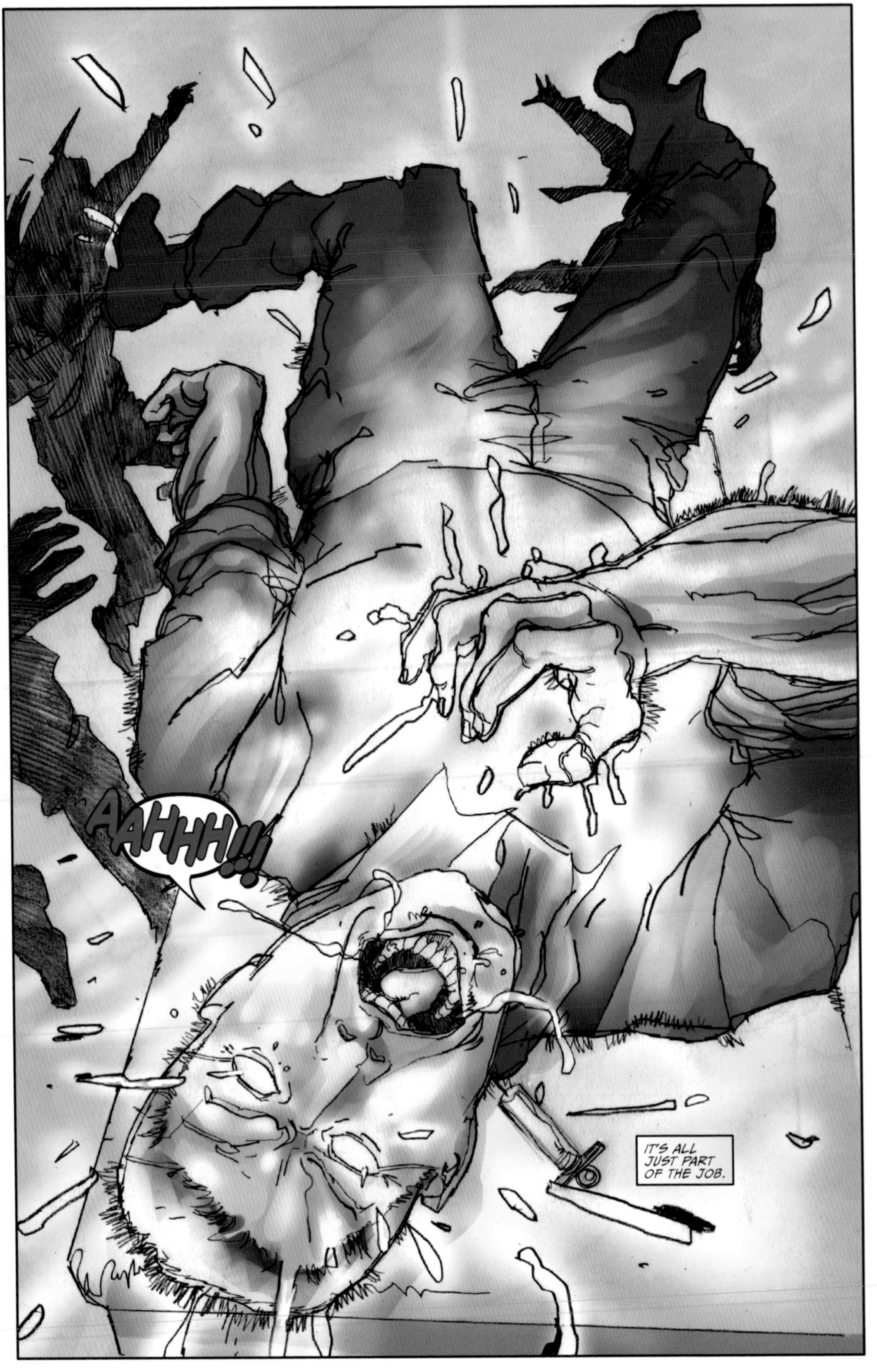
AAHHH!!!
IT'S ALL JUST PART OF THE JOB.

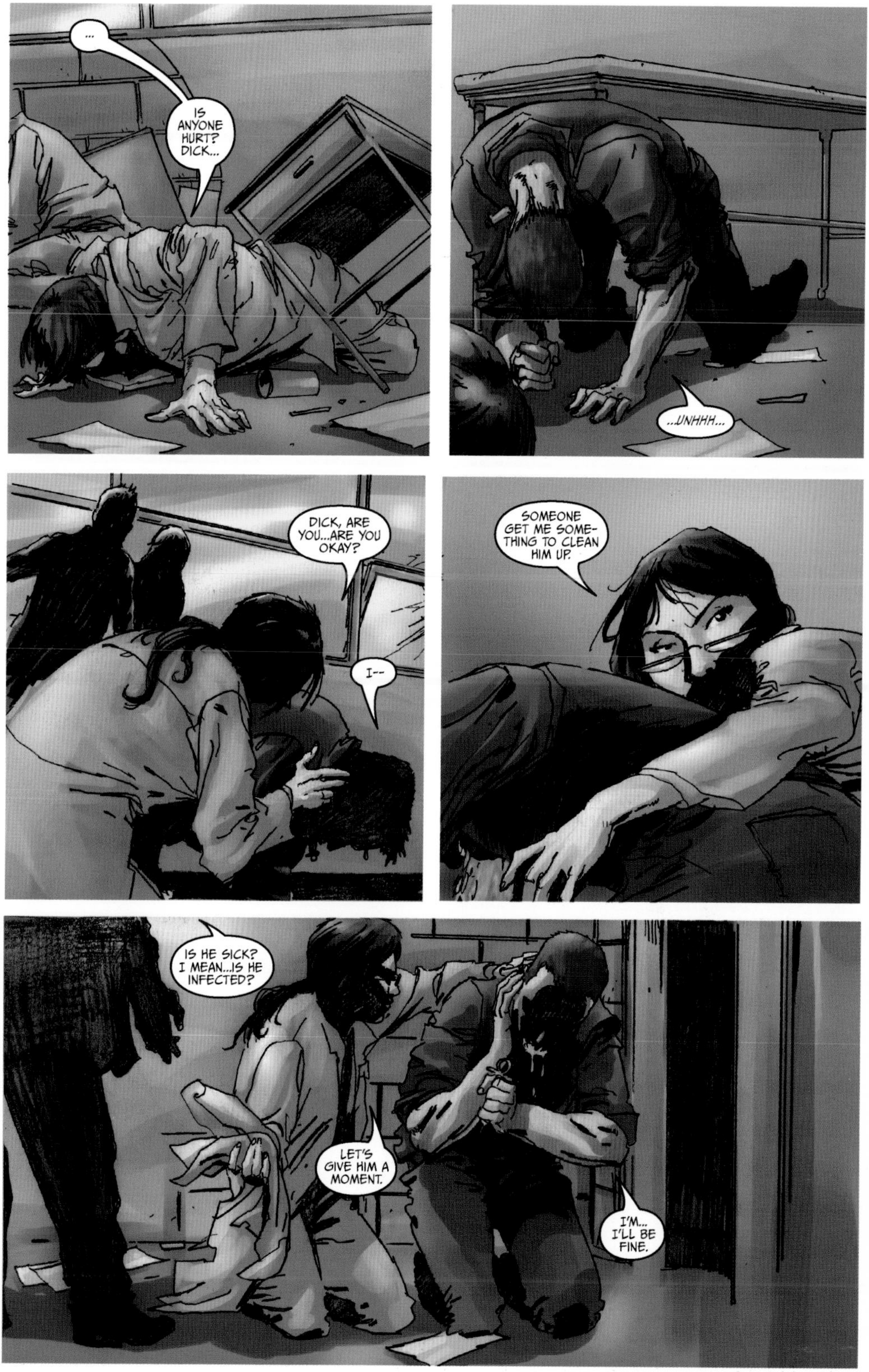
...
IS ANYONE HURT? DICK...
...UNHHH...
DICK, ARE YOU...ARE YOU OKAY?
I--
SOMEONE GET ME SOME-THING TO CLEAN HIM UP.
IS HE SICK? I MEAN...IS HE INFECTED?
LET'S GIVE HIM A MOMENT.
I'M... I'LL BE FINE.

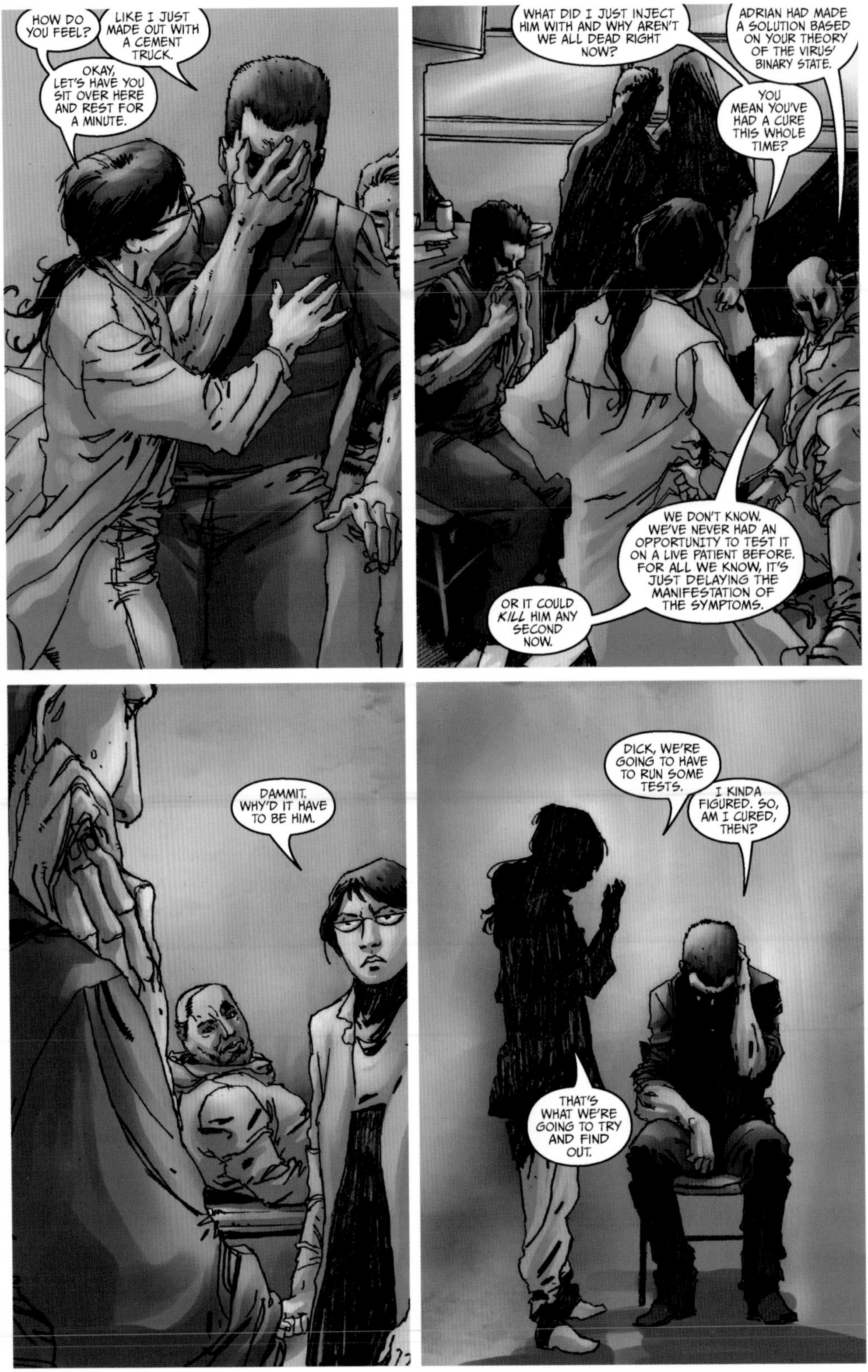
HOW DO YOU FEEL?
LIKE I JUST MADE OUT WITH A CEMENT TRUCK.
OKAY, LET'S HAVE YOU SIT OVER HERE AND REST FOR A MINUTE.
WHAT DID I JUST INJECT HIM WITH AND WHY AREN'T WE ALL DEAD RIGHT NOW?
ADRIAN HAD MADE A SOLUTION BASED ON YOUR THEORY OF THE VIRUS' BINARY STATE.
YOU MEAN YOU'VE HAD A CURE THIS WHOLE TIME?
WE DON'T KNOW. WE'VE NEVER HAD AN OPPORTUNITY TO TEST IT ON A LIVE PATIENT BEFORE. FOR ALL WE KNOW, IT'S JUST DELAYING THE MANIFESTATION OF THE SYMPTOMS.
OR IT COULD KILL HIM ANY SECOND NOW.
DAMMIT. WHY'D IT HAVE TO BE HIM.
DICK, WE'RE GOING TO HAVE TO RUN SOME TESTS.
I KINDA FIGURED. SO, AM I CURED, THEN?
THAT'S WHAT WE'RE GOING TO TRY AND FIND OUT.

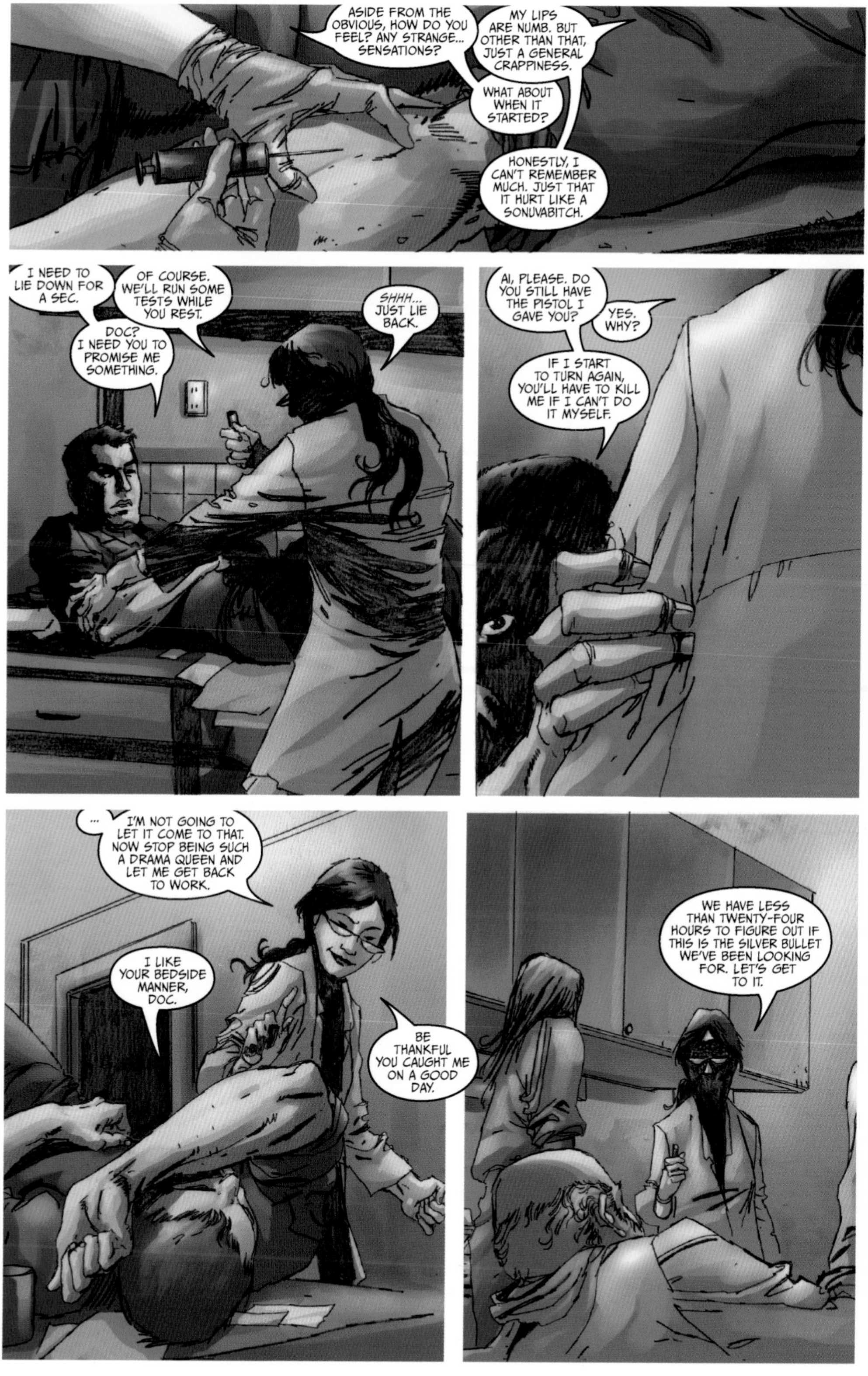

ASIDE FROM THE OBVIOUS, HOW DO YOU FEEL? ANY STRANGE... SENSATIONS?
MY LIPS ARE NUMB. BUT OTHER THAN THAT, JUST A GENERAL CRAPPINESS.
WHAT ABOUT WHEN IT STARTED?
HONESTLY, I CAN'T REMEMBER MUCH. JUST THAT IT HURT LIKE A SONUVABITCH.
I NEED TO LIE DOWN FOR A SEC.
OF COURSE. WE'LL RUN SOME TESTS WHILE YOU REST.
DOC? I NEED YOU TO PROMISE ME SOMETHING.
SHHH... JUST LIE BACK.
AI, PLEASE. DO YOU STILL HAVE THE PISTOL I GAVE YOU?
YES. WHY?
IF I START TO TURN AGAIN, YOU'LL HAVE TO KILL ME IF I CAN'T DO IT MYSELF.
...
I'M NOT GOING TO LET IT COME TO THAT. NOW STOP BEING SUCH A DRAMA QUEEN AND LET ME GET BACK TO WORK.
I LIKE YOUR BEDSIDE MANNER, DOC.
BE THANKFUL YOU CAUGHT ME ON A GOOD DAY.
WE HAVE LESS THAN TWENTY-FOUR HOURS TO FIGURE OUT IF THIS IS THE SILVER BULLET WE'VE BEEN LOOKING FOR. LET'S GET TO IT.

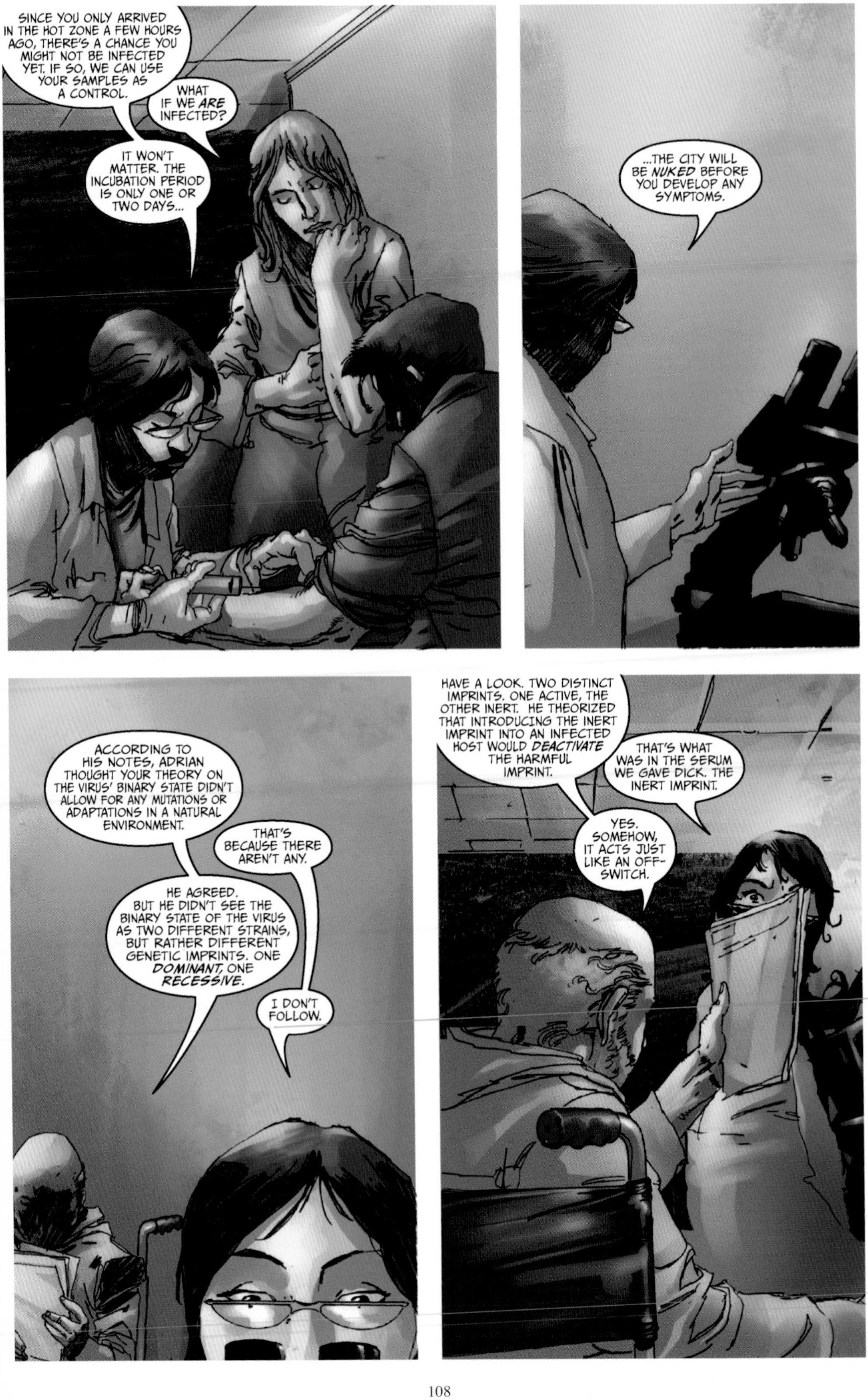
SINCE YOU ONLY ARRIVED IN THE HOT ZONE A FEW HOURS AGO, THERE'S A CHANCE YOU MIGHT NOT BE INFECTED YET. IF SO, WE CAN USE YOUR SAMPLES AS A CONTROL.
WHAT IF WE *ARE* INFECTED?
IT WON'T MATTER. THE INCUBATION PERIOD IS ONLY ONE OR TWO DAYS...
...THE CITY WILL BE *NUKED* BEFORE YOU DEVELOP ANY SYMPTOMS.
ACCORDING TO HIS NOTES, ADRIAN THOUGHT YOUR THEORY ON THE VIRUS' BINARY STATE DIDN'T ALLOW FOR ANY MUTATIONS OR ADAPTATIONS IN A NATURAL ENVIRONMENT.
THAT'S BECAUSE THERE AREN'T ANY.
HE AGREED. BUT HE DIDN'T SEE THE BINARY STATE OF THE VIRUS AS TWO DIFFERENT STRAINS, BUT RATHER DIFFERENT GENETIC IMPRINTS. ONE *DOMINANT,* ONE *RECESSIVE*.
I DON'T FOLLOW.
HAVE A LOOK. TWO DISTINCT IMPRINTS. ONE ACTIVE, THE OTHER INERT. HE THEORIZED THAT INTRODUCING THE INERT IMPRINT INTO AN INFECTED HOST WOULD *DEACTIVATE* THE HARMFUL IMPRINT.
THAT'S WHAT WAS IN THE SERUM WE GAVE DICK. THE INERT IMPRINT.
YES. SOMEHOW, IT ACTS JUST LIKE AN OFF-SWITCH.

SO WE'LL HAVE TO INJECT EVERYONE WITH THE INERT IMPRINT.

THAT'S NOT FEASIBLE. IT WAS MANUFACTURED USING ALIEN TECHNOLOGY. WE HAVE NO IDEA HOW TO REPLICATE IT, AND WE DON'T HAVE THE TIME TO FIND ENOUGH SAMPLES IN THE WILD.

TRUE. AND THERE'S NO TELLING HOW LONG THE "CURE" WOULD LAST, OR EVEN IF IT WOULD KILL MORE PEOPLE THAN IT SAVED.

BUT SOMETHING ABOUT ALL THIS BOTHERS ME.

ACCORDING TO HIS NOTES, THE INERT IMPRINT DOESN'T REPLICATE. ONLY THE ACTIVE DOES. SO IN ORDER FOR THIS "VIRUS" TO SURVIVE, THE ACTIVE IMPRINT *SHOULD* BE DOMINANT, BUT IT'S NOT.

IT DOESN'T MAKE SENSE.

OF COURSE IT DOES.

DICK. YOU SHOULD BE RESTING.

I'M FINE. WELL, BETTER ANYWAY. BESIDES, I'M NOT GOING TO LIE ON MY BACK WHILE THIS CITY BURNS.

WHAT WERE YOU GOING TO SAY, DICK?

YOU SAY THIS VIRUS IS ALIEN TECHNOLOGY, RIGHT? THAT MEANS THEY BUILT IT. BUT WHY? IT HAS TO BE A WEAPON. LIKE OUR OWN BIOLOGICAL AND CHEMICAL WEAPONS.

BUT WHY WOULD THEY MAKE THE DOMINANT IMPRINT OF THE VIRUS THE HARMLESS ONE? IF IT TRULY IS A WEAPON, WOULDN'T THEY WANT IT THE OTHER WAY AROUND?

IF THEY WANTED TO KILL EVERYONE, THEN YEAH. BUT THINK ABOUT IT. IT'S LIKE DR. JOHNSON SAID. THE VIRUS HAS AN OFF-SWITCH.

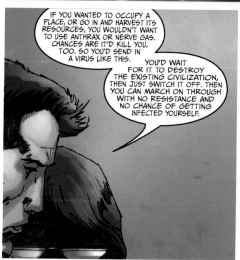

IF YOU WANTED TO OCCUPY A PLACE, OR GO IN AND HARVEST ITS RESOURCES, YOU WOULDN'T WANT TO USE ANTHRAX OR NERVE GAS. CHANCES ARE IT'D KILL YOU, TOO. SO YOU'D SEND IN A VIRUS LIKE THIS.

YOU'D WAIT FOR IT TO DESTROY THE EXISTING CIVILIZATION, THEN JUST SWITCH IT OFF. THEN YOU CAN MARCH ON THROUGH WITH NO RESISTANCE AND NO CHANCE OF GETTING INFECTED YOURSELF.

THAT ACTUALLY MAKES SENSE. I WONDER--

DR. JOHNSON, DR. TANAKA. YOU'RE GOING TO WANT TO SEE THIS.

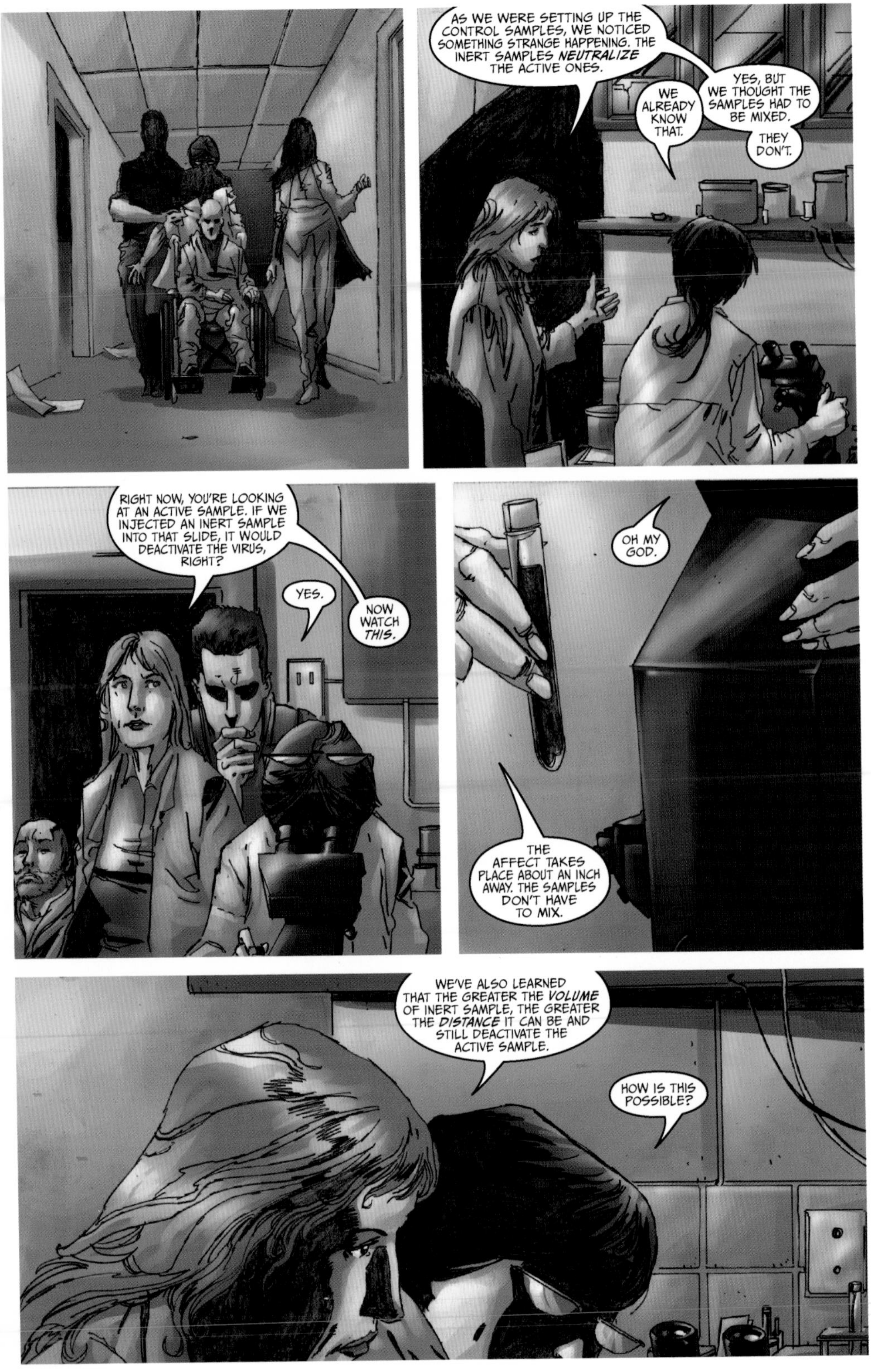

AS WE WERE SETTING UP THE CONTROL SAMPLES, WE NOTICED SOMETHING STRANGE HAPPENING. THE INERT SAMPLES *NEUTRALIZE* THE ACTIVE ONES.
WE ALREADY KNOW THAT.
YES, BUT WE THOUGHT THE SAMPLES HAD TO BE MIXED.
THEY DON'T.
RIGHT NOW, YOU'RE LOOKING AT AN ACTIVE SAMPLE. IF WE INJECTED AN INERT SAMPLE INTO THAT SLIDE, IT WOULD DEACTIVATE THE VIRUS, RIGHT?
YES.
NOW WATCH *THIS*.
OH MY GOD.
THE AFFECT TAKES PLACE ABOUT AN INCH AWAY. THE SAMPLES DON'T HAVE TO MIX.
WE'VE ALSO LEARNED THAT THE GREATER THE *VOLUME* OF INERT SAMPLE, THE GREATER THE *DISTANCE* IT CAN BE AND STILL DEACTIVATE THE ACTIVE SAMPLE.
HOW IS THIS POSSIBLE?

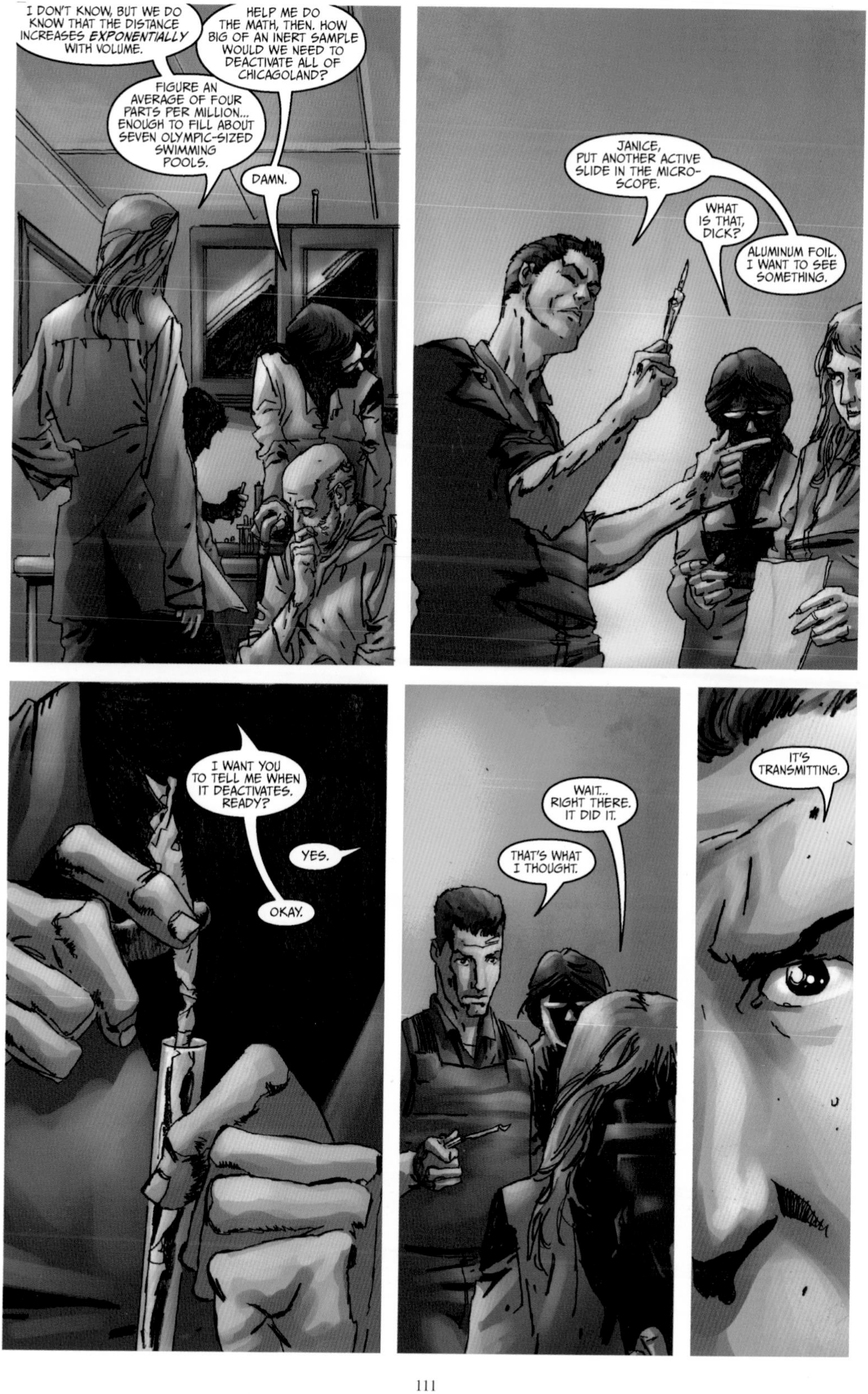
I DON'T KNOW, BUT WE DO KNOW THAT THE DISTANCE INCREASES EXPONENTIALLY WITH VOLUME.
HELP ME DO THE MATH, THEN. HOW BIG OF AN INERT SAMPLE WOULD WE NEED TO DEACTIVATE ALL OF CHICAGOLAND?
FIGURE AN AVERAGE OF FOUR PARTS PER MILLION... ENOUGH TO FILL ABOUT SEVEN OLYMPIC-SIZED SWIMMING POOLS.
DAMN.
JANICE, PUT ANOTHER ACTIVE SLIDE IN THE MICRO-SCOPE.
WHAT IS THAT, DICK?
ALUMINUM FOIL. I WANT TO SEE SOMETHING.
I WANT YOU TO TELL ME WHEN IT DEACTIVATES. READY?
YES.
OKAY.
WAIT... RIGHT THERE. IT DID IT.
THAT'S WHAT I THOUGHT.
IT'S TRANSMITTING.

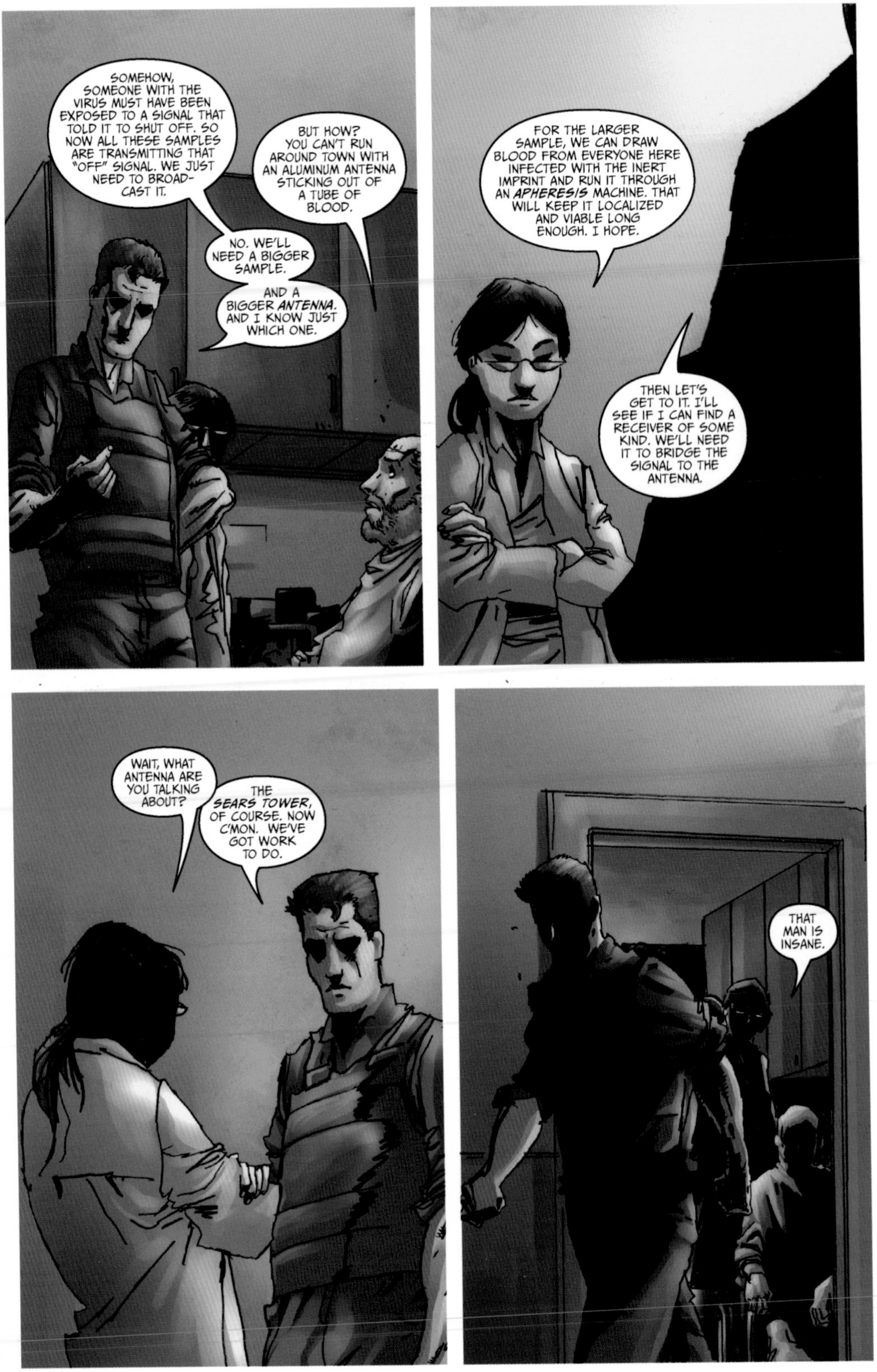
SOMEHOW, SOMEONE WITH THE VIRUS MUST HAVE BEEN EXPOSED TO A SIGNAL THAT TOLD IT TO SHUT OFF. SO NOW ALL THESE SAMPLES ARE TRANSMITTING THAT "OFF" SIGNAL. WE JUST NEED TO BROAD-CAST IT.
BUT HOW? YOU CAN'T RUN AROUND TOWN WITH AN ALUMINUM ANTENNA STICKING OUT OF A TUBE OF BLOOD.
NO. WE'LL NEED A BIGGER SAMPLE.
AND A BIGGER *ANTENNA*. AND I KNOW JUST WHICH ONE.
FOR THE LARGER SAMPLE, WE CAN DRAW BLOOD FROM EVERYONE HERE INFECTED WITH THE INERT IMPRINT AND RUN IT THROUGH AN *APHERESIS* MACHINE. THAT WILL KEEP IT LOCALIZED AND VIABLE LONG ENOUGH. I HOPE.
THEN LET'S GET TO IT. I'LL SEE IF I CAN FIND A RECEIVER OF SOME KIND. WE'LL NEED IT TO BRIDGE THE SIGNAL TO THE ANTENNA.
WAIT, WHAT ANTENNA ARE YOU TALKING ABOUT?
THE *SEARS TOWER*, OF COURSE. NOW C'MON. WE'VE GOT WORK TO DO.
THAT MAN IS INSANE.

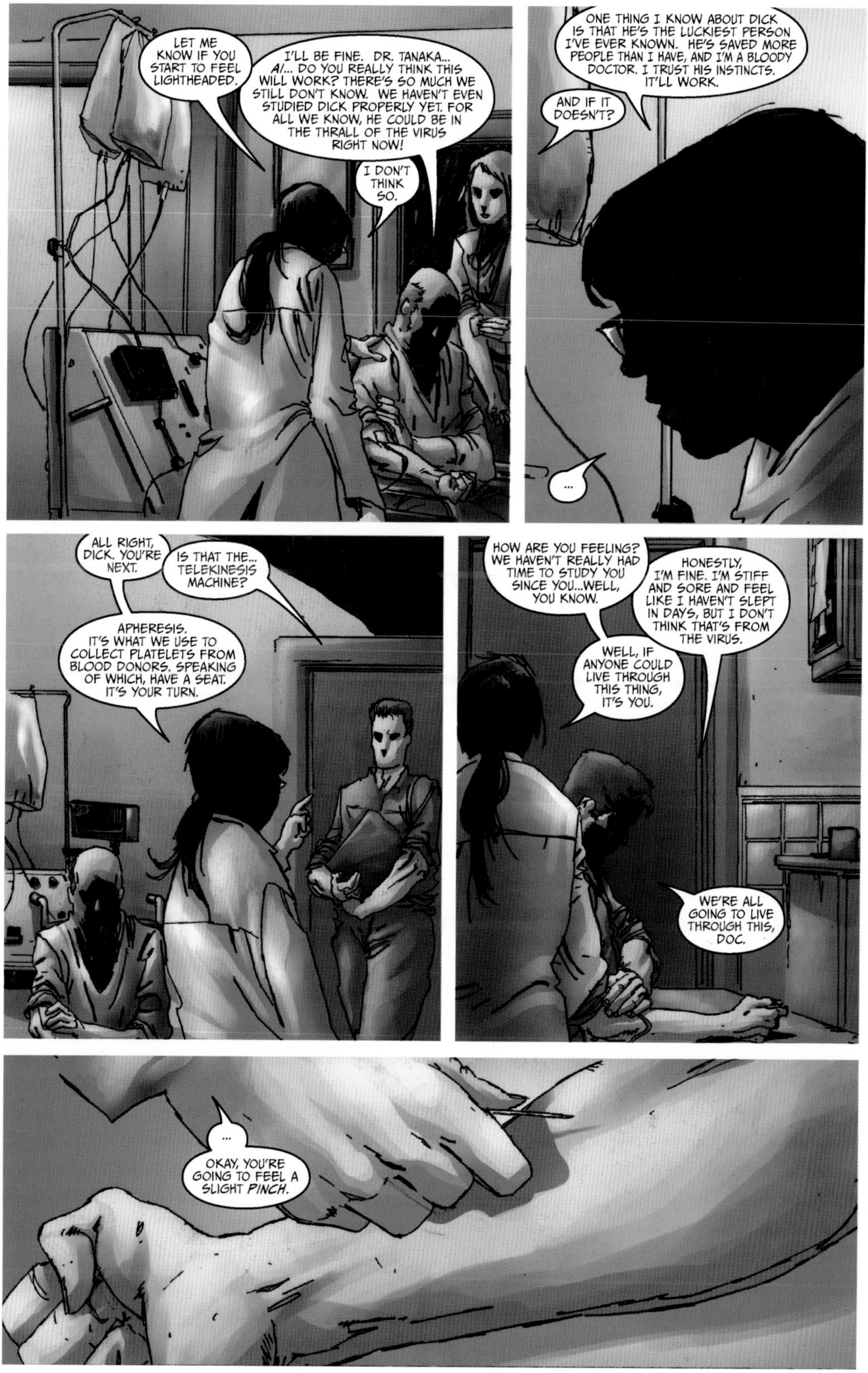
LET ME KNOW IF YOU START TO FEEL LIGHTHEADED.
I'LL BE FINE. DR. TANAKA... *AI*... DO YOU REALLY THINK THIS WILL WORK? THERE'S SO MUCH WE STILL DON'T KNOW. WE HAVEN'T EVEN STUDIED DICK PROPERLY YET. FOR ALL WE KNOW, HE COULD BE IN THE THRALL OF THE VIRUS RIGHT NOW!
I DON'T THINK SO.
ONE THING I KNOW ABOUT DICK IS THAT HE'S THE LUCKIEST PERSON I'VE EVER KNOWN. HE'S SAVED MORE PEOPLE THAN I HAVE, AND I'M A BLOODY DOCTOR. I TRUST HIS INSTINCTS. IT'LL WORK.
AND IF IT DOESN'T?
...
ALL RIGHT, DICK. YOU'RE NEXT.
IS THAT THE... TELEKINESIS MACHINE?
APHERESIS. IT'S WHAT WE USE TO COLLECT PLATELETS FROM BLOOD DONORS. SPEAKING OF WHICH, HAVE A SEAT. IT'S YOUR TURN.
HOW ARE YOU FEELING? WE HAVEN'T REALLY HAD TIME TO STUDY YOU SINCE YOU...WELL, YOU KNOW.
HONESTLY, I'M FINE. I'M STIFF AND SORE AND FEEL LIKE I HAVEN'T SLEPT IN DAYS, BUT I DON'T THINK THAT'S FROM THE VIRUS.
WELL, IF ANYONE COULD LIVE THROUGH THIS THING, IT'S YOU.
WE'RE ALL GOING TO LIVE THROUGH THIS, DOC.
...
OKAY, YOU'RE GOING TO FEEL A SLIGHT *PINCH*.

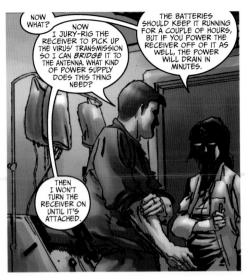

NOW WHAT?

NOW I JURY-RIG THE RECEIVER TO PICK UP THE VIRUS' TRANSMISSION SO I CAN *BRIDGE* IT TO THE ANTENNA. WHAT KIND OF POWER SUPPLY DOES THIS THING NEED?

THE BATTERIES SHOULD KEEP IT RUNNING FOR A COUPLE OF HOURS, BUT IF YOU POWER THE RECEIVER OFF OF IT AS WELL, THE POWER WILL DRAIN IN MINUTES.

THEN I WON'T TURN THE RECEIVER ON UNTIL IT'S ATTACHED.

YOU MEAN "WE." I'M COMING WITH YOU.

WHAT? NO, YOU'RE STAYING HERE. I HAVE NO IDEA WHAT'S GOING TO HAPPEN BETWEEN HERE AND THERE. YOU'LL BE SAFER HERE.

YOU DON'T KNOW HOW TO OPERATE THIS THING. IF SOMETHING GOES WRONG WITH IT, WE'RE SCREWED. EVERYONE IS SCREWED. I'M COMING WITH YOU, AND THAT'S FINAL.

ALL RIGHT, DOC. HERE, THEN. YOU HOLD ONTO THIS. WE WON'T BE ABLE TO TURN ON THE RECEIVER WITHOUT THIS. DON'T LOSE IT.

IT DOESN'T HAVE AN "ON" SWITCH?

HEY, I STILL CAN'T WRAP MY HEAD AROUND AN MP3, SO DON'T ASK ME TO EXPLAIN WHY THEY MAKE THINGS THAT CAN'T OPERATE WITHOUT A REMOTE.

DR. JOHNSON, GET ON THE HORN TO SOMEBODY OUTSIDE OF THE CITY AND TELL THEM WHAT WE'VE LEARNED.

DO YOU THINK THAT WILL KEEP THEM FROM NUKING THE CITY?

THEY WON'T NUKE THE CITY. THEY HAVE PLENTY OF OTHER TOYS THAT CAN DO THE JOB WITHOUT ANY FALLOUT.

GOOD LUCK, DICK. DR. TANAKA.

THANKS. WE'LL SEE YOU IN A FEW HOURS.

WE BETTER.

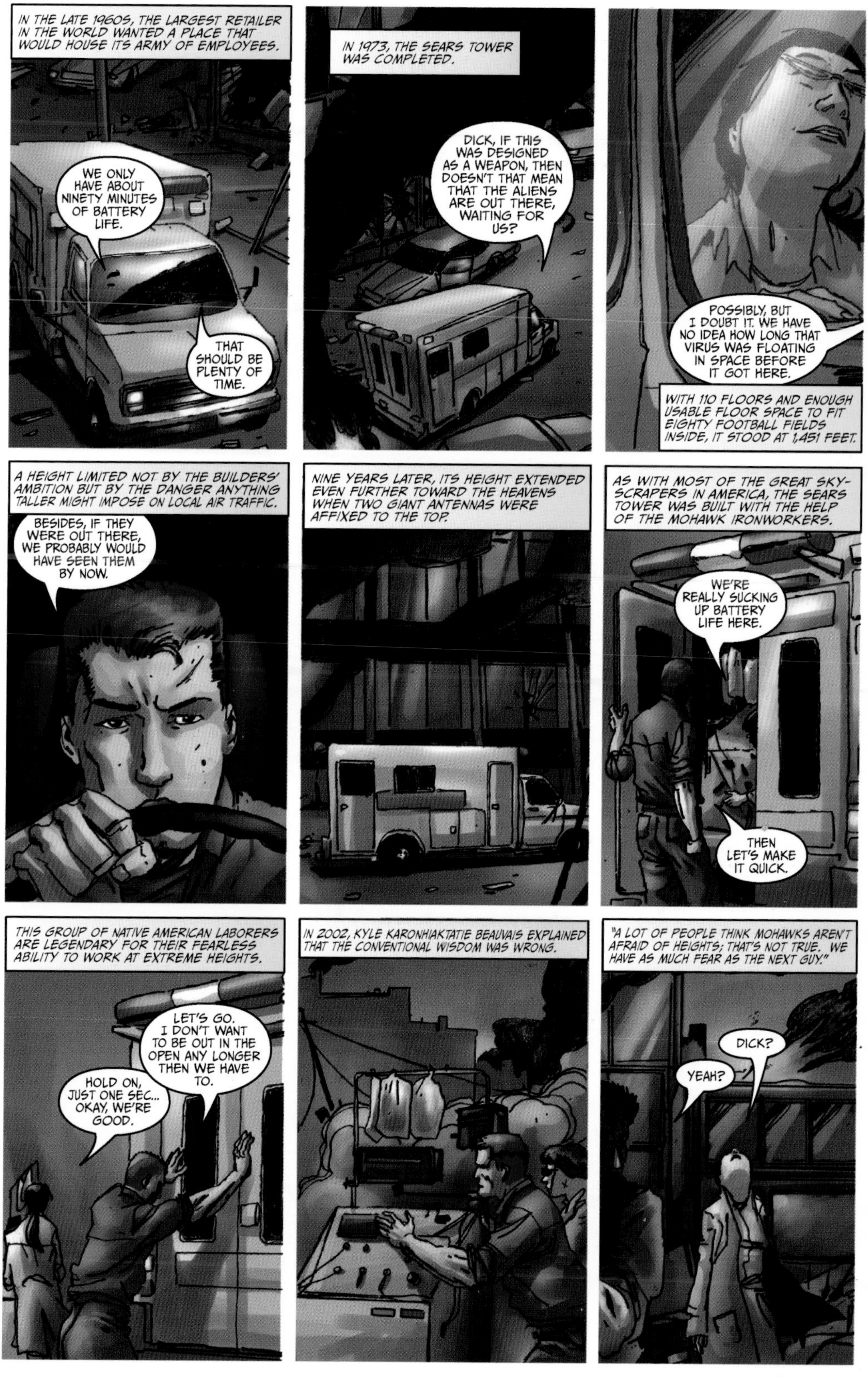
IN THE LATE 1960S, THE LARGEST RETAILER IN THE WORLD WANTED A PLACE THAT WOULD HOUSE ITS ARMY OF EMPLOYEES.
WE ONLY HAVE ABOUT NINETY MINUTES OF BATTERY LIFE.
THAT SHOULD BE PLENTY OF TIME.
IN 1973, THE SEARS TOWER WAS COMPLETED.
DICK, IF THIS WAS DESIGNED AS A WEAPON, THEN DOESN'T THAT MEAN THAT THE ALIENS ARE OUT THERE, WAITING FOR US?
POSSIBLY, BUT I DOUBT IT. WE HAVE NO IDEA HOW LONG THAT VIRUS WAS FLOATING IN SPACE BEFORE IT GOT HERE.
WITH 110 FLOORS AND ENOUGH USABLE FLOOR SPACE TO FIT EIGHTY FOOTBALL FIELDS INSIDE, IT STOOD AT 1,451 FEET.
A HEIGHT LIMITED NOT BY THE BUILDERS' AMBITION BUT BY THE DANGER ANYTHING TALLER MIGHT IMPOSE ON LOCAL AIR TRAFFIC.
BESIDES, IF THEY WERE OUT THERE, WE PROBABLY WOULD HAVE SEEN THEM BY NOW.
NINE YEARS LATER, ITS HEIGHT EXTENDED EVEN FURTHER TOWARD THE HEAVENS WHEN TWO GIANT ANTENNAS WERE AFFIXED TO THE TOP.
AS WITH MOST OF THE GREAT SKY-SCRAPERS IN AMERICA, THE SEARS TOWER WAS BUILT WITH THE HELP OF THE MOHAWK IRONWORKERS.
WE'RE REALLY SUCKING UP BATTERY LIFE HERE.
THEN LET'S MAKE IT QUICK.
THIS GROUP OF NATIVE AMERICAN LABORERS ARE LEGENDARY FOR THEIR FEARLESS ABILITY TO WORK AT EXTREME HEIGHTS.
LET'S GO. I DON'T WANT TO BE OUT IN THE OPEN ANY LONGER THEN WE HAVE TO.
HOLD ON, JUST ONE SEC... OKAY, WE'RE GOOD.
IN 2002, KYLE KARONHIAKTATIE BEAUVAIS EXPLAINED THAT THE CONVENTIONAL WISDOM WAS WRONG.
"A LOT OF PEOPLE THINK MOHAWKS AREN'T AFRAID OF HEIGHTS; THAT'S NOT TRUE. WE HAVE AS MUCH FEAR AS THE NEXT GUY."
DICK?
YEAH?

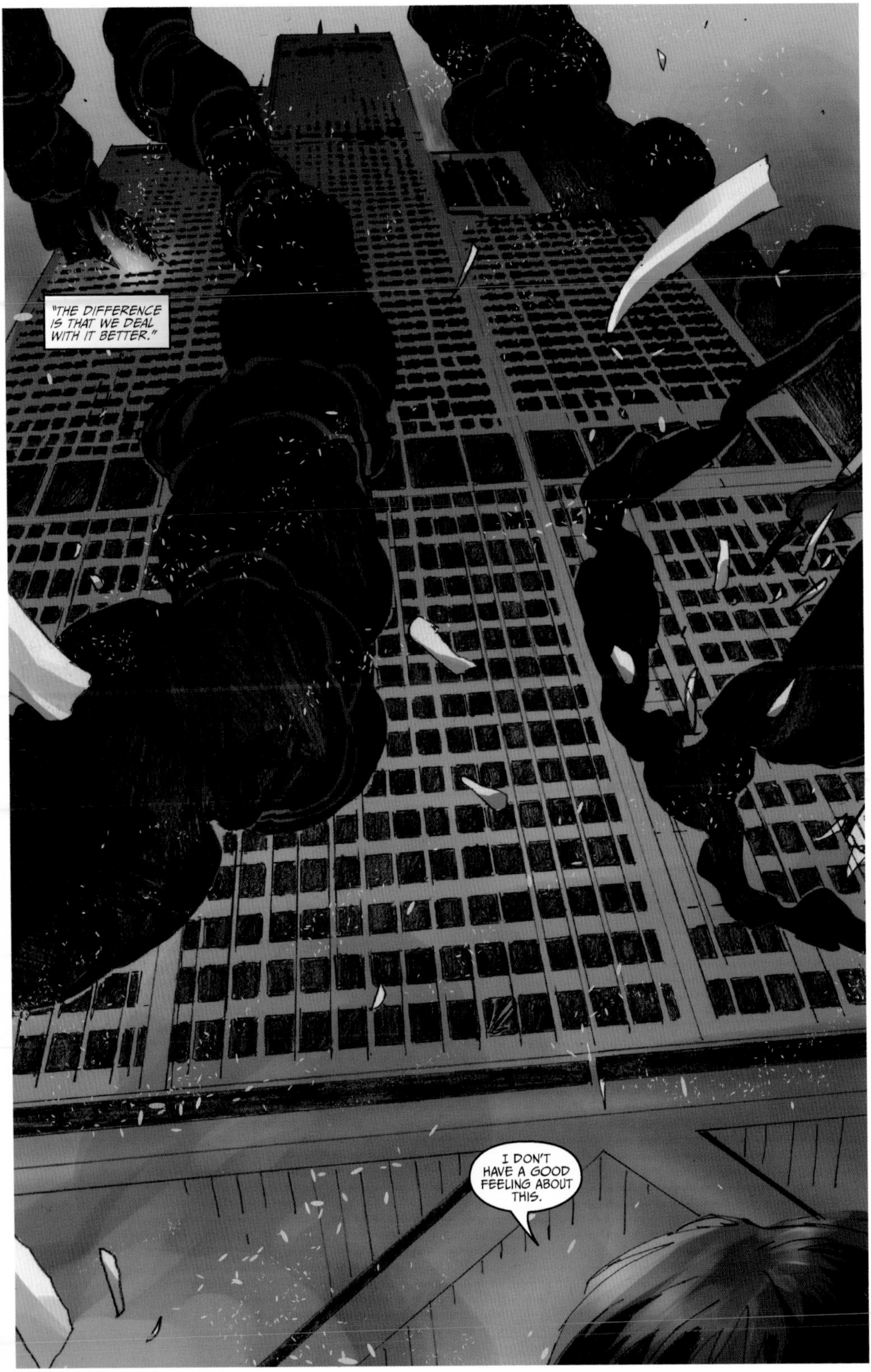
"THE DIFFERENCE IS THAT WE DEAL WITH IT BETTER."
I DON'T HAVE A GOOD FEELING ABOUT THIS.

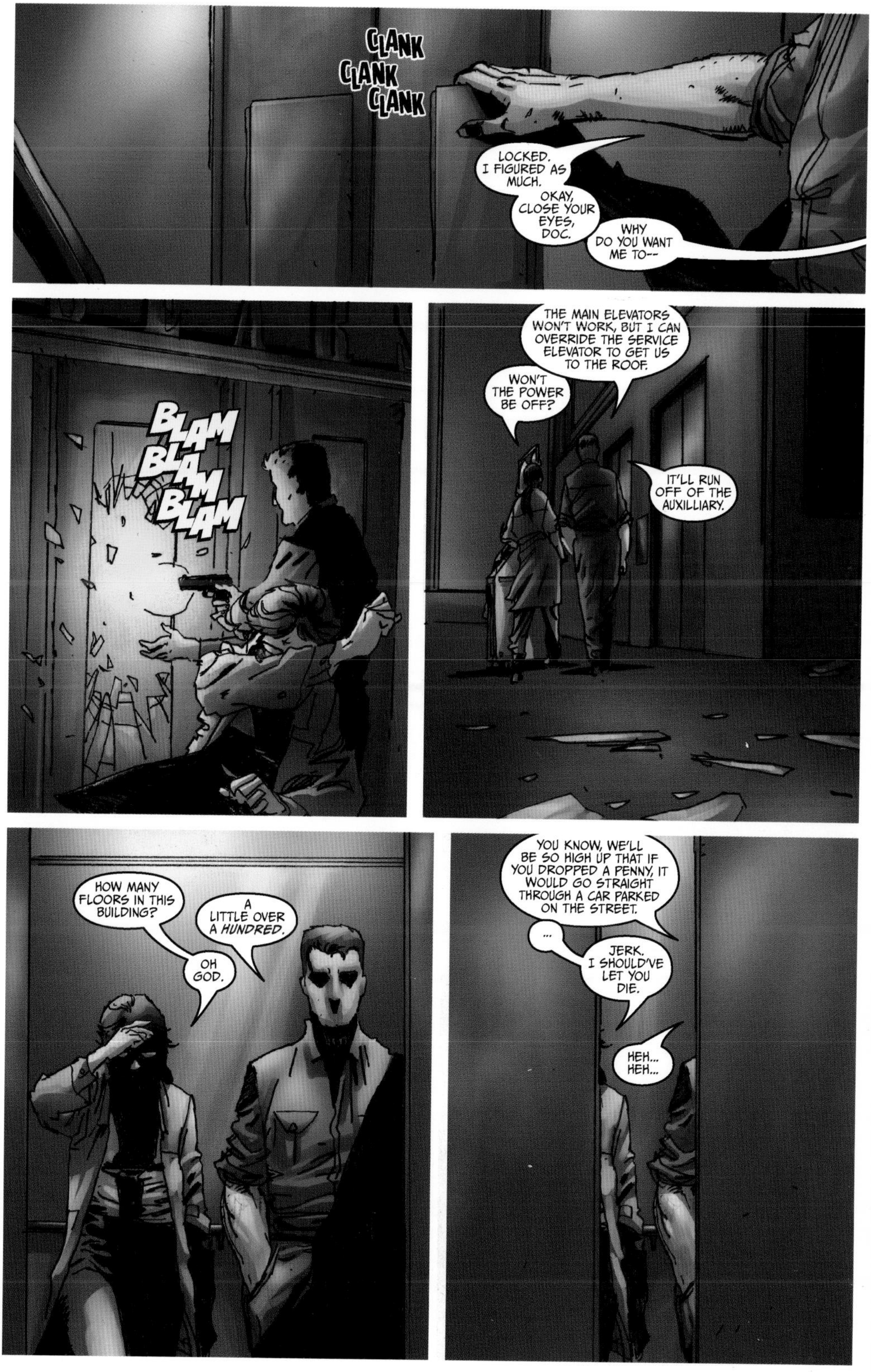
CLANK
CLANK
CLANK
LOCKED. I FIGURED AS MUCH.
OKAY, CLOSE YOUR EYES, DOC.
WHY DO YOU WANT ME TO--
BLAM
BLAM
BLAM
THE MAIN ELEVATORS WON'T WORK, BUT I CAN OVERRIDE THE SERVICE ELEVATOR TO GET US TO THE ROOF.
WON'T THE POWER BE OFF?
IT'LL RUN OFF OF THE AUXILLIARY.
HOW MANY FLOORS IN THIS BUILDING?
A LITTLE OVER A *HUNDRED*.
OH GOD.
YOU KNOW, WE'LL BE SO HIGH UP THAT IF YOU DROPPED A PENNY, IT WOULD GO STRAIGHT THROUGH A CAR PARKED ON THE STREET.
...
JERK. I SHOULD'VE LET YOU DIE.
HEH... HEH...

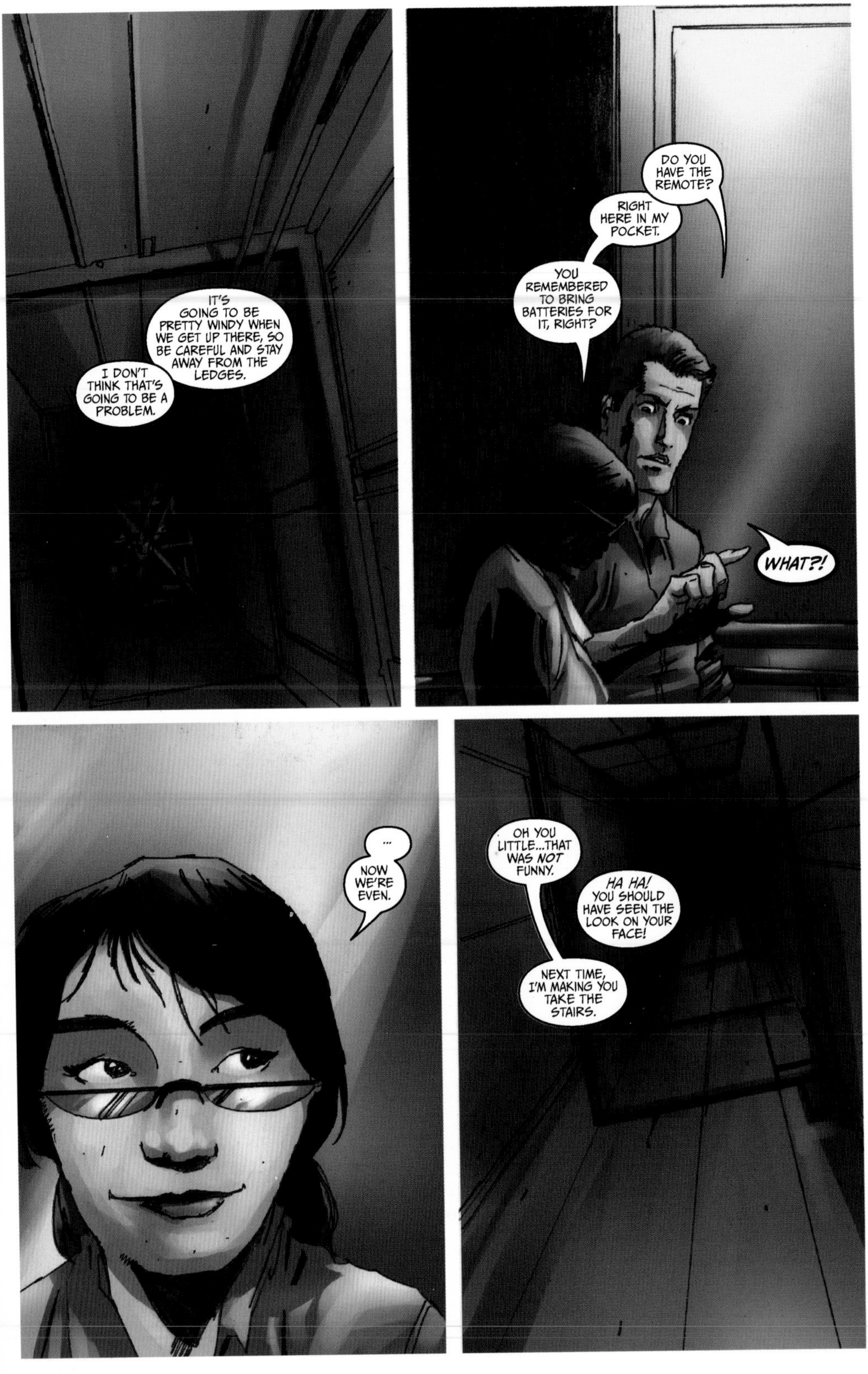
IT'S GOING TO BE PRETTY WINDY WHEN WE GET UP THERE, SO BE CAREFUL AND STAY AWAY FROM THE LEDGES.
I DON'T THINK THAT'S GOING TO BE A PROBLEM.
DO YOU HAVE THE REMOTE?
RIGHT HERE IN MY POCKET.
YOU REMEMBERED TO BRING BATTERIES FOR IT, RIGHT?
WHAT?!
...
NOW WE'RE EVEN.
OH YOU LITTLE...THAT WAS *NOT* FUNNY.
HA HA! YOU SHOULD HAVE SEEN THE LOOK ON YOUR FACE!
NEXT TIME, I'M MAKING YOU TAKE THE STAIRS.

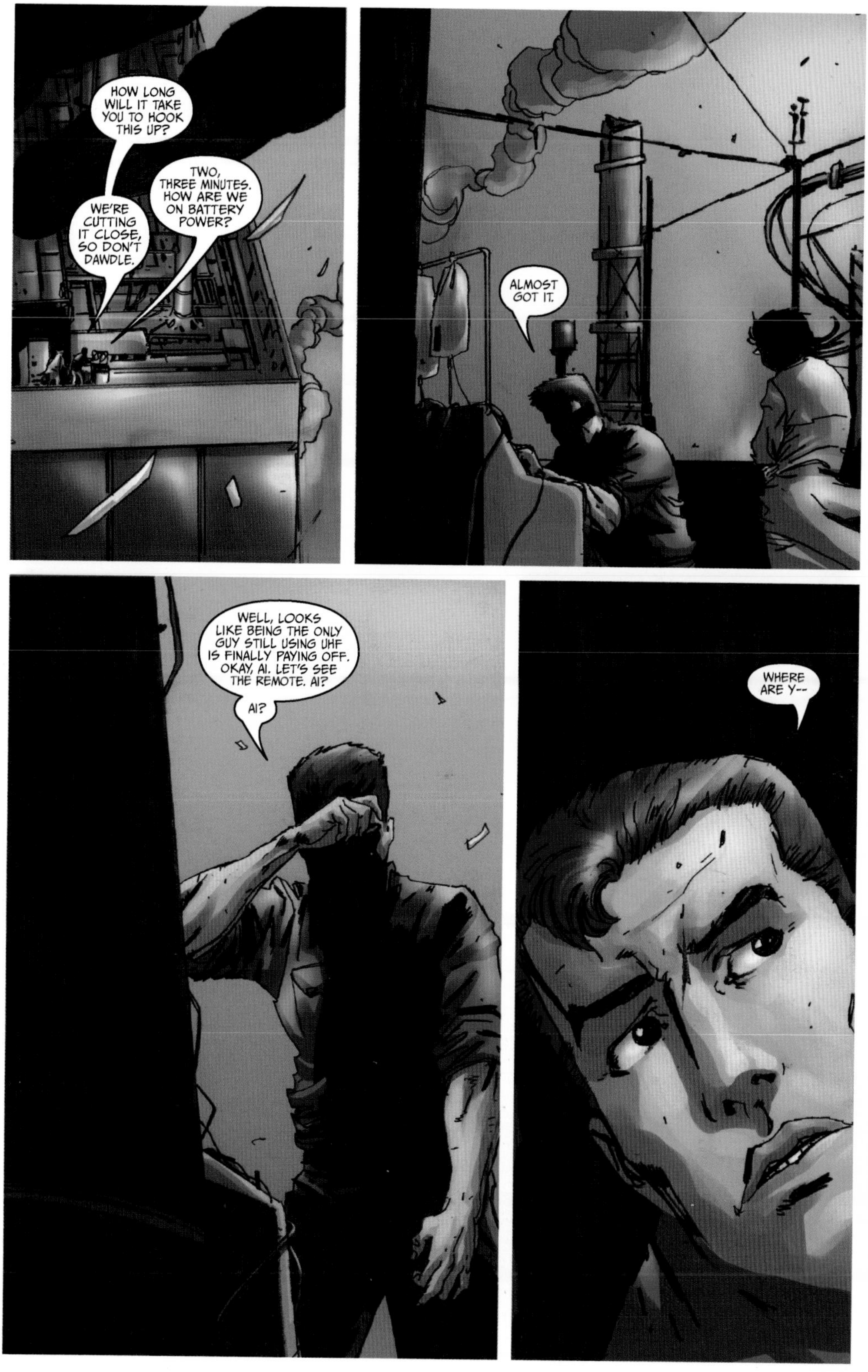
HOW LONG WILL IT TAKE YOU TO HOOK THIS UP?
TWO, THREE MINUTES. HOW ARE WE ON BATTERY POWER?
WE'RE CUTTING IT CLOSE, SO DON'T DAWDLE.
ALMOST GOT IT.
WELL, LOOKS LIKE BEING THE ONLY GUY STILL USING UHF IS FINALLY PAYING OFF. OKAY, AI. LET'S SEE THE REMOTE. AI?
AI?
WHERE ARE Y--

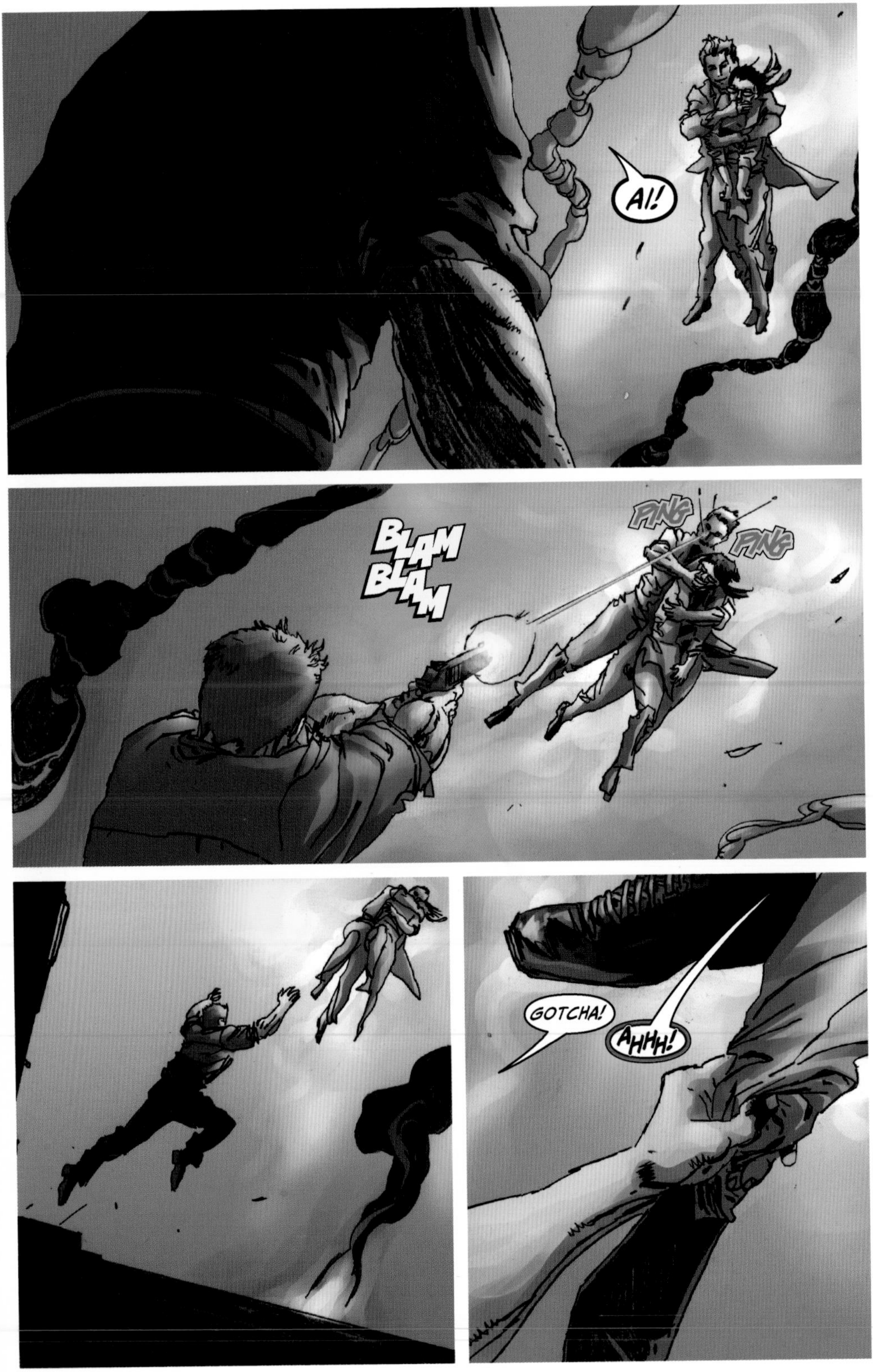
AI!
BLAM BLAM
PING
PING
GOTCHA!
AHHH!

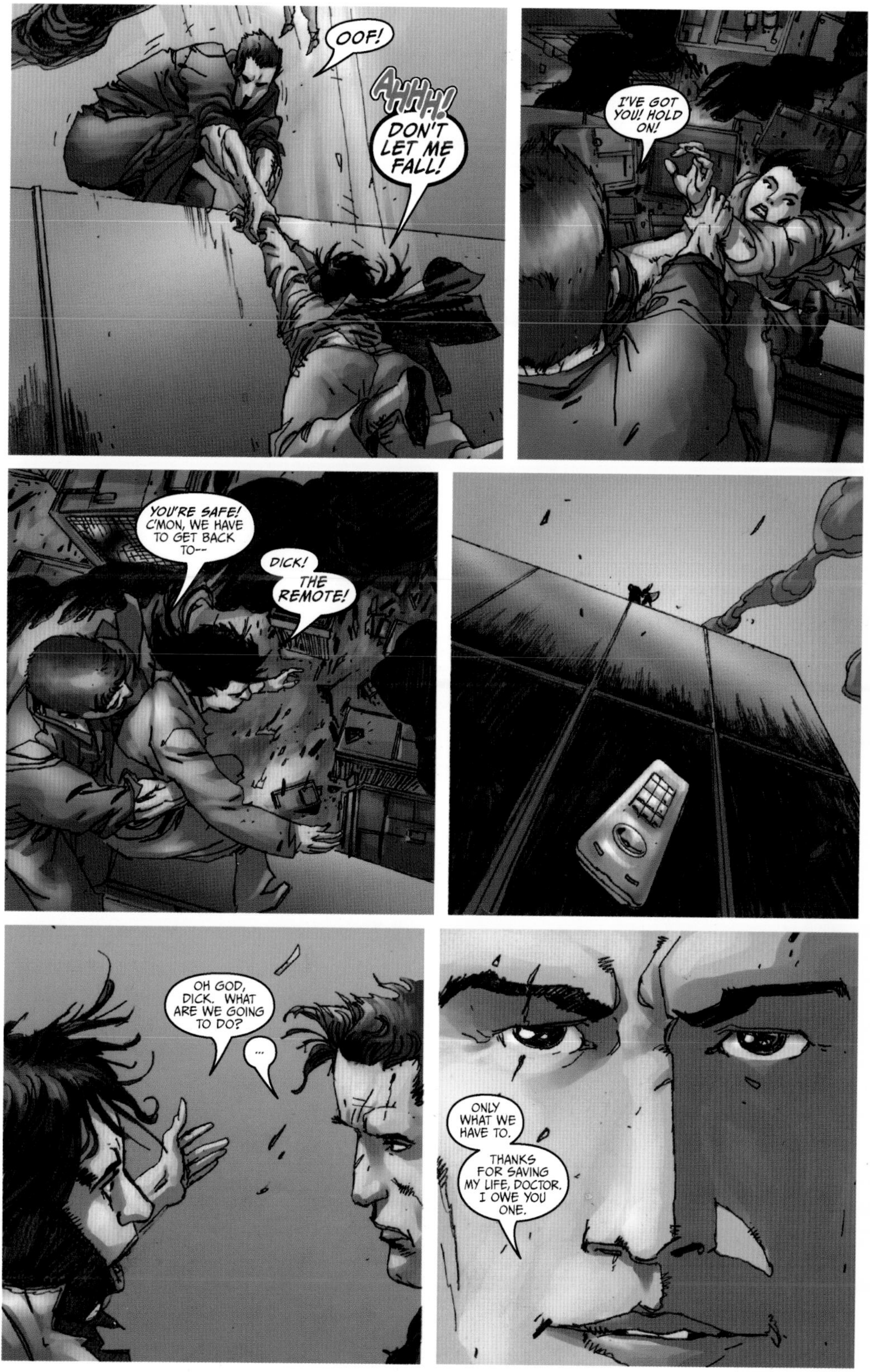
OOF!
AHHH! DON'T LET ME FALL!
I'VE GOT YOU! HOLD ON!
YOU'RE SAFE! C'MON, WE HAVE TO GET BACK TO--
DICK! THE REMOTE!
OH GOD, DICK. WHAT ARE WE GOING TO DO?
...
ONLY WHAT WE HAVE TO.
THANKS FOR SAVING MY LIFE, DOCTOR. I OWE YOU ONE.

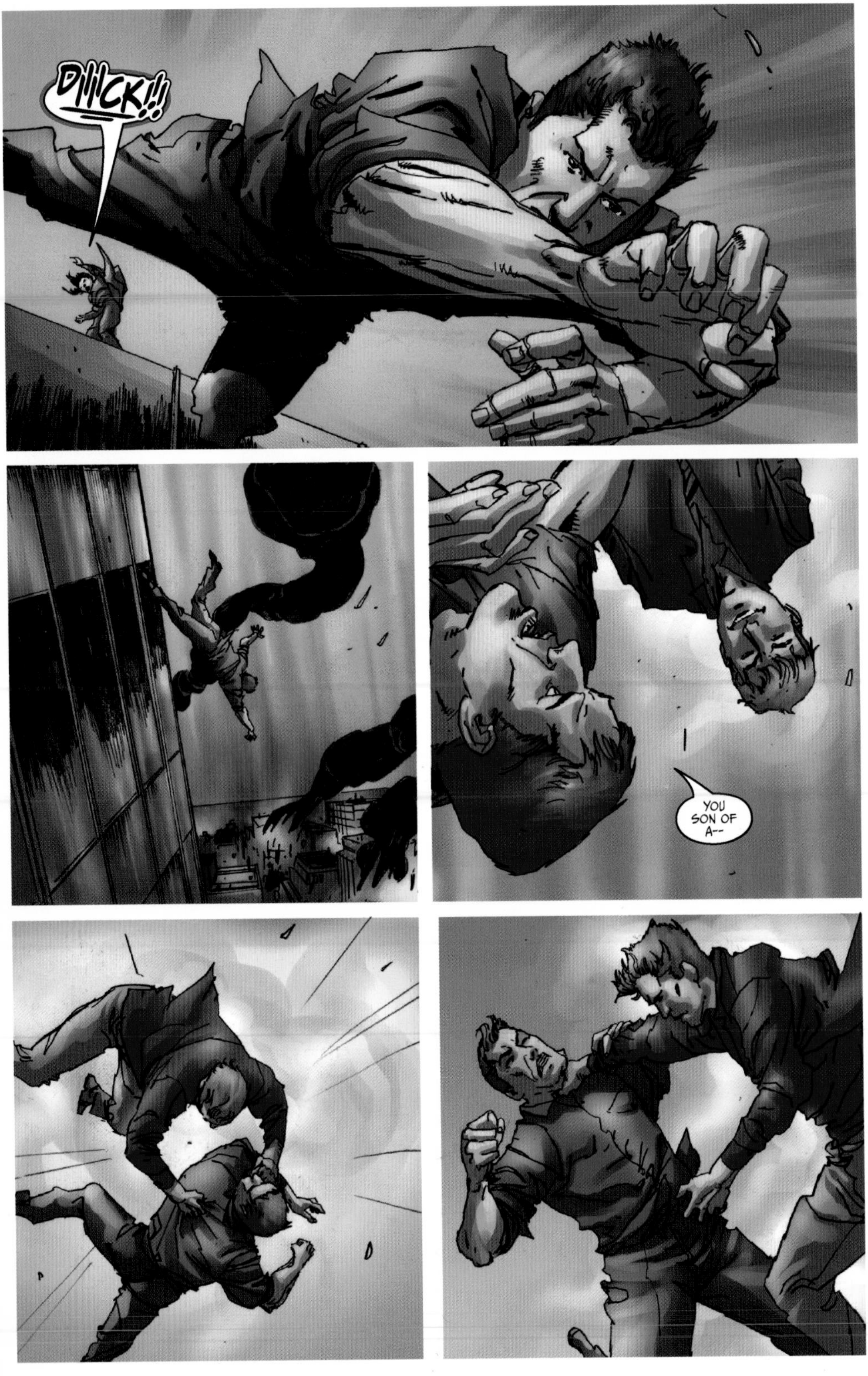
DIIICK!!
YOU SON OF A--

GIFFEN · DEMATTEIS · ABRAHAM
HERO 2
SQUARED

HERO SQUARED VOLUME 1

Written by Keith Giffen
and J.M. DeMatteis
Drawn by Joe Abraham
$14.99, full color, 136 pages

ISBN13: 978-1-934506-00-4

Collecting the sold-out X-Tra Sized Special one-shot - which was such a success that it lead to a three issue miniseries - this book is packed with extras. In print for the first time will be the popular web comic promotion that Keith Giffen plotted and penciled, and which DeMatteis scripted along with Giffen's original character designs and Joe Abraham's concept sketches. Also in print for the first time is a Keith Giffen plot, which can now be compared side-by-side with DeMatteis' final script!

ZOMBIE TALES
JOHNSON

ZOMBIE TALES

written and drawn by various
$14.99, full color, 144 pages

ISBN13: 978-1-934506-02-8

The best-selling zombie anthology finally gets collected, featuring work from the best of the best: material written by Mark Waid, Keith Giffen, Eureka creator Andrew Cosby, Transformers The Movie writer John Rogers, Eureka TV show writer Johanna Stokes, Fall of Cthulhu writer Michael Alan Nelson, and more! Artists featured are a non-stop constellation of names: Keith Giffen, Fallen Angel's J.K. Woodward, Painkiller Jane's Lee Moder, 100 Bullets' Dave Johnson, Mark Badger, and many many more! This edition collects Zombie Tales #1, Zombie Tales: Oblivion, and Zombie Tales: The Dead. Don't wait 28 days later for the new dawn of the walking dead!

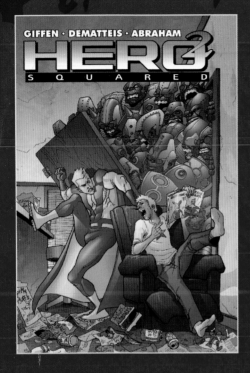

STARDUST KID

written by J.M. DeMatteis
drawn by Mike Ploog
$14.99, full color, 128 pages

ISBN13: 978-1-934506-04-2

From the best-selling creative team behind Abadazad comes the collection of their conceptual sequel! Last night, when Cody DiMarco went to bed, life was the same as it's always been. This morning, when he woke up, the world he knew...was gone. A Magic older than Time. An ancient evil. And four children whose only chance to restore their families, and their world, is to solve the mystery of...The Stardust Kid. Twelve year old Cody DiMaro's best friend is Paul Brightfield and Paul Brightfield isn't human: He's the last of The Old Ones, ancient elemental beings from The Time Before.

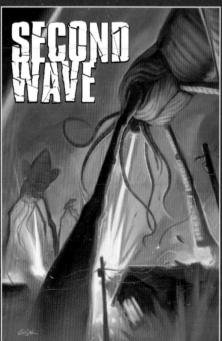

SECOND WAVE

written by Michael Alan Nelson
drawn by Chee
$14.99, full color, 144 pages

ISBN13: 978-1-934506-06-6

Mankind held the first invasion back. But then the second wave came... Mitch was an ordinary man living an ordinary suburban life, but alien invaders took his home and his wife away. Now that they're back, how have they grown immune to mankind's defenses? And what key role does Mitch play in the invasion? What's his link to this extra-terrestrial threat? This edition collects issues 1 to 6 of the critically acclaimed series.

TRADE PAPERBACKS

DEATH VALLEY

written by Johanna Stokes
and Andrew Cosby
drawn by Rhoald Marcellus
cover by Kaare Andrews
$14.99, full color, 128 pages

ISBN13: 978-1-934506-08-0

Samantha's graduating from high school in the Valley - getting together with her pals to throw an End of the World party to celebrate, everyone ends up accidentally locked in a bomb shelter. When Samantha and her pals emerge, they find that the entire world has changed, and the dead now walk the Earth... It's Dawn of the Dead by way of The O.C.! From EUREKA TV show writers writers Andrew Cosby and Johanna Stokes (Mr. Stuffins and The Savage Brothers)!

PLANETARY BRIGADE

written by Keith Giffen
and J.M. DeMatteis
drawn by various
$14.99, full color, 128 pages

ISBN13: 978-1-934506-10-3

More Giffen and DeMatteis Bwaha-ha-ha hilarity! From the hit-writers of Justice League International comes their own, quirky, turn on a league of super-heroes! The Planetary Brigade is a group of heroes fronted by Hero Squared's Captain Valor and Grim Knight. Meet Mr. Brilliant - Earth has never met a smarter, or more smug, hero. Earth Goddess - by day, she's a sweet, unassuming wallflower, but when the Earth needs her, she turns into a gargantuan guardian of the planet. Purring Pussycat -sweet, sexy... what's she hiding? The Third Eye - spiritual mystic. The Mauve Visitor - strange visitor from another world, or cute little Smurf-like dude? Together, they're in a league all their own.

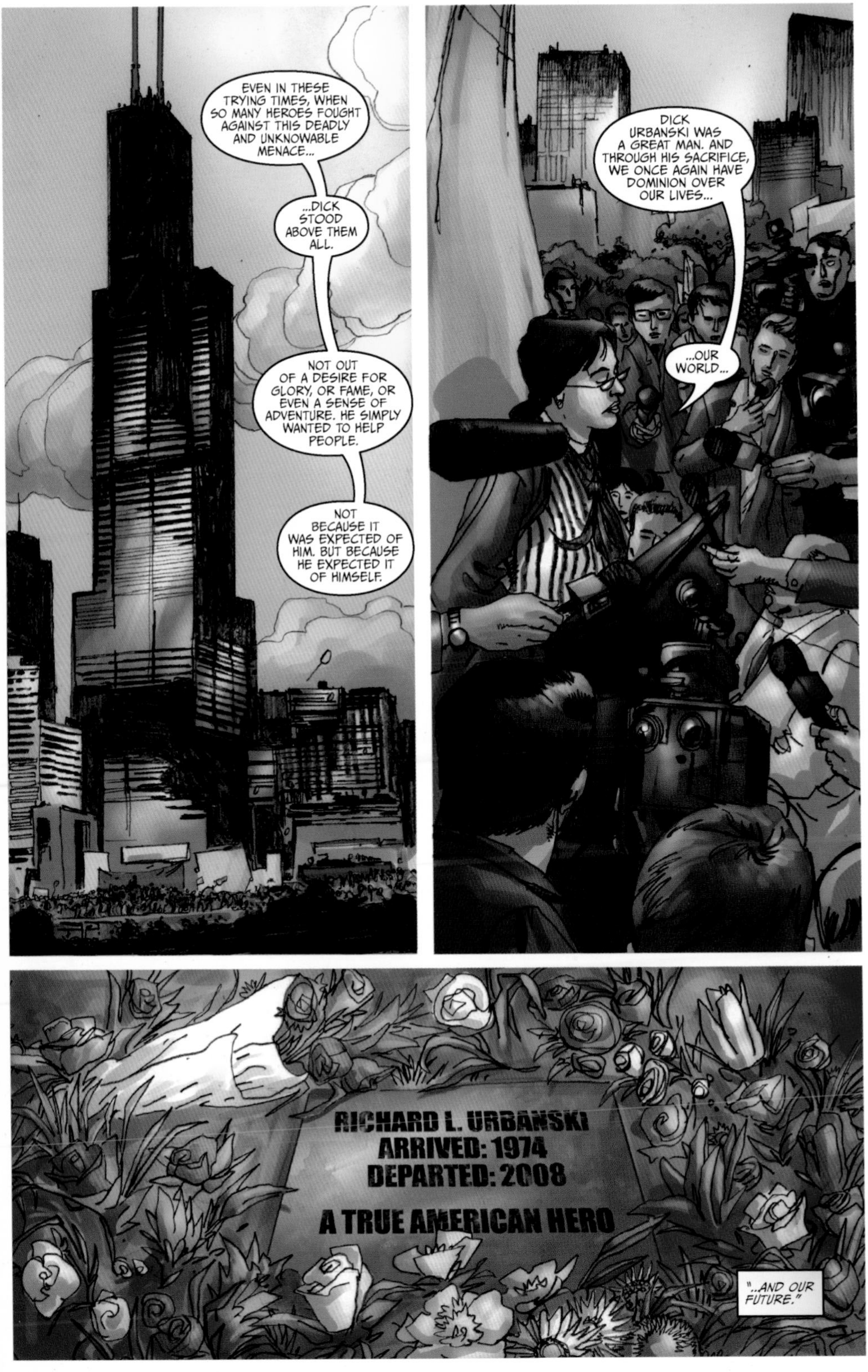
EVEN IN THESE TRYING TIMES, WHEN SO MANY HEROES FOUGHT AGAINST THIS DEADLY AND UNKNOWABLE MENACE...
...DICK STOOD ABOVE THEM ALL.
NOT OUT OF A DESIRE FOR GLORY, OR FAME, OR EVEN A SENSE OF ADVENTURE. HE SIMPLY WANTED TO HELP PEOPLE.
NOT BECAUSE IT WAS EXPECTED OF HIM. BUT BECAUSE HE EXPECTED IT OF HIMSELF.
DICK URBANSKI WAS A GREAT MAN. AND THROUGH HIS SACRIFICE, WE ONCE AGAIN HAVE DOMINION OVER OUR LIVES...
...OUR WORLD...
RICHARD L. URBANSKI
ARRIVED: 1974
DEPARTED: 2008
A TRUE AMERICAN HERO
"...AND OUR FUTURE."

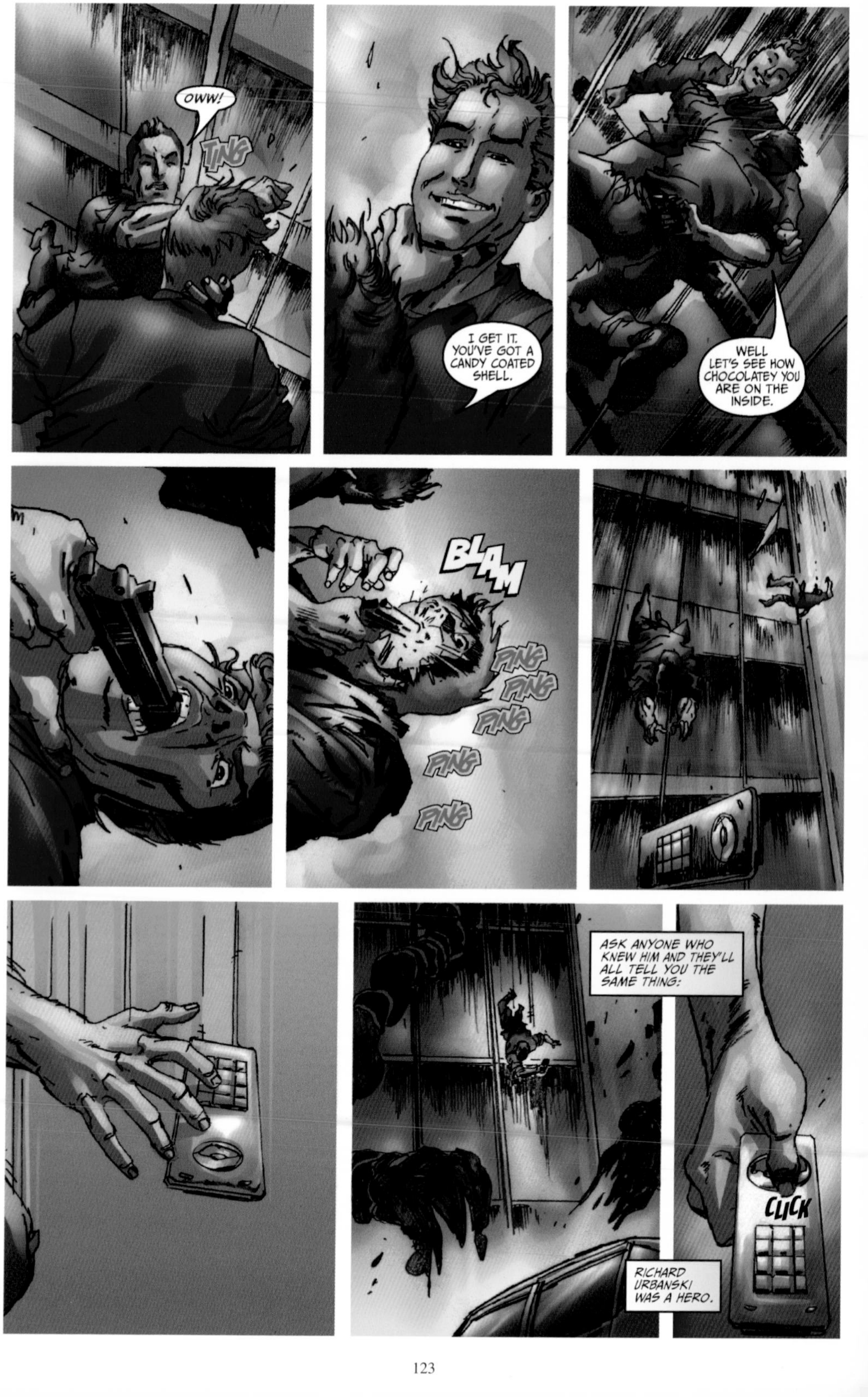
OWW!
TING
I GET IT. YOU'VE GOT A CANDY COATED SHELL.
WELL LET'S SEE HOW CHOCOLATEY YOU ARE ON THE INSIDE.
BLAM
PING
PING
PING
PING
PING
ASK ANYONE WHO KNEW HIM AND THEY'LL ALL TELL YOU THE SAME THING:
CLICK
RICHARD URBANSKI WAS A HERO.